MYSTICISM & SPACE

MYSTICISM & SPACE

Space and Spatiality in the Works of Richard Rolle,

The Cloud of Unknowing Author, and

Julian of Norwich

CARMEL BENDON DAVIS

THE CATHOLIC UNIVERSITY OF AMERICA PRESS
Washington, D.C.

Library of Congress Cataloging-in-Publication Data
Davis, Carmel Bendon.
Mysticism and space : space and spatiality in the works
of Richard Rolle, The cloud of unknowing author, and
Julian of Norwich / Carmel Bendon Davis.
p. cm.
Includes bibliographical references and index.
ISBN 978-0-8132-1522-8 (cloth : alk. paper)
1. English literature—Middle English, 1100–1500—
History and criticism.   2. Space perception.   3. Mysticism
and literature.   4. Religious literature, English—History and
criticism.   5. Rolle, Richard, of Hampole, 1290?–1349—
Criticism and interpretation.   6. Julian, of Norwich, b. 1343.
7. Mysticism—England—History.   8. Mysticism—
History—Middle Ages, 600–1500.   9. Space
and time in literature.   I. Title.

PR275.T45D38 2008
820.9'37—dc22   2007035855

To my mother, Mercia Bendon

1927–2006

CONTENTS

ACKNOWLEDGMENTS

The writing and preparation of this book did not, to use a spatial metaphor, happen in a vacuum and its existence would not have been possible without the help and encouragement of several people. To them I extend my deepest thanks.

To Macquarie University, Sydney, for its supportive research environment; to Professor John Stephens who generously shared his expertise in the project's early stages; to Associate Professor Peter Goodall for invaluable advice on the preparation of the manuscript and for his encouragement and interest throughout; to my colleagues in the Department of English, especially Dr. Teresa Peterson, Dr. Alison Scott, and Lee O'Brien, for being willing sounding boards for my ideas and such dependable friends.

To the editors of the *Australasian Universities Language and Literature Association (AUMLA)* journal and *Peaceworks Proceedings* I extend my gratitude for permission to republish here a version of a section of Chapter Three that appeared with the title "The Language of Space: Presence, Representation and Inexpressibility" in *AUMLA,* No. 106 (November 2006) and a version of a part of another section of Chapter Three, "God in a poynt" which appeared, in electronic form, under the title "God in a poynt: What Julian of Norwich Knew about Modern Science," in *PeaceWorks: 3rd Triennial Conference for Women Scholars of Religion and Theology* (January 2004).

To my brother, Dr. Michael Bendon (Ritsumeikan University, Kyoto), for introducing me some years ago to Michel Foucault's essay on space which was to start me thinking in a very different direction.

To Professor Denis Renevey (University of Lausanne, Switzerland) and to Professor Denise Baker (University of North Carolina) who read the manuscript in an earlier incarnation and offered invaluable advice on ways to improve it, and who encouraged me to publish what were then new and untried ideas.

To David McGonagle and Theresa Walker at the Catholic University of America Press for their interest in the project and for their clear and patient editorial guidance, and for providing such excellent readers, Associate Professor Anne Savage (McMaster University, Ontario) and the other anonymous reader, for my submission to the press. The readers' astute observations and generous advice have improved the book immeasurably and I thank them wholeheartedly.

To my parents, James and Mercia Bendon, for their love and interest over many years. To my mother, especially, who passed away before this book was completed, I give thanks for her unstinting love, her faith, her drive, and her unfailing belief in whatever I undertook.

To my daughter, Erin, for taking just the right photo for this project, and to Daniel Murdolo for his generous help in digitally enhancing the photograph; to my daughters Laura, Erin (again), and Bridget for their loving support over the many long years of my studying and writing.

Most of all, I thank my husband, Adrian, who has always supported and encouraged me and has always allowed me space.

ABBREVIATIONS

Cl.	*The Cloud of Unknowing*
Com.	*The Commandment*
E.D.	*Ego Dormio*
F.L.	*The Form of Living*
Fire	*The Fire of Love*
LT.	Long Text (of Julian of Norwich)
Med.	*Meditations on the Passion*
P.C.	*The Book of Privy Counselling*
ST.	Short Text (of Julian of Norwich)

NOTE ON TRANSLATION

The translations of all the Middle English quotations appearing in the notes of this book are my own. In most instances I have favored the medieval idiom, and even word order, over strict grammatical accuracy in modern terms. This is because I did not want to superimpose any of my own (conscious and unconscious) biases on the original expression of the words. Readers who are interested in etymological details are advised to consult the *Middle English Dictionary* and critical editions of the individual texts.

MYSTICISM & SPACE

INTRODUCTION

The most profound and sublime experience of which man is capable is the awareness of the mystical. In it lies the seeds of true science.

(*Albert Einstein*)

MYSTICISM AND SPACE

Space and *mysticism* are conceptually loaded terms. Through the ages, space has been broadly understood as being either (or both) a receptacle *for* things or an attribute *of* the things contained. Though it has been characterized by boundlessness and by infinite divisibility, the actuality of space is elusive in definition. At the everyday level, we have appropriated space, pairing the term with such diverse qualifiers as "outer," "personal," and "parking." Theoretically, space has been the focus of inquiry from earliest times; through the centuries it has challenged philosophers, theologians, mathematicians, and, more recently, physicists, cosmologists, and sociologists. The medieval conception of space, based on the theories of Aristotle and Ptolemy, provided a springboard for the conceptual exploration of space that now reaches beyond the edges of the vast universe and into the gaps between the quarks of subatomic physics.

Likewise, while mysticism might properly be defined as a personal, unmediated approach to, and attainment of, a direct apprehension of God, the concept of mysticism is not straightforward.[1] Today

1. While all the major world religions have a mystical element, the basis of Christian mysticism can be traced to early Jewish thought and to Greek (especially Neo-

the term *mysticism,* and the associated terms *mystic* and *mystical,* are used loosely and often in a pejorative sense to refer to a range of unusual experiences that are deemed to be beyond ready explanation. The true origin of the words, as Ewart H. Cousins explains, are to be found in the

Indo-European root *mu* (imitative of inarticulate sounds). From this root are derived the Latin *mutus* (mute, dumb, silent) and the Greek verb *myein* (to close the eyes or lips), from which comes the nouns *mysterion* (mystery) and *mystes* (one initiated into the mysteries) as well as the adjective/substantive *mystikos* (mystical, mystic). (1992, 236)

Furthermore, David Knowles notes that the standard understanding of *mystic* and *mystical* from the early Middle Ages to the sixteenth century "derived its currency from the title of the short treatise by the pseudo-Denis which he entitled *Theologia Mystica.* Literally this means the secret knowledge of God. . . . Mystical theology is thus distinguished from what is called natural theology and from dogmatic and speculative theology" (1961, 2).

The application of the words *mystic* and *mysticism* to fourteenth-century persons is also problematic. In recent years there has been scholarly debate on whether the term "mystic" should still be used in regard to vernacular writings of the period.[2] At the time, it was more likely that those whom we now refer to as *mystics* would have been referred to as "meditative" and "contemplative" individuals. Confusion about the term has not necessarily been lessened by the number

---

platonist) philosophy. However, it is generally considered that it is with Origen in the early third century that "we begin to discuss specifically Christian mystical theology" (Louth 1981, 52). Underhill believes that the Christianization of Greek thought was initiated by Origen's teacher, Clement of Alexandria (c. A.D. 160–220) (1911, 455). The theological, philosophical, and historical underpinnings of Christian mysticism have already been well documented; see, e.g., Hirsh 1995, McGinn 1991, Grant 1983, and Louth 1981.

2. E.g., Nicholas Watson (1995), following Bernard McGinn, prefers the "catch-all" term "vernacular theology" as a way of referring to, and incorporating, the wide variation in religiously centered texts of the period.

of recent studies that examine the mystical texts from one of several sharply focused theoretical perspectives. Often such perspectives have resulted in a polarized view of mystics and their texts as being either authentic in the experiences that they represent or as socially constructed phenomena with little evidence of spiritual value at their core.

Grace Jantzen, for example, regards mysticism as "a social construction . . . [that] has been constructed in different ways at different times" (1995, 12). This view echoes an earlier one expressed by Laurie Finke that mysticism is "not a manifestation of the individual's internal affective state but a set of cultural and ideological constructs that both share in and subvert orthodox religious institutions" (1993, 29). This view is sharply at odds with theologians such as Edmund Colledge and James Walsh who uphold the orthodox view that

God can reveal himself . . . to an individual person; and he can give to the recipient a sufficient certitude of the divine origin of this personal experience by internal or external criteria. Such revelations are called private not because they are intended simply for the spiritual benefit of an individual but because they are addressed through the beneficiary to the whole church. . . . Authentic private revelation . . . is imperative; it is a specific command, a manifestation of the divine will inspired in a member of the Church which is to affect conduct of the Church or of some of its members in a concrete situation. (1978, 70)

That is, the orthodox view sees authentic mystical experience as neither shaped by cultural phenomena nor experienced and revealed with the intention of subverting authority, but, on the contrary, as an experience capable of shaping and contributing to the continuing revelation of orthodoxy. Gender-focused studies of medieval religion and mysticism generally counter that power and orthodoxy were male-centered and marginalized female participation to the extent that medieval women were denied access to the means of producing culture (Finke 1992, 3). Theorists who consider gender to be performative make the link between the cultural construction of mysticism and the exclusion of women from the power structures of the Church, finding that the expression by women of mysticism in the Middle Ages was, in itself, a means of redressing the power balance.[3] Support for this view is garnered from the distinction made between *sacramentum* and *propheta:* while the male priesthood required literacy, and therefore education, prophecy required no special training but was "merely the privilege of being chosen as God's mouthpiece" (Holloway et al. 1990, 3). That is, though the Church and its authority were a strictly male preserve, women could appeal to a higher authority in God and thus transcend "cultural restrictions on their behavior, self-image and influence despite their lack of books [and] rudimentary education" (Lagorio 1984, 162).

Given the divergent views on the authenticity of mysticism as a phenomenon and the hitherto nonspecific use of the term *space,* it is not surprising, then, that, to date, scholarly inquiry has not brought the concepts of space and mysticism into juxtaposition, let alone synthesis. While this is the first study of Middle English mystics from a spatial perspective, the inclusion of a consideration of space in relation to religious texts and issues has not been entirely ignored. As early as 1969, for example, Thomas Torrance addressed the issue of time and space in relation to the Incarnation but he did not consider mystical texts. More recently, Brant Pelphrey (1998) and Vincent Gillespie and Maggie Ross (1992) have included some discussion on aspects of quantum physics and particle theory in relation to the revelations of Julian of Norwich; Denis Renevey has considered the "geography of the reclusorium" (1997, 55) in his study of anchoritic texts, finding that the "fundamental design of the anchorhold" (ibid.) has a role to play in the facilitation of the anchoresses' meditation; and the space of enclosure and its relationship to gender have been considered in a collection of essays edited by Liz Herbert McAvoy and Mari Hughes-Edwards (2005). The focus of these studies, however, has been on the physical parameter of space. My undertaking differs in that it also incorporates medieval cos-

3. See, e.g., Biddick 1993.

mological and modern philosophical conceptions of space and the social and textual parameters of spatiality. By applying this broad spatial perspective to the works of Richard Rolle, the *Cloud* author, and Julian of Norwich, I reveal new insights into both the texts and the endeavors of the three mystics.

My juxtaposing of mysticism and space is, in part, a response to the call by Michel Foucault some decades ago for an "epoch of space." Edward Soja took up and reiterated Foucault's call, observing that

[a]n essentially historical epistemology continues to pervade the critical consciousness of modern social theory. It still comprehends the world primarily through the dynamics arising from the emplacement of social being and becoming in the interpretive contexts of time. . . . This enduring epistemological presence has preserved a privileged place for the "historical imagination" in defining the very nature of critical insight and interpretation. (1993, 136)

Here, of course, Soja is referring to the need for a spatial perspective in social theory, but it seems to me that his observation can be usefully extrapolated to suggest a broad-based approach to many disciplines including the study of medieval mystics and their texts.

A spatial perspective permits the incorporation of multiple levels, including the mystics' physical and social environment, as well as their individual mystical experiences and the elaboration of those experiences in textual form. Thus I regard a spatial perspective as capable of defusing divisive epistemological conceptions of mysticism that act against the reconciliation of the theological and the social parameters of mystical experience. That is, the spatial perspective that I apply allows mysticism to be understood as both a social construct in its exterior representations and yet, interiorly, as an authentic experience of God. This is achieved by considering the mystical experience as being not only an exclusively "inner" apprehension but also an embodied one that takes place in what I designate as *mystical space*. This is the multifaceted space of mystical experience and its subsequent representations (social and textual). It incorporates all aspects of the mystics' life conditions: their personal experience of God; their physical environment; social influences, past and present; the influences of the communities in which they lived and wrote; their religious enculturation; and, additionally, their texts and the language of those texts. Broadly, then, mystical space may be conceptualized as a space encompassing, and being encompassed by, physical space, social space, and textual space, with the possibility of God both "outside" all those spaces as the initiator of mystical experience, and at the core of all spaces as the focus of the experience and, additionally, as present within all the other spatial strata.

In conception, then, I propose that mystical space can be considered as analogous to the literary figure of the *mise en abîme,* an impression of infinite regress that duplicates within all its layers the qualities of the larger, initiating structure without.[4]

The concept of *mise en abîme* is particularly applicable to an investigation of spatial concerns in the mystical texts because, in its definition, it allows textual, spatial, and mystical application. For example, as Neil Hertz explains,

There is no term in English for what French critics call a *mise en abîme*—a casting into the abyss—but the effect itself is familiar enough: an illusion of infinite regress can be created by a writer or painter by incorporating within his own work a work that duplicates in miniature the larger structure, setting up an apparently unending metonymic series. (1979, 311)

Though the technical term, as applied to literature, is usually rendered *mise en abyme* (i.e., with the "y" spelling), critics such as Hertz retain the *abîme* spelling. The latter spelling is apt in relation to mysticism in that it is the equivalent of the English word *abyss* which has the (spatial) denotation of an immense gap and the connotation, in relation to some expressions of mystical theology, of the unbreachable gap between God and humanity. The continental (medieval) mystic John Ruysbroeck, for example, refers to the "Unplumbed

---

4. For an elaboration of the literary *mise en abîme/abyme,* see Dällenbach 1989. See also Macris 2003 for a specific application of the literary notion.

Abyss" and his contemporary John Tauler speaks of the mystic's spirit as being "sunk and lost in the Abyss of the Deity [where it] loses the consciousness of all creature distinctions" (Underhill 1995/1911, 84). Denis Renevey describes how St. Anselm of Canterbury, in offering advice on meditation to William the Conqueror's youngest daughter, indicated that "the abyss which separates the contemplative from God" can be bridged by "a chain made up of holy representatives" (1997, 40). The image of the "abyss" of separation and the linking "chain" is an apt analogy for the overall concept inherent in my deployment of the *mise en abîme* as a primary perspective paradigm.

In that deployment I am not using the term in its strict literary sense but as a model to elucidate spatial ideas that happen to be represented in textual form.[5] My reconceptualization of the *mise en abîme,* then, aims to educe the idea of successive, perhaps concentric, layers of space as analogous to the various strata of experience that are constitutive of mystical space.

The distinction between these strata is not clear-cut. The various spatial perspectives are not mutually exclusive but frequently interact with, and overlap, each other. Most obviously, and importantly, God is to be found deep within the mystical space, within the mystic's soul, and is therefore the very center of the mystical *mise en abîme.* However, God is not only contained within the human soul but is the "container" of all humanity. That is, God is both within and outside space and spatiality; He is in the most enclosed layer of the *mise en abîme* of mystical space and is present within all its strata. At the same time, He is outside all space.

My elaboration of mystical space finds theological reflection in the image of God as the container for all humanity and as that which is contained most deeply within the human soul. Further reflection is found in the medieval philosophical and cosmological views of space

---

5. I use the *abîme* spelling throughout to reflect the appropriateness of the application of both connotations to the idea of mystical space except when directly quoting authors who use the *abyme* spelling in their elaborations.

which, resting on a combination of Aristotelian and Ptolemaic theories, yielded the broad definition of space as either a receptacle *for* things or an attribute *of* the things contained.

The reflection of theological and cosmological ideas in the Middle Ages is hardly surprising because space has been variously conceptualized through the centuries. Thus, as Margaret Wertheim has neatly pointed out, "the medieval world picture encompassed both a physical and a spiritual realm—it incorporated a space for body and a space for soul. This was a genuinely *dualistic* cosmology, consisting of both a physical order and a spiritual order" (1999, 33).

Wertheim's further designation of the medieval physical realm as *body-space* and the spiritual realm as *soul-space* provides a useful means for us, as modern observers of the medieval world picture, to distinguish between that which was then considered to be *of* the material world and that which was not. Useful, too, is Wertheim's view that, today, space is conceived only in geometricophysical terms to the extent that our view of space is "a purely *monistic,* physical view" (38) in which any concept of spiritual space has been virtually erased. While this summation of the current situation is certainly an oversimplification, it does point to a general trend in the conception of space since the time of René Descartes who, as Wertheim again points out, "rejected void space per se, preferring, with Aristotle, to see the universe as a *plenum* in which matter filled the entire volume" (146). In this view Descartes differed from Isaac Newton in whose earlier opinion space was an intrinsically void, though real, receptacle.

Most recently, the view of space has been expanded by the new insights of cosmology on the grand scale and by physics on the quantum scale.[6] It has moved far beyond the theoretical explanations provided by Einstein's general and special theories of relativity and his proposal that space and time are linked in a "spacetime" that is curved according to the objects within it. Spacetime currently is be-

6. On the subject of quantum physics and current cosmological trends, see, e.g., Paul Davies 1982, 1984, 1992, and 2003; and Davies, Barrow, and Harper 2004.

lieved to be boundless but finite and, at some places, to wrap and fold back on itself, encasing multiple dimensions. And Descartes's "matter" has been relegated to second position as a category of reality because space, at least experimentally, seems to be the main constituent of matter (Wertheim, 214).

However, while the sciences have tended to dominate our modern worldview, interest in space on a more personal and social level has been increasing, and it is perhaps not surprising that one of the most comprehensive modern examinations of space comes not from the field of physics or astronomy but from philosophy.

Henri Lefebvre's comprehensive and seminal work *The Production of Space* (1991/1974) propounds, as its basic premise, the theory that space is a social production. On the one hand, such a conception is problematic when applied to the medieval worldview in general and to mysticism in particular because the idea of God is a central consideration. And while, notionally and theologically, God can be contained within the human soul, He is also the container in which humanity finds its being. Of course to unbelievers God can be considered as a social production but, to the faithful of the Middle Ages, God was the producer, not the production, and this presupposition underlies my approach to mysticism and space.

On the other hand, Lefebvre's basic contention is illuminating when applied to a consideration of the texts of Rolle, the *Cloud* author, and Julian of Norwich and aspects of social life that are discernible therein. That is, the mystics can be viewed as "products" of their society and, in turn, their texts are products formed and disseminated in that society.

David Harvey, in his "Afterword" to the English edition of Lefebvre's *The Production of Space*[7] comments that

---

7. This and all subsequent references to and quotations from Lefebvre's work are from Henri Lefebvre, *The Production of Space,* trans. Donald Nicholson-Smith (1974; Oxford: Blackwell, 1991).

[t]he reader will find here not only innumerable lines of thought to be followed up, but tacit or implicit criticisms of structuralism, of critical theory and deconstruction, of semiotics, of Foucault's views on the body and
power, and of Sartre's existentialism. Yet Lefebvre never rejects such formulations outright. He always engages with them in order to appropriate and
transform the insights to be gained from them in new and creative ways.
(1991, 431)

Harvey's comment sums up, in a way, the reason that I have engaged
with Lefebvre's theory of space. Because it is the most comprehensive
theory of space to date and therefore cannot be overlooked, its inclusion in my argument is essential at some level. And though its application to the medieval period in general and to the mystics in particular presents some difficulties and inconsistencies, Lefebvre's theory
permits several aspects of the spatiality that is inherent in the texts of
Rolle, Julian, and the *Cloud* author to be more thoroughly elucidated.

Particularly useful in regard to the mystics and their texts is Lefebvre's elaboration of social space as consisting of the conceptual triad
of *spatial practice, representations of space,* and *representational spaces.*
Lefebvre evades precise definition of these concepts, tending instead
to express each in relation to its function and contents. This is because he sees his theory not as an abstract "model" of space but as
the "perceived-conceived-lived" spatial triad with interconnections
between the three tiers and in which "an individual member of a giv-
en group may move from one to another without confusion" (40).[8]
Spatial practice refers to the "perceived" space that "embodies a close

8. Lefebvre, despite the imprecise nature of the definitions of his own terms, is
critical of the way that the word *space* in general is poorly defined. He criticizes, for
example, Noam Chomsky for proposing a linguistic space that is "a mental space endowed with specific properties—with orientations and symmetries . . . [which] completely ignores the yawning gap that separates this linguistic mental space from that
social space wherein language becomes practice" (5) and Foucault for declaring that
"knowledge is the space in which the subject may take up a position" (4) without defining "space." In a way his criticism is fair—the term is not well defined. But neither
are other words in their theories. In general, we intuit by context the meaning to be
applied to the terms. As I have suggested, Lefebvre could just as fairly be criticized

association ... between daily reality (daily routine) and urban reality (the routes and networks which link up places set aside for work, 'private' life and leisure)" (38).

Thus *spatial practice* primarily involves a negotiation of material rather than conceptual space. In applying the definition to the Middle Ages specifically, Lefebvre states that "[then], *spatial practice* embraced not only the network of local roads close to peasant communities, monasteries and castles, but also the main roads between towns and the great pilgrim and crusaders' ways" (45). As applied to the mystics, *spatial practice* would have involved, most often, the deciphering of their own small private space of seclusion, and perhaps the traversing of that space as was required by their daily office and practices of dedication.[9]

In the second category, *representations of space* are "conceptualized space, the space of scientists, planners ... and social engineers ... all of whom identify what is lived and what is perceived with what is conceived" (38). The Aristotelian and Ptolemaic models of the medieval cosmos are examples of this type of space in Lefebvre's formulation. However, as I have already explained, in my reconceptualization I have posited social space as a category within conceptualized space, in direct contrast to Lefebvre's view which posits, of course, that we would not have a conception of space without a society to produce and uphold the conception. Indeed, the potential for shifting and expanding the way categories signify is already implicit in Lefebvre's formulation of the third category, *representational spaces*. In explaining that *representational spaces* "with certain exceptions, ... tend towards more or less coherent systems of non-verbal

---

for failing to provide definitions for pivotal terms in his project. Most notably, he does not offer a definition of *society*. His point is valid, however, when we consider how frequently we use the word *space* and other "spatial terms" in general and academic discourse. It seems we are far freer in applying the terms today.

9. Contemporaneous guides to anchoritic life, in particular *Ancrene Wisse,* may offer some clues as to the ways in which enclosed contemplatives negotiated their daily lives in general and the material space of the anchorhold in particular.

symbols and signs" (39), Lefebvre opens the category to the possibility of significances that are beyond the obvious representations in social space. He further suggests that in the medieval period *representational spaces* "determined the foci of a vicinity: the village church, graveyard, hall and fields, or the square and the belfry. Such spaces were interpretations, sometimes marvellously successful ones, of cosmological representations. Thus the road to Santiago de Compostela was the equivalent, on the earth's surface, of the way that led from Cancer to Capricorn on the vault of the heavens" (45). This suggestion implies that the social application followed the cosmological conception and not the reverse. Furthermore, *representational space* is the "lived" space of Lefebvre's triad, the space alive with the multiple "products" of social space that, to the medieval mentality, were symbolic of a variety of other possibilities. That is, the mystics may be seen to be both representing and subverting the "non-verbal symbols and signs" of *representational space* in aid of the expression of their mystical experiences. In accepting the signs, the mystics were partaking, as were other members of medieval society, in a social world that was beyond the physical world yet linked to it and made manifest in earthly signs. In subverting them, they were imbuing those symbols with significances beyond those current in the social world. Thus, for example, in the case of Julian of Norwich, the crucifix, a central symbol for Christianity, becomes additionally the means by which she is precipitated into mystical experience.

A concept within Lefebvre's argument that, though additional to his categories, in part enables the three categories to be opened up in a way that is particularly useful for discussing the mystics and their space is that of "decrypting." This polysemous term encompasses a range of ideas that revolve around of the notion of "emergence" (260) of that which was previously hidden. Lefebvre argues that, in the early medieval period, "Christianity . . . was a great worshipper of tombs" (254). In line with this, he suggests that space was also "encrypted" in the dual sense that there was a focus on death and its representations in religion, and that perceived and lived space were literally not open to receive light. In contrast, Lefebvre considers that

[t]he urban landscape of the Middle Ages turned the space which had preceded it, the space of the "world," upon its head. It was a landscape filled with broken lines and verticals, a landscape that leapt forth from the earth bristling with sculptures. In contrast to the maleficent utopia of the subterranean "world," it proclaimed a benevolent and luminous utopia where knowledge would be independent, and instead of serving an oppressive power would contribute to the strengthening of an authority grounded in reason. What do the great cathedrals say? They assert an inversion of space as compared with previous religious structures. . . . They "decrypt" in a vigorous (perhaps more than rigorous) sense of the word: they are an emancipation from the crypt and from cryptic space. (256)

The relationship of the notion of "decryption" to mysticism, I would argue, lies in the manner in which the mystics both experienced something that was "hidden" and then brought it to light in the sharing of the experience in their texts. That is, mysticism and space both have the potential of decrypting that which is, or has been, hidden. Presumably, many texts, not only those from the medieval period, are absorbent of the notion of decrypting and elaboration by means of application of a spatial paradigm. Of necessity, however, the examination here is limited.

TEXTS TO BE CONSIDERED

Ego Dormio, The Commandment, Form of Living, and *The Fire of Love* by Richard Rolle; *The Cloud of Unknowing* and *The Book of Privy Counselling* by the *Cloud* author; and *Revelations* (or *Showings*) *of Divine Love* by Julian of Norwich are my focus. Brief reference will also be made to *Meditations on the Passion.* (Although attribution of authorship has not been established definitively, both Hope Emily Allen [1931] and Nicholas Watson [1991] offer a strong case for Rolle's authorship which I accept.) All these works, with the exception of *The Fire of Love,* were written originally in English.

My decision to include *The Fire of Love* is prompted both by its autobiographical elements and because it has "considerable influence on some of the English [works]" (Watson 1991, 277). *The Fire of Love* was written originally in Latin by Rolle and translated into English by Richard Misyn in 1435. It is Misyn's translation (Early English Text Society) that will be my primary reference. It was chosen in preference to the original Latin in an effort to establish some modicum of linguistic parity between this text and the other vernacular texts under consideration. Linguistic parity is important in this project as I am examining spatial concepts. Such concepts can alter dramatically over time. Modern translations of all the texts, for example, are far freer in their use of spatial words when the translator is really translating a temporal concept.

I am aware that Misyn's translation of *Incendium Amoris* is considered by some to weaken, even distort, Rolle's original intention (Riehle 1981) but any semantic shifts seem minor in comparison to modern English translations. Rita Copeland considers that Misyn's translation "regards the style of Rolle's text as integral with its proper meaning so he reproduces its technique to the extent that his own talents will allow" (1980, 75). Of course, the artifice of Rolle's Latin cannot be reproduced in English, and therefore I offer Misyn's own qualification to his translation as the rationale of my choice: "The whilk boke, in sentence ne substance I þink to chaunge, bot treuly aftyr myn vnderstandynge to wryte it in gude exposicione" (*Fire,* Misyn's Pro.1: 9–11).[10] I have used the H. E. Allen edition of Rolle's English works based on MS Cambridge Dd.v.64 in preference to the Early English Text Society's (1988) version, edited from the MS Longleat 29 by S. J. Ogilvie-Thomson in response to Ogilvie-Thomson's own advice that "[MS Longleat 29] has never been considered as a base text for an edition because of its non-Northern dialect" (1988, xv).

The Cloud of Unknowing and *The Book of Privy Counselling* are

---

10. "This book, neither in sentence nor in substance, do I intend to change, but to the best of my understanding, to offer a good exposition of it."

the main texts of the *Cloud* author to be considered. All reference to these texts is from the Early English Text Society edition, edited by Phyllis Hodgson, whose choice of basic text was BM. MS. Harleian 674.

The account of Julian's revelations is extant in two forms, which are now referred to as the Short Text and the Long Text. Generally, the Short Text is regarded as having been written shortly after Julian received the revelations while "the longer version came later and incorporates her growth in understanding over the subsequent twenty years" (Glasscoe 1993, 217).[11] That is not to dismiss the relevance of the Short Text which, having being written as a "first impression" account, contains much of the immediacy and wonder of the revelations.[12] The unique copy of the Short Text is preserved in BL MS Additional 37790 and "was made sometime after 1435 from an exemplar dated 1413" (Barratt 1995, 27). Selections from the Long Text, dated around 1500, are found in Westminster Treasury MS 4, but "the only complete manuscripts of the Long Text are post-Reformation" (ibid.). Principal among these are the Bibliothèque Nationale Fonds anglais MS 40 and the BL MS Sloane 2499. While it seems to me that the Short and the Long Texts are aspects of the same mystical experience, the former experienced more immediately, the latter a result of frequent re-visioning and reexperiencing, I cite primarily from the Long Text in the interest of ease of reference for the reader.[13]

The editorial problem that surrounds Julian of Norwich's *Revelations,* the Long Text specifically, magnifies the difficulties in ana-

11. Glasscoe flags the possibility that the Short Text is a later contraction of the Long Text but concludes, as most other scholars have, that "the nature of the passages unique to the longer version render it extremely unlikely that it predated the shorter account" (1993, 217–18).

12. Nicholas Watson's argument for a later dating for the composition of the Short Text leads him to regard the Short Text "as a vastly more interesting text than its neglect by scholars suggests" (1993, 674).

13. Exception is made only when a relevant quotation or passage either does not appear in the Long Text or is more pertinently expressed in the Short Text.

lyzing Julian's work.[14] While acknowledging that the Sloane BL MS 2499 may sometimes be preferable to the Paris MS Fonds anglais 40, I have chosen to work from the latter for reasons of editorial parity.[15] That is, I have used the Colledge and Walsh edition of both the Short Text (MS BM Additional 37790) and the Long Text.[16]

The form of citations will be as follows (with "page" referring to the page number in the editions detailed above):

Richard Rolle:

The Fire of Love (*Fire,* Book.Chapter.Page: line).
Meditations on the Passion (Med. Page: line).
Ego Dormio (E.D. Page: line).
The Commandment (Com. Page: line).
The Form of Living (F.L. Page: line).

The Cloud author:

The Cloud of Unknowing (Cl. Chapter.Page: line).
The Book of Privy Counselling (P.C. Page: line).

Julian of Norwich:

Long Text (LT. Chapter.Page: line).
Short Text (ST. Chapter.Page: line).

14. For an overview of editorial considerations, particularly in regard to the Long Text, see Barratt (1995) and Glasscoe (1989).

15. An anthology of essays on Julian of Norwich 1998 features more authors using the Paris than the Sloane manuscript as the base Long Text, but a perfunctory overview of all relevant literature shows opinion to be about equally divided.

16. Felicity Riddy summarizes the main differences between the two Long Text copies as (a) the language of Sloane has more northerly features than that of the Paris manuscript; (b) the Sloane manuscript has chapter headings summarizing the contents of each chapter; (c) in both manuscripts scribes have modernized the language, but this is less frequent in Sloane than in the Paris manuscript (hence Glasscoe's and Crampton's decision to use it as their copytext); (d) Sloane frequently lacks short passages that are included in the Paris manuscript, some of which may be not expansions in Paris but rather contractions in Sloane; (e) they occasionally disagree about where chapter divisions come; and (f) there are very many, apparently minor, textual divergences, some of which have interpretative implications (1998, 109–10).

OTHER SPATIAL PARAMETERS

Other ways of "decrypting" that which is hidden in the texts are by the application of several contemporary theories that either explicitly include, or implicitly intimate, an interest in spatial parameters. In particular, these include Pierre Bourdieu's elaboration of *habitus,* Mikhail Bakhtin's notion of the *grotesque,* Michel Foucault's *heterotopias,* Arnold van Gennep's *rites of passage,* and Margaret Wertheim's *body-space* and *soul-space* distinction. The applicable features of these theories will be elaborated as they become relevant within the course of this work. By way of brief overview, however, the following chapter summaries indicate the main areas of focus.

Chapter One considers the representations of the medieval conception of physical space and cosmology in the mystics' texts and the negotiating of, and interaction with, physical space by Richard Rolle, the *Cloud* author, and Julian of Norwich. Solitude, enclosure, and stillness are considered in the context of the space in which they are experienced. Architecture and architectural imagery are shown to serve specific purposes in the texts; this part of the examination is underpinned by the theories of Henri Lefebvre in particular and to a lesser extent Erwin Panofsky. Representations of the body, and the importance of the body in the mystical experience, are examined from a variety of theoretical perspectives, in particular Bakhtin's elucidation of *grotesque* realism.

Chapter Two examines the social parameters of space as represented in the texts. While accepting the idea that space is a social production, the chapter offers a case for the mystics as unique occupants of social space, most particularly through the application of Bourdieu's notion of *habitus.* The chapter elaborates the ways in which medieval society viewed and valued the mystics and mystical experience and, in reflection, the ways in which the mystics valued their society. The idea of the mystic, and the *place* of the mystic, as simultaneously *other* and socially representative, will be considered through the theoretical perspectives of Foucauldian *heterotopias* and van Gennep's *rites of passage* in the context of which I propose that the mystics' spiritual "journey" was undertaken on behalf of all society.

Textual space and the language of space are the interests of Chapter Three. Here I posit a link between the specific idea of the book in the Middle Ages and the medieval conceptions of cosmology. Textual representations of apophatic and cataphatic mysticism are considered as part of a dialectical relationship that are shown to be metaphorically representative of the notion of God's containment in the human soul and the containment of humanity within God. Spatial language is defined in terms of the evocation of impressions of space and spatiality rather than exclusively in terms of individual spatial images. Thus the gap between presence and representation is shown to have spatial connotations. A central question is whether language is capable of reliably depicting the mystical experience, but language is shown to have a role beyond mere signification, especially in its function of spiritual transformation. The expression of God in spatial terms is shown to be related to His "completeness." The frequent disavowal of literal signification for (spatial) prepositions in particular is suggested as effecting a detachment of the usual signification from words and images that is reflective of the contemplative's own necessary experience of detachment from earthly things.

Chapters Four, Five, and Six are concerned with the individual mystical spaces of Richard Rolle, the *Cloud* author, and Julian of Norwich, respectively. Rolle's mystical space is expounded as being representative of the medieval worldview in which there is an eluctable interconnection between soul-space and body-space, leading to Rolle's evocative descriptions of spiritual phenomena in sensual metaphors. His threefold mystical experience of *calor, dulcor,* and *canor* is posited as having links to medieval cosmology, Pythagorean theory, medieval music theory, and the modern theory of buccal perception. Rolle's careful categorizations are shown to be indicative of a man whose mystical experience is far more thoughtfully and sensitively conceived and expressed than is often acknowledged.

The *Cloud* author's mystical space is expounded in dialogue with the overarching paradigm of the *mise en abîme* which facilitates the view that the mystical space is an empty space, full of God, in a reflection of the author's recommendation that contemplative aspirants be empty of all ego and desire for materiality and yet full of the hope of union with God. This view is consolidated by the examination of the idea of the *mirror* and, in particular, the elaboration of the mirror-image qualities of the *mise en abîme.*

Julian of Norwich's mystical space is elucidated in partial dialogue with Lefebvre's theoretical categories and by means of a consideration of Wertheim's body-space, soul-space nexus to reveal Julian's clarity of perception that enables her to distinguish between the multiple levels of her visionary experiences and yet simultaneously to elaborate a space in which God's completeness is revealed. The completeness is shown, often, to be reflective of a dissolution of common binaries, particularly those that are gender-related.

This dissolution of common binaries is, in fact, a quality that is discernible in the texts of Richard Rolle and the *Cloud* author too. Like Julian, they offer an insight into lives that straddled the usual human distinctions between body and spirit, knowing and being, immanence and transcendence, the immediate and the infinite. That is, they experienced the rarified and extraordinary space of mystical union while simultaneously inhabiting the physical actuality of fourteenth-century England.

Chapter One

PHYSICAL SPACE

This litel spot of erthe that with the se
Embraced is

    (Geoffrey Chaucer, Troilus and Criseyde *5.1815–16)*

DEFINING MEDIEVAL SPACE

In the paradigm of the *mise en abîme* that I have suggested as being an apt figurative analogy for the concept of mystical space, physical space at first might be considered as an "outer" layer of experience in which bodies and material objects exist, social life is enacted, texts are produced and circulated, language is exchanged and inscribed, and religious practice takes place. However, because the *mise en abîme* is a figure of infinite regress and duplication in all its strata, physical space also can be conceived of as being intrinsic to mystical space and present within it, in a variety of representations. Most obviously, Richard Rolle, the *Cloud* author, and Julian of Norwich do not separate themselves physically from the space of their material lives when they are "with" God and/or when they are relating their experience of God in their texts for the edification of others. On the contrary, their texts indicate both that aspects of physical space have helped facilitate their approach to God and that images and metaphors of physical space offer an effective means of describing mystical experience.

For Henri Lefebvre, physical space is "the space of nature and the Cosmos" (1991/1974, 11) and of all created things. It relates to natural, cosmological, material, and bodily things as opposed to those that might be considered as belonging to the mental, moral, spiritual, or imaginary realm. Lefebvre's deceptively simple definition of physical space, however, fails to alert us to the fact that space has been variously conceptualized throughout the ages. Obviously, the physical space of the Middle Ages, for example, was very different from the physical space of the twenty-first century.

The medieval views of space, place, and cosmology basically rested on the theories of Aristotle and Ptolemy. Aristotle had proposed that space was a receptacle[1] and that place was "the immobile body which is the term with respect to which one can recognize and determine the movement of bodies" (Duhem 1985, 142).

In cosmological terms, the Ptolemaic universe reigned securely. At its very center was the Earth which, in turn, was surrounded by the seven progressively larger concentric spheres of the Moon, Mercury, Venus, the Sun, Mars, Jupiter, and Saturn. Beyond the planetary spheres were, firstly, the *stellatum* (the area of fixed stars), and then the *primum mobile* that was the boundary of the physical universe. Beyond this outermost sphere and "literally *outside* the universe, was the Empyrean Heaven of God ... [which] was beyond space and time, both of which were said to end at the primum mobile" (Wertheim 1999, 35). However, in the Christianized account of space, the place of God was not only *beyond,* but also most deeply *within,* spatiality, as C. S. Lewis explains that "what is in one sense 'outside the heaven' is now, in another sense, 'the very Heaven,' *caelum ipsum,* and full of God" (1964, 97). This spatial paradox is reflected not only in the postulation of God's immanence and transcendence but also in the understanding that all souls are enclosed within God while simultaneously God is enclosed within each individual soul. The par-

---

1. Plato had first used the "receptacle" idea "to designate the pregiven space with which the Demiurge must begin" (Casey 1997, 32).

adox is also reflective of the two basic medieval understandings of
space that were to dominate thinking and provoke differences in spatial conceptions until the present day. That is, that space is either a
receptacle *for* things or an attribute *of* the things contained. The medieval mind accommodated both notions, though not without dis-
putation at the philosophical level.

Averroës, the commentator on Aristotle, elaborated and clari-
fied Aristotle's viewpoint by concluding that "[p]lace is immobile
essentially; in fact, place is that towards which something moves or
in which something rests" (Duhem, 142). Aristotle's conclusion that
"the rotation of heaven requires the existence of an immobile central
body" (ibid.) was used by Averroës to dispute Ptolemy's system of ec-
centrics whereby Ptolemy proposed that celestial movements required
several centers, or epicycles. Averroës concluded that "if celestial
movements required several centres, there would have to be several
heavy bodies external to the Earth" (ibid.) and he could not conceive
of this. Nevertheless, as Duhem points out, "at the beginning of the
fourteenth century, the astronomical system of Ptolemy reigned un-
contested [particularly] among Franciscans who followed Duns Sco-
tus and among the masters of the Faculty of Arts at University of Paris" (ibid.). Theologically, however, debate took another turn. In 1277,
under the direction of Pope John XXI, "Etienne Tempier, Bishop of
Paris . . . issued a series of 219 condemnations of doctrines that denied
or limited the power of God, including the power to move the world
into a different place than it currently occupies" (Casey 1997, 106–7).
The effects of these condemnations were profound but perhaps the
most momentous was that they ". . . reopen[ed] the vista of the possible infinity of space" (ibid., 107). In 1328 Bradwardine was to upset
things further with his *Treatise on Proportions* in which he mathema-
tized the idea of motion through space and substituted *impetus* for
Aristotle's idea of motion in space as "change." This opened the way
to the conception of the universe as mechanical (Medcalf and Reeves
1981, 73) and led Ockham subsequently to refute the notion that had

previously enabled argument from the created to the Creator and to deny the possibility of "the description of God in terms of reason" (Medcalf and Reeves 1981, 75). Both Bradwardine and Ockham, however, were to agree that "the only point of contact between God and man lay in the action of God's will" (ibid.). Though the vicissitudes of philosophy during the twelfth and thirteenth centuries may have caused disputes in the universities and an apparent triumph of nominalist thinking may have laid the foundation for a split between theology and science, the triumph was by no means complete. William Courtney stresses that nominalism "was hardly dominant in the second quarter of the fourteenth century, and . . . it lost out to realism in 1350" (quoted in Ruud 1995, 34)[2] and the medieval world was to retain its belief in a harmonious order under God for some time to come. This basic confidence in a harmonious order included a view of physical space that drew little or no distinction between the space of material experience and the space of spiritual experience. That is, both spheres of experience were understood to coexist. For example, the understanding of the body's physiology reflected the elements of the cosmos. Lewis explains that "[t]he human body . . . is built out of the four contraries. . . . [T]hese combine to form the elements— fire, air, water, earth. But in our bodies they combine to form the Hu-

2. Though the conflicting philosophies of the realists and the nominalists, and the subsidiary disputes between Thomists, Scotists, and Ockhamists, are obviously of some tangential interest here, there is not the scope in this book for detailed discussion of the issues and therefore I will confine my use of the terms to directly relevant matter. For a thorough overview of the arguments, see, e.g., Frederick C. Copleston, *Medieval Philosophy* (New York: Harper, 1961). Equally, I am aware of scholarly works that discuss the convergences and divergences of mysticism and nominalism in particular but do not regard these as necessarily germane to the present argument and will make reference to them only when directly pertinent to a point. See, e.g., Erwin Panofsy, *Gothic Architecture and Scholasticism* (New York: Meridian Books, 1967) for an elaboration of the view that mysticism and nominalism are ". . . nothing but opposite aspects of the same thing. Both . . . cut the tie between faith and reason" (14). Ruud (1995) offers a balanced view of the issues with particular respect to Julian of Norwich.

mours. Hot and Moist make Blood; Hot and Dry, Choler; Cold and Moist, Phlegm; Cold and Dry, Melancholy" (1964, 169–70).

Mikhail Bakhtin expounds the link more fully, stating that,

[t]he medieval cosmos ... was based on the precept of the four elements (earth, water, air and fire), each of which had its special rank in the structure of the universe. According to this theory all the elements were subject to a definite order from top to bottom. The nature and the movement of each element were determined according to its position in relation to the center of the cosmos. Nearest of all to this center is the earth, and any part separated from the earth tends to move back to the center along a straight line. . . . Fire moves in the opposite direction; it continually tends upward, therefore away from the center. Water and air lie between earth and fire. . . . [A]bove the earthly world there rises the world of celestial bodies, not ruled by this law. . . . Celestial bodies, as the most perfect, are endowed with pure movement only, the circular movement around the center of the earth. . . . The characteristic trait of this picture was that all degrees of value correspond strictly to the position in space, from the lowest to the highest. The higher the element on the cosmic scale (that is, the nearer to the "immovable motor"), the more nearly perfect was this element's quality. The conceptions and the images of the higher and lower stratum as expressed in space value become the flesh and blood of medieval man. (1984/1968, 362–63)

This belief in an ordered universe under God, together with the predominant medieval ideas of space and cosmology, are variously reflected in contemporaneous literature and in the works of the mystics. Medcalf and Reeves, for example, remark on the unique nature of Dante's vision "when he passes beyond the fixed stars and the Primum Mobile" (1981, 60), and point out that "Dante's extraordinary intuition rests on the assumption that the Middle Ages took from Boethius that the true view of the universe is perceived not from where we are but from where God is" (ibid.). Such a "true view" is echoed by Chaucer in his *Troilus and Criseyde,* when he gives the dead Troilus the perspective that shows the world to be "this litel spot of erthe that with the se embraced is" (5.1815–16).[3]

3. "this little spot of earth that is surrounded by the sea"

Julian of Norwich is also given such a view of "this litel erthe" and describes it within the context of her first revelation:

And in this he shewed me a little thing, the quantitie of an haselnott, lying in þe palme of my hand, as me semide, and it was as rounde as a balle. I looked theran with the eye of vnderstanding, and thought: What may this be? And it was answered generaelly thus: It is all that is made. I marvayled how it might laste, for me thought it might sodenly haue fallen to nawght for littlenes. And I was answered in my vnderstanding: It lasteth and ever shall, for god loueth it; and so hath all thing being by the loue of god. (LT. 5.299: 9–300: 16)[4]

In that moment Julian is granted both a physically and a mentally heightened view of creation. In fact, she seems to be sharing God's view of creation, for just as creation "lasteth and ever shall, for god loueth it," so Julian is afforded the passing privilege of also holding creation in the palm of her hand and preserving it for that moment. She seems to see with the superior all-encompassing view of the Creator, explaining that "the cause why it shewyth so lytylle to my syght was for I saw it in the presence of hym that is the maker. For a soul that seth the maker of all thyng, all that is made semyth fulle lytylle" (LT. 8.317: 10–18: 13).[5] In addition, her description invites the reader to also experience a vastly heightened and different perspective on creation. In that moment, too, Julian has traveled metaphorically in space, has been translocated to a place outside creation, and that vantage point to which she is raised seems to be the Empyrean.

---

4. "And in this he showed me a little thing, the size of a hazel nut, lying in the palm of my hand, as it seemed to me, and it was as round as a ball. I looked on it with the eye of my understanding, and thought: What can this be? And I was answered generally thus: It is all that is made. I marveled that it endured, for I thought it might suddenly have fallen into nothingness because it was so little. And I was answered in my understanding: It endures and always shall, for God loves it; and so all things have being by the love of God."

5. "the reason that it looked so little to my sight was because I saw it in the presence of him who is the Creator. For a soul that sees the Creator of all things, all that is created seems very little."

Similarly, the *Cloud* author, while certainly insisting that "Alle þe reuelacions þat euer sawe any man here in bodely licnes in þis liif, þei haue goostly bemenynges" (Cl. 58.107: 11–12),[6] still calls on a particular medieval conception of space to elaborate his points, showing that he accepts the Ptolemaic model of physical cosmology but warning against the application of that actual model to spiritual experience. Thus when he strives to castigate those who misinterpret the word "up" when they attach a literal meaning to a spiritual concept, he explains that "Þe sonne & þe mone & alle þe sterres, þof al þei be abouen þe body, neuer þeles ʒit þei ben beneþe þi soule" (Cl. 62.114: 18–19).[7] That is, he defers to the medieval conception of cosmological order but insists that it is inferior to things of the spirit. Likewise, Aristotle's notion of space as a receptacle is also invoked as physically actual but inapplicable spiritually when the *Cloud* author describes as "presumptuous goostly disciples" (Cl. 57.105: 4)[8] those who seek to find God in an entirely physically located heaven when they "sumtyme wiþ þe coriouste of here ymaginacion peerce þe planetes, & make an hole in þe firmament to loke in þerate" (ibid., 10–11).[9]

Rolle presents a subtle allusion to the cosmological world when he says that "þai have na mare syght of þe lufe of God in þaire sawle þen þe egh of a bak has of þe sonne" (Com. 74: 24–25).[10] Rolle, too, elucidates the metaphorical brightness of the hierarchical orders of angels in terms of a comparison to other sources of light in the natural world, relating it particularly to a quantitative comparison of observable objects in the cosmos:

6. "All the visions that anyone has seen in bodily form in this life have spiritual meanings."

7. "the sun, the moon and all the stars, though they are above the body, nevertheless are beneath the soul."

8. "presumptuous spiritual disciples"

9. "sometimes in their curious imagination reach the planets, and make a hole in the sky to look through."

10. "they have no more sight of the love of God in their soul than the back of the eye has of the sun."

In heven er neyn orders of aungels, þat er contened in thre ierarchies . . . þe heest ierarchi, þat neest es to God, contenes thronos, cherubyn, and seraphyn. Þe lawest es aungels, þe heest es seraphyn; and þat order, þat leste es bryght, es seven sythe sa bryght als þe sonn es bryghtar þan a kandele, þe kandel bryghtar þan þe mone, þe mone bryghtar þan a sterne. (E.D. 61: 18–62: 27)[11]

In *Meditations on the Passion,* Rolle uses cosmological imagery to refer to the sufferings and wounds of Christ in His Passion:

þan was þy body lyk to hevyn. For as hevyn is ful of sterris, so was þy body ful of woundes; bot, Lord, þy woundes bene bettyr þan sterris, for sterres shynen bot by nyght, and þy woundes bene ful of vertu day and nyght. Al þe sterris by nyȝt lygheten bot lite, and oon cloud may hide ham alle; bot oon of þy woundes, swete Jhesu, was and is inogh to do away þe cloudes of al synful men, and to clere þe conscience of al synful men. . . . Also, swet Jhesu, þe sterres ben cause of euche þynge þat is grene, or groweth or bereth fruyt. Now, swet Jhesu, mak me grene in my beleve, growynge in grace, berynge fruyt of good workes. Also, sterris ben cause of mynys, metaill, and of precious stonys. Now swet Jhesu, mak me togh as metaille ayeyns temptacions, and precious as perle into þe heigh degre of charite. (Med. 34: 232–35: 250)[12]

11. "In heaven there are nine orders of angels which are organized into three hierarchies. . . . the highest hierarchy, which is nearest to God, contains thrones, cherubim, and seraphim. The lowest is the angels, who are [also] called seraphim; and that order which is the least bright, is seven times as bright as the sun compared to a candle, the candle brighter than the moon, the moon brighter than a star."

12. "Then your body was like the heavens. For just as the heavens are full of stars, so your body was full of wounds; but, Lord, your wounds are better than stars, because stars shine only at night, but your wounds are full of virtue both day and night. All the stars lighten the night but a little, and one cloud may hide them all; but one of your wounds, sweet Jesus, was and is enough to take away the cloud of all sinners, and to clear the conscience of all sinners. . . . Also, sweet Jesus, the stars are responsible for every [living] thing that is green, or grows or bears fruit. Now, sweet Jesus, make me green in my belief, growing in grace and bearing the fruit of good works. Also, stars are the cause of mines, metal and precious stones. Now sweet Jesus, make me as tough as metal against temptations, and as precious as pearls in the high degree of charity."

Here, too, Rolle establishes a connection between the observable physical space of his own time and the metaphorical spatiality of Christ's body, thereby effecting an alignment of medieval body-space and soul-space in the juxtaposing of the physical space of cosmology with the spiritual and physical space of Christ's Passion. Additionally, Rolle exemplifies some of the medieval beliefs in the interconnectedness of different aspects of medieval physical space. For example, in stating that the "sterris ben cause of mynys, metaill and of precious stonys," Rolle admits of the medieval belief in stars' and planets' influence on the production of metals. The planet Saturn, for example, was believed to produce lead in the Earth, while Venus produced copper, Jupiter produced tin, and Mars iron (Lewis 1964, 105ff.).[13] The stars, too, are shown to have an influence on the greening and growth of the Earth's vegetation. These cosmological influences are reinscribed so that Jesus becomes Rolle's means of "growynge in grace and berynge fruyt of good workes." And it is Jesus who is invoked to prove Rolle's "metaille ayeyns temptacions." Simultaneously, then, Rolle verifies his acceptance of the medieval belief in cosmological influences and attests to a recognition of a greater influence from God.

Thus, the *Cloud* author, Julian, and Rolle indicate in their texts an awareness of physical and cosmological space. Equally, they exhibit an awareness of God as the source of that space and cosmology, and presumably it is this faith that prompted Rolle, the *Cloud* author, and Julian to assume lives that were dedicated to God.

---

13. Personality and appearance were also susceptible to arrangement and subject to a "higher" rule. E.g., the relationship between astrological bodies and human health and dispositions was strong. Albertus Magnus writes that "Taurus rules over the neck, Gemini over the shoulders, Cancer over the hands and arms; Leo over the breast, the heart and the diaphragm; Virgo over the stomach; Libra takes care of the second part of the back; Scorpio is responsible for those parts that belong to lust" (quoted in Lefebvre, 45–46). Personal constitutions were elaborated psychophysiologically according to the combinations of different humours in the body. Personalities, therefore, could be "read" in people's complexions and physical appearance.

THE ENCLOSED SPACE OF CONTEMPLATION

Prominent among the physical modes of expression of a life dedicated to God was the solitary contemplative life. Central to the idea of the contemplative life was the spatially loaded notion of "enclosure." The word *enclosure,* in its general denotation of being that which is surrounded or encompassed, suggests a means by which physical space is divided. The boundary of enclosure need not be a physical wall or building. Indeed, as the early Desert Fathers exemplified, the desert acts as a most effective enclosure, the expanse of uninhabited space representing a real physical barrier to the outside world.[14] In medieval England, enclosure of a type of "isolation" was practiced but by the twelfth century it had become almost exclusively the preserve of men. Elizabeth Freeman has examined the differing experiences of English male and female Cistercians in the medieval period and notes that, unlike their male counterparts,

... the women's houses do not use the language of wilderness and desert. In principle the desert and vast solitude was a universal positive of Christianity, available to both male and female. But in the Cistercian context, in England, the desert's benefits were gendered and these benefits were not a realistc goal for women to aspire to. Before the women's communities could use a play on words to argue for their metaphorical distance from culture they needed to insert themselves within this culture at a practical level. This takes us to the premise behind renunciation. One can renounce only when one possesses in the first place. (2005, 74)

Thus, in sharp contrast to their continental sisters,[15] for English women the space of solitude and enclosure existed only within the social sphere where enclaustration was practiced within towns. Sharon Elkins notes that, by the last half of twelfth century,

14. For a new view on this topic, see Totah (1998).
15. See Mulder-Bakker (2005) for details of continental medieval urban recluses.

the only known [English] eremitic women were strictly enclosed recluses. . . . [T]he elimination of the less-structured eremitism, common earlier
in the century, was in part a result of the increased number of monasteries
that could meet the needs of religious women. But also the distrust that had
grown of [previous male-dominated] informal arrangements led to the cur-
tailment of a way of life that depended on close contact between female and
male religious. Hermitesses had ceased to live alongside their hermit friends
. . . [and] the eremitism they chose . . . had become a defined and distinct
form of religious life. (1988, 151)

Even those males who pursued a hermitic life were involved in their
society to the extent that they worked for their living, and their hermitages, however sparse, were known and supported by other local
residents.[16] In fourteenth-century England, then, solitude was a relative term insofar as it suggested a solitary but not socially or physically isolated mode of living and, at the same time, it was a synonym for
the contemplative life insofar as it referred to a mode of living that
emphasized a nonactive, noncommunal dedication to God.

Though solitude was not the only lifestyle in which contemplation could be undertaken and mystical experience possibly attained,
the texts of Richard Rolle and Julian of Norwich give evidence that
their own mystical attainments were linked to solitude and the contemplative life, at least for some stages of their lives.[17] Rolle, in particular, advocates the solitary life for his readers, assuring them in *The
Form of Living* that the solitary life will lead to spiritual advancement
and reward:

16. For an overview of patronage for anchorites in medieval England, see Warren (1985).
    17. Pollard (1997) quite correctly points out that "the writings of mysticism and
devotion that grace the Middle English period of English literature present no single
paradigm for spirituality. Hermits and anchorites, monks and nuns, prelates and lay
people all contributed to that literature" (iv). The observation can be extrapolated
to the modes of living of the mystical writers. However, as far as Julian of Norwich,
Richard Rolle, and the *Cloud* author are concerned, evidence points to solitude as
the predominant way of living.

For þat þou has forsakyn þe solace and þe joy of þis world, and taken þe to
solitary lyf. . . . I trowe treuly þat þe comforth of Jhesu Criste and þe swetnes
of his love with þe fire of þe Haly Gast, þat purges all syn, sall be in þe and
with þe, ledand þe . . . so þat in a few ȝers þou sall have mare delyte to be
by þi nane, and speke till þi luf and to þi spows Jhesu Crist, þat hegh es in
heven, þan if þou war lady here of a thowsand worldes. (F.L. 89: 1–10)[18]

Here Rolle is alluding to the assumption that contemplative life leads
to some degree of mystical experience and union with God.[19] In *The
Fire of Love* he is more explicit, stating that

& þe more þat lyf with-oute mans solace to take þa drede not, þe more sall
be gyfyn with godis comforthinge to be glad. Gostly visitacion forsoth oft-
tyms þa take þe whilk in cumpany set playnly knawes not—wharfore to a
lykand saule it is said: *Ducam eam in solitudinem & ibi loquar ad cor eius,*
/ þat is to say: "I sall it lede to wyldernes & þer sall I speke vnto his hartt."
(*Fire*, 1.14.29: 22–27)[20]

18. "Since you have forsaken the solace and joy of this world, and taken up the
solitary live . . . I trust that the comfort of Jesus Christ and the sweetness of his love
together with the fire of the Holy Spirit that purges all sin, shall be in you and with
you, leading you . . . so that in a few years you shall have more delight in being alone,
and speaking to your love and your spouse, Jesus Christ, who is high in heaven, than
if you were the lady of a thousand worlds here."

19. At times, Rolle's works have prompted discussion on the extent to which he
himself actually promoted the solitary life. In regard to this, Denise Baker comments
that

[w]hile [Nicholas] Watson demonstrates how Rolle's own writings develop
as he attempts to provide instruction for his disciples rather than a defense
of himself, it would be a mistake to conclude that he proposes the mixed life,
either in its traditional Gregorian version or in his own modification of it, for
others. Although Rolle's epistles increasingly acknowledge the needs of his
readers, including those in active life, he maintains . . . the preeminence of the
solitary throughout his career. (1998, 88)

20. "And the more that you do not fear a life without human company, the more
of God's comforting gladness will you be given. Spiritual visitations, too, are often received that those in company know nothing of. Therefore to a loving soul it is said:
Ducam eam in solitudinem & ibi loquar ad cor eius, that is to say: 'I shall lead you into
the wilderness and there I shall speak to your heart.'"

Rolle's own quest for, and attainment of, a solitary life is clearly, if somewhat melodramatically, described in the *Legenda* prepared in anticipation of his canonization.[21] Details of his "flight to solitude" will be considered in the following chapter. Here, suffice it to say that he offers a personal and pointed statement of his own solitary life when he declares that

Truly I fled in to wildyrnes, for with men I myght not accorde, for sikirly fro Ioy þai lett me oft & because I dyd not as þai dyd, errour & indignacion þai put to me, & þerfor tribulacion & sorow I haue fun, bot our lordys name I ay ha worschippyd. (*Fire*, 1.28.60: 13–16)[22]

This, of course, is a somewhat loaded statement, pointing as it does to an admission by Rolle that his flight to solitude was not prompted solely by a desire to be alone with God but rather by personal difficulties in the social sphere. Nevertheless, his own writings convey the idea that he prized the contemplative way of life. Moreover, the original addressees of his epistles *Ego Dormio, The Commandment,* and *The Form of Living* were all anchoresses. Inclusive language in these epistles strengthens the probability that Rolle was still living in some form of seclusion at the time of his writing. For example, in *The Form of Living,* when detailing the benefits of solitary life, he uses plural pronouns, pointing to his own life state:

Men wenes þat we er in pyne and in penance grete, bot we have more joy & more verray delyte in a day þan þei have in þe worlde all þair lyve. Þai se oure body; bot þai se noght oure hert, whare oure solace es. If þai saw þat, many of þam wold forsake all þat þai have, for to follow us. (F.L. 89: 12–17)[23]

21. Rolle's followers' hopes for his canonization were not fulfilled though he continued to be revered long after his death. In addition, "[I]t is claimed that there are more manuscripts of his works extant than of any other medieval English writer" (Medcalf and Reeves 1981, 82).

22. "Truly I fled to the wilderness, for with men I could not agree, for certainly from joy they often led me and because I did not do as they did, they heaped error and indignation upon me, and therefore I found sorrow and tribulation, but I have always honored our Lord's name."

23. "Men think that we are in great pain and penance, but we have more joy and

The *Cloud* author, though we have no biographical knowledge of him, shows himself in his texts to be an ardent supporter of the contemplative life.[24] In *The Cloud of Unknowing* he devotes almost a quarter of that work to extolling the contemplative life. In addition, like Rolle, he initially addresses his work to a young person (probably male) who is embarking on the solitary life. The only direct allusion to the author's own mode of life—apart from the few examples of inclusive addresses, such as "goostly freende"[25]—is given at the end of Chapter 73 of *The Cloud of Unknowing,* when he implores his reader that "Siþen we ben boþe clepid of God to worche in þis werk, I beseche þee for Goddes loue fulfille in þi partye þat lackiþ of myne" (Cl. 73.129: 10–12).[26]

Julian's embrace of the solitary life is more overtly attested though it cannot be firmly ascertained that her enclosure predated the revelations. She is known to have been an anchoress for a large part of her life. There are records of three bequests made to "Julian, anchoress" in Norwich during Julian's known lifespan. The last recorded bequest is in 1416, confirming that she was alive until at least that year. Julian's contemporary, Margery Kempe, referring to herself always in the third person, specifically mentions Julian in her *Book* when she describes visiting her: "Þan sche was bodyn be owyr Lord for to gon to an ankres in þe same cyte [Norwich] whych hyte Dame Ielyan" (BMK.18.42: 7–9).[27] Julian's enclosure, in an anchorhold attached

---

more true delight in a day than they have all their lives living in the world. They see our body; they do not see our heart, where our solace is. If they saw that, many of them would forsake all that they have in order to follow us."

24. There is some evidence to suggest a Carthusian association for the *Cloud* author, but in the absence of an identity, this cannot be established. See, e.g., William O. Gregg, "Presence of the Church in *The Cloud of Unknowing,*" *American Benedictine Review* 43, no. 2 (1992): 184–206, and Marion Glasscoe, *English Medieval Mystics: Games of Faith* (London: Longman, 1993), 167.

25. "spiritual friend"

26. "Since we have both been called by God to this work, I implore you for the love of God to make up any part in which I am lacking."

27. "Then she was bidden by our Lord to go to an anchoress in the same city [Norwich] who was called Dame Julian."

to a church in the busy town of Norwich, represented a powerful physical sign of spiritual dedication to the faithful of that society. In terms of Lefebvre's categories of space, the anchorhold is a *representational space,* a physical symbol with a spiritual meaning. The symbolism in the location and physical presence of places of religious retirement is well attested. Roberta Gilchrist observes, for example, that "[m]onastic landscapes were invested frequently with very specific meanings so that the more austere landscapes were associated with the more eremitic hermitages and Cistercian monasteries" (1994, 63).[28] Lefebvre finds that cloisters, too, in general are

a gestural place [that] has succeeded in mooring a mental space—a space of contemplation and theological abstraction—to the earth, thus allowing it to express itself symbolically and to become part of a practice, the practice of a well-defined group within a well-defined society. Here, then, is a space in which a life balanced between the contemplation of the self in its finiteness and that of a transcendent infinity may experience happiness composed of quietude and a fully accepted lack of fulfilment. As a space for contemplatives, a place of promenade and assembly, the cloister connects a finite and determinate locality—socially particularized but not unduly restricted as to use, albeit definitely controlled by an order or rule—to a theology of the finite. (217)

Cloisters, then, too, are a *representational space,* a place in which the cloister walls represent the physical division between the physical and the religious space. Similarly, the assuming of the contemplative life by Rolle, Julian, and the *Cloud* author represented, in their own physical space, a spiritual focus. On a deeper symbolic level, in the connection between body-space and soul-space, a decision to assume a life of solitude also meant that the physical enclosure was the outward sign of the individual's spiritual enclosure in God.

28. Jean-Francois Leroux-Dhuys observes that "Cistercian [architecture] makes us meditate not only on the coherence between the taming of natural space and the social organisation that underlies it, but also on the coherence between the ethics of life and the aesthetics of the works that are its products" (1998, 7).

Though in the Christianized Ptolemaic account, God was to be found beyond the *primum mobile* in unbounded space,[29] for the Christian in general and for the contemplative in particular, God was also to be found within that space that is physically most bounded: the soul within the body.[30] "Enclosure" had multiple representations in the Middle Ages, most of which were based on scriptural precedents. Johnston confirms that "the image of the soul dwelling in God or God dwelling in the soul, is an image widespread in the Bible, [and] is frequently used to express this mystical union" (1978/1967, 130). Augustine had expressed the paradox in his *Confessions,* questioning, accepting, and marveling at it simultaneously:

> Since then you do fill the heaven and earth, do they contain you? Or do you fill and overflow them, because they cannot contain you? . . . Or is it rather that you are wholly present everywhere, yet in such a way that nothing contains you wholly? (Con. 1.3)

Here Augustine intimates the spatial notion of God as both container and that which is contained. Similarly, for the mystic, God is both the initiator and the goal of mystical experience, the beginning and the end of the seeking. He is both "enclosed" within the mystic's soul and he is the "enclosure" that the mystic enters spiritually. .

---

29. Thomas Torrance stresses that "the mythological synthesis of God and the cosmos, with its confusion between the presence of God and upper space, is to be found in the anonymous *De Mundo* (falsely attributed to Aristotle) that gained currency in the second and third centuries and corrupted proper understanding of Ptolemaic cosmology" (1969, 3). Russell traces the confusion to a mixed origin, noting that "the poet Pindar (fifth century B.C.E.) identified the ruler of the Islands of the Blest with Cronos (Saturn), the king of the golden Age, thus conflating blessed time with blessed place" (1997, 22) and that, earlier, "The Pythagoreans (sixth century B.C.E.) were the first Greek philosophers to advance the doctrine of immortality in the heavens" (ibid.).

30. Russell (1997) makes the very important point that, since Christianity preaches a resurrection of the body, a rejoining of body and soul, after Judgment Day, then "[t]he role of space and time in the concept of heaven is related to the presence of bodies there which requires that it be in some sense a place" (15).

The *Cloud* author emphasizes the "God as enclosure" view by foregrounding the idea that the seeking of a personal union with the Divine is initiated by God's grace. He explains:

For first þou wote wel þat when þou were leuyng in þe comoun degree of Cristen mens leuyng in companie of þi wordely freendes, it semeþ to me þat þe euerlasting loue of his Godheed ... kyndelid þi desire ful graciously, & fastnid bi it a lyame of longing, & led þee bi it in-to a more special state & forme of leuyng, to be a seruaunt of þe special seruauntes of his where þou mi ȝtest lerne to liue more specialy & more goostly in his seruise þan þou dedist, or miȝtest do, in þe comoun degree of leuyng bifore. ... Seest þou nouȝt how lystly & how graciously he haþ pulled þee to þe þrid degre & maner of leuing, þe whiche hiȝt Synguleer ? in þe which solitari forme & maner of leuyng þou maist lerne to lift up þe fote of þi loue, & step towardes þat state & degre of leuyng þat is parfite, & þe laste state of alle. (Cl. 1.13: 18–14: 15)[31]

Julian more directly expresses the notion of God as both the "enclosed" and the "enclosure" when she elucidates the reciprocal indwelling of God in the soul and the soul in God:

Hyely owe we to enjoye þat god dwellyth in oure soule; and more hyly we owe to enjoye that oure soule dwellyth in god. Oure soule is made to be goddys dwellyng place, and the dwellyng of oure soule is god, whych is vnmade. A hye vnderstandyng it is inwardly to se and to know that god, whych is oure maker, dwellyth in oure soule, and a hygher vnderstandyng it is and more, inwardly to se and to know oure soule that is made dwellyth in god in substance, of whych substance by god we be that we be. (LT. 54.561: 9–562: 16)[32]

---

31. "Firstly, you know well that when you were living in the common degree of Christians in the company of your worldly friends, it seems to me that the everlasting love of God ... kindled your desire very graciously, and fastened it by a leash of longing, and led you by it into a more special state and form of living, to be a servant of among his special servants, where you might learn to live more specially and more spiritually in his service than you did, or could do, in your former common degree of life. ... Do you not see how quietly and graciously he pulled you toward the third degree and manner of living, which is called Singular? In this solitary form and manner of living you can learn to lift up the feet of your love and step toward that perfect state and degree of living that is the last of all."

32. "We should highly rejoice that God dwells in our soul; and more highly we

This statement juxtaposes more than the idea of God in the soul and the soul in God. First, Julian adds that there is a mutual joy at the indwelling. "Made" and "vnmade" are also juxtaposed, though the idea of the soul as "made" denotes a materiality that is at odds with the general idea of the soul as a spiritual entity. Its spiritual nature is, in fact, reestablished when she aligns the "substance" of "oure soule" with the basic idea of being. Furthermore, while the notion of the soul as a dwelling place can approach Lefebvre's category of *representational space,* Julian's elucidation of the reciprocal indwelling, which is essentially the same as Rolle's and the *Cloud* author's elucidations of it, inverts Lefebvre's formulation. That is, the soul, which has no substance, becomes the symbol for the "solid" building of a dwelling, equal on the spiritual scale to a church or cathedral in the material world. However, a church is an observable *representational space* in which an unseen, uncreated God may dwell while a soul is an unseen, immaterial space. In fact, Julian overlays the whole notion of reciprocal indwelling with architectural imagery, thereby combining spiritual and physical aspects:

That wurschypfull cytte þat oure lorde Jhesu syttyth in, it is oure sensual-yte, in whych he is enclosyd; and oure kyndly substance is beclosyd in Jhesu, with þe blessyd soule of Criste syttyng in rest in the godhed. (LT. 56.572: 23–25)[33]

Thus, the metaphorical, spatially expressed, idea that God is both the container and the contained is given a tangible expression by Julian as she applies the architectural image of a "wurschypfull cytte" to the

---

should rejoice that our soul dwells in God. Our soul is made to be God's dwelling place, and the dwelling of our soul is God, who is uncreated. It is a heightened understanding to inwardly see and know that God, who is our creator, dwells in our soul, and an even higher understanding to inwardly see and know that our created soul dwells in God in substance, of which substance, through God, we are what we are."

33. "That honorable city that our Lord sits in, it is our sensuality, in which he is enclosed; and our natural substance is enclosed in Jesus, with the blessed soul of Christ sitting in rest in the Godhead."

soul. In a way, it is the reverse of Lefebvre's *representational space* that allows the endowment of physical structures with spiritual meaning. Here Julian endows the spiritual "structure" of the soul with a very physical (metaphorical) symbol. It seems, too, that the physical actuality of the enclosed life gave observable expression to the spiritual actuality and that architectural imagery has a particular role to play in the mystics' texts as it enables the translation of the spiritual undertaking and achievement into a tangible form.

PHYSICAL SPACE AND ARCHITECTURAL IMAGERY

Architectural imagery so abounds in religious texts that its scope and application have become increasingly interesting to scholars. Tessa Morrison (2006), for example, examines the symmetry of the heavenly Jerusalem as presented in Revelations and Christiana Whitehead (2003) demonstrates the importance and variety of application of such imagery in the medieval period. As Jill Mann points out,

> [T]he building is an important symbol of achievement and aspiration in both the Old and New Testament; there is the temple of Solomon, built as a resting-place for the Ark of God (I Kings vi–vii); there is Ezekiel's imaginary re-creation of the Solomonic temple in vision (Ezekiel xl–xliv) and there is the description of the heavenly Jerusalem in the Book of Revelation (xxi). (1994, 192)

The image of the temple (and, indeed, the Ark of the Covenant) features in the mystics' texts and will be discussed later in this section. Prominently, though, the *Cloud* author, Julian, and Rolle make use of other architectural images that are more representative of their own time. I refer, in particular, to the figure of the church. Spatially, church architecture reflected the idea that God was everywhere, both beyond the known universe and within each Christian. The medieval cathedral soared skyward, its spires pointing in the direction of heaven, God's transcendent dwelling place (Frayling 1995, 39). Enclosed within the aspiration, however, was the iconography of the human,

suffering, immanent God, Christ crucified. In contemplating the latter, one was drawn inevitably to the former, so that inside the cathedral medieval humanity experienced the power and mystery of God,
of Christ's sacrifice both on the cross on Calvary and daily repeated in the Eucharist. And God was understood to be truly present in
every church and within every soul. Thus, personal apprehension of
God was available to everyone, at least in theory.

Rolle intimates this idea when he points to the indwelling of God
by allusion to architectural imagery. In *The Fire of Love,* he aligns the
solitude of contemplation and the tabernacle and house of God when
he interpolates Psalms 43:3 and tells his reader that "Of whilk solitary
þe psalme in songe of lufe spekis sayand: 'I sall go in-to þe place of þe
meruellus tabernakyll, in-to þe hous of god'" (*Fire,* 1.14.30: 26–28).[34]
In *The Commandment* he advises the reader that

[Christ] es noght funden in þair lande þat lyves in fleschly lustes. Hys moder, when he was willed fra hyr, scho soght hym gretand arely and late ymang
hid kynredyn and hirs; bot scho fand hym noght, for al hyr sekyng, til at þe
laste scho come intil þe tempyl, and þare scho fand hym syttand ymange þe
maysters, herand and answerand. Swa behoves þe do, if þou wil fynd hym:
seke hym inwardly, in trouth and hope and charite of haly kyrk. (Com. 76:
113–77: 121)[35]

The "holy kyrk" refers primarily, of course, to the institution of the
Church. Rolle here implores his reader to keep stringently within
its guidelines. But the close juxtaposing of "tempyl" and "kyrk" also
evokes the concept of the actual edifice of a church. As the body is
also considered to be the "temple" of the soul and the soul, in turn,

34. "It is of the solitary that the psalmist in the songs of love speaks when he says:
I shall go into the place of the marvelous tabernacle, into the house of God."
35. "[Christ] is not found in the land of those who live lives of fleshly lusts. His
mother, when he strayed from her, sought him tearfully, early and late among his
kindred and hers; but she did not find him, despite all her seeking, until at last she
came to the temple, and there she found him sitting among the masters, listening and
answering. So you are required to do, if you will find him: seek him inwardly, in the
faith and hope and charity of holy Church."

the temple of God, there is here a suggestive alignment of edifice, body, soul, and humility (represented by the image of the humble "crib") as receptacles of God. Again, Rolle effects several juxtapositions of physical and spiritual notions here. Most obviously, he aligns the reader with Christ's mother in the shared role of seeker for Christ. Of course, Mary was seeking Christ in his physicality while the reader seeks for him spiritually. Likewise, the reader is advised that she, too, will find Christ, spiritually, by looking "inwardly." The adverb, however, points to both the focusing of attention on inner concerns and, equally, though more literally, to within the "haly kyrk" for, just as Christ was found within a temple, listening and teaching, Rolle intimates that Christ is also continuing to listen to the faithful and to teach them through the Church. The pairing of the two edifices, temple and church, offers the reader two solid physical images on which to focus as she turns her attention spiritually inward.

Rolle reinforces these physical, spiritual, and metaphorical architectural links by further recommending to the reader that she "Dyght þi sawle fayre, and make þarin a towre of lufe til Goddes sonn, and gar þi will be covaytous to receyve hym als gladly as þou walde be at þe commyng of a thyng þat þou lufed mast of al thyng" (Com. 79: 212–16).[36] Rolle's recommendation contains not only an alignment of the body-space and the soul-space with architectural imagery but also an inverted development of his earlier idea. That is, while initially the reader is required to visualize Christ within the temple and within the church, she is then required to metaphorically translocate Christ's position to her own soul and there to "construct" her own spiritual edifice—"a towre of lufe."

Julian implies a similar association between contemplative life and the enclosing of God within the soul and uses the image of a house in her comparison, when she says that

36. "Dress your soul fairly, and make therein a tower of love to God's son, and make your will as eager to receive him as you would be at the arrival of something that you loved most of all."

Our lorde seyde: I thangke the of thy servys and of thy travelle of thy yow-yth. And in thys my vuderstondyng was lyftyd vppe in to hevyn, wher I saw our lorde god as a lorde in his owne howse, whych lorde hayth callyd alle hys derewurthy frendes to a solempne fest. (LT. 14.351: 1–7)[37]

In the larger implication of the vision, of course, Julian is detailing the heavenly reward that she and others who have given service in their lives will receive in heaven. However, the vision, as are all of Ju-lian's revelations, is outside of time because she is seeing the joyful reward of heaven in the moment, during her lifetime, as she contem-plates God within her understanding.

The *Cloud* author uses the exact figure of the Ark of the Cove-nant to highlight the importance of the contemplative life. He de-scribes that "þis grace of contemplacion is figurid by þe Arke of þe Testament in þe olde Lawe, & þe worchers in þis grace ben figurid by hem þat most medelid hem aboute þis arke" (Cl. 71.126: 18–20).[38] He then draws an analogy between the soul and the temple, the jewels of which are contained within the Ark, stating that "mans soule . . . is þe goostly temple of God" (Cl. 71.126: 24).[39] That is, contemplation, like the Ark, holds within it the "jewels," the prize of the temple, the promise of God, just as the soul also holds God within it. The Ark, the soul, and contemplation are thus equally posited as the proper domain of God. In *The Book of Privy Counselling* the author takes the analogy further by explaining that

For þis same werk, ȝif it be verrely conceyuid, is þat reuerent affeccion & þe frute departid fro þe tre þat I speke of in þi lityl pistle of preier. Þis is þe cloude of unknowyng; þis is þat priue loue put in purete of spirit; þis is þe

---

37. "Our Lord said: I thank you for your service and the work of your youth. And in this my understanding was lifted up into heaven, where I saw our Lord God as a lord in his own house, a lord who has called all his dear friends to an important feast."

38. "This grace of contemplation is prefigured/metaphorically represents the Ark of the Covenant in the Old Testament, and the workers in this grace are prefigured by those who were concerned with the Ark."

39. "man's soul . . . is the spiritual temple of God."

Arke of þe Testament. Þis is Denis deuinite, his wisdom & his drewry, his
liȝty derknes & his unknown kunnynges. Þis is it þat settiþ þee in silence as
wele fro þouȝtes as fro wordes. (P.C. 154: 13–19)[40]

Here the "Ark" is the only material object acting as vehicle for the
figure in the signification series. While not exactly an architectural
image, the Ark is a three-dimensional container in which resides the
promise of God. Whitehead observes that

[t]his Ark … is also … the text of the *Cloud* itself—that thing which the
author puts literally into the hands of the reader. The text has become the
Ark of contemplation. It demands a meditative beholding. It has overcome
the unsuitable linearity of the medium in which it finds itself by reconven-
ing as a three-dimensional vessel inherently suited to the indwelling of God.
(1998, 205)

That is, the text, like the Ark, is a material representation of the spiritual goal. Some internalization of the text's contents could be seen, then,
as part of the practice of contemplation and could assist the reader toward achieving perfect contemplation.

Denis Renevey points to an expanded application of architectural
imagery in the practice of contemplation when he explains that

[b]uilding imagery features pervasively in devotional and mystical writings.
In the *Didascalicon,* Hugh of St. Victor compares divine scripture to a building with special reference to its foundation and structure. Richard of St. Victor follows on by setting up an architectonic of the mystical life based on the
monumental ark of the covenant. Mnemonic visualization of the building
allows for a careful memorization of the six degrees of the contemplative
life. (1997, 55)[41]

---

40. "For this work, if it is correctly understood, is the reverent love and the fruit
separated from the tree that I spoke of in your little epistle of prayer. This is 'the cloud
of unknowing'; this is the secret love that comes from a purity of spirit; this is the
Ark of the Covenant. This is Dionysius's theology, his wisdom, and his dowry, his
shining darkness and his unknowing knowing. This is that which makes you silent,
far from thoughts and words."

41. Rebecca Leuchak (1997) refers to Cicero's *Ad Herennium,* which influenced

This memory function seems to be particularly discernible in the manner in which Rolle, the *Cloud* author, and Julian categorize and group their main ideas for ease of assimilation by their readers.

Rolle, in particular, has frequent recourse to categorization. For example, in addition to detailing the hierarchies of the nine orders of angels for his reader, Rolle also categorizes all his epistles in some way. *Ego Dormio, The Commandment,* and *The Form of Living* all feature the progressive degrees of love: "insuperable," "inseparable," and "syngulere."[42] He also makes the usual division between the active and the contemplative life but further divides contemplative life into a lower and a higher part. In *The Form of Living,* Rolle offers "seuen experimentes er, þat a man be in charite" (114: 212),[43] "seuen gyftes of þe hali Gaste" (116: 1),[44] and advises of "thre wrechednes" (85: 2)[45] that bring sinners to hell. As Rolle is writing for enclosed, solitary women, the quantitative divisions are, very probably, in part, an aid to memory with a view to assisting these women in structuring their daily life and prayers.

Such categorizations, while not necessarily presented in architectural images, nevertheless find a resonance with architectural notions in the theories of Erwin Panofsky. He posits a link between text and architecture in the form of the particular medieval habit of thought termed "Scholasticism." Panofsky begins his argument by noting that

---

medieval metaphysicians to adopt " . . . the physical, architectural structures and spaces as their most common paradigm for memory. According to Cicero's technique and medieval practice, memorization worked through a series of 'places' or rooms into which the individual was mentally able to enter and navigate. This mentally constructed place for storing memories was a mapped and comfortable terrain that could be visited at will, time and again" (357 n. 25). For a thorough study of the memory section of *Ad Herrenium,* see Yates (1966).

42. Literally, "impossible to surmount," "unable to be separated (from)," and "singular/exceptional." In practice, Rolle uses these terms with much wider connotations to apply to categories of the contemplative life.

43. "seven tests . . . that a man is in charity"

44. "seven gifts of the Holy Spirit"

45. "three [sorts of] wickedness"

artistic perspective did not emerge until around the time of Giotto and Duccio, suggesting that it only gained true currency between 1330 and 1340 (1951, 16). He stresses, though, that perspective is not only a device of the two-dimensional arts but that sculpture and architecture were becoming, by the later Middle Ages, representative of a "comprehensive picture space" (17). He takes the idea of comprehensiveness even further, positing a direct cause-and-effect relationship between Scholasticism and gothic art, particularly religious architecture. Panofsky notes that gothic architecture was prepared in Benedictine monasteries (22), its formation there having been affected by the *habitus* of Scholasticism. He summarizes the reason for the appearance of this alignment thus:

Like the High Scholastic *Summa,* the High Gothic cathedral aimed, first of all, at "totality" and therefore tended to approximate, by synthesis as well as elimination, one perfect and final solution. . . . In its imagery the high Gothic cathedral sought to embody the whole of Christian knowledge, theological, moral, natural and historical, with everything in its place and that which no longer found its place, suppressed. (44–45)

Lefebvre is contemptuous of such an alignment, arguing that a habit of thought cannot have begotten gothic architecture. He finds something "problematic" in Panofsky's conviction that the "spatial arrangement of the Gothic church . . . 'reproduces' [the *Summa Theologiae*], embodying as it does a reconciling of opposites, a tripartite totality and the organizational equilibrium of a system whose component parts are themselves homologues" (258). The main problem seems to be that Panofsky is equating visual perspective and spatial understanding. In the Middle Ages, as now, there was a gap between (in Lefebvrian terms) *representations of space* and *representational spaces.* That is, the world of art was representational and, therefore, not required to obey the "rules" of the conceptions of space that "are shot through with knowledge" (Lefebvre, 41). Lefebvre, however, does credit Panofsky with "discovering" the idea of a "visual logic," though he considers that Panofsky did not take the idea far enough.

Lefebvre therefore expands the idea to involve a "production of space" and "not merely a space of ideas, an ideal space, but a social and mental space. An emergence. A decrypting of the space that went before" (260). Such an emergence, according to Lefebvre, would involve a degree of subsuming of the oral world for the visual. It is in this context that Lefebvre understands the advent of the gothic cathedral—as a production of a luminous space, one that admits more light, thereby causing "the dark" and "the realm of death . . . to retreat before the intense onslaught of visualisation" (261). Such a production, Lefebvre argues, was the inevitable reversal of late antiquity's obsession with the realm of the dead and the cult of saints (254ff.).[46] Although this is a proposition of enormous implications, the majority of which are beyond the scope of this current work, I draw here only on Lefebvre's general notion of reversal in order to suggest that mysticism, too, shows a certain reversal of "dark" and "light" and an exchange of "encrypted" spaces in the physical world for "luminous" spiritual spaces. Initially, and most clearly, this exchange is apparent in the assuming of the solitary life by the mystics. That is, in becoming a contemplative, an individual exchanged the apparently "light" material world for the "dark" interior of a solitary cell. For individuals embracing such a life, however, the perspective was inverted. That is, though it might appear that they were "dead" to the world, they were "alive" to spiritual possibilities. The dark enclosures, therefore, were spiritually luminous places.

I want now to explore this exchange of the worldly for the spiritual, and the reversal of the notions of dark and light, by considering Julian's, Rolle's, and the *Cloud* author's explicit and implicit understanding of the roles of their bodies in the mystical process.

---

46. See Peter Brown (1981) for an examination of the connection between the Christian church and the dead, their tombs, and their relics in the western Mediterranean in late antiquity.

THE SPACE OF BODIES

The notion of "body" is central to a spatial consideration of mysticism as it is the body that contains the soul, and the body that is also the vehicle or conduit through which mystical experience is filtered and subsequently conveyed back to the public arena. Whether that body is male or female is, obviously, an issue of considerable importance. Much valuable recent work has focused on the points of intersection and difference between the religious experiences of medieval men and women. Since Roberta Gilchrist's seminal study (1994) on the archaeology of places inhabited by religious women, scholarly interest in space as a gendered entity has also grown. However, as I am unable to do justice to the scope of this scholarship and as my interest here is more directly concerned with the body in mystical space (of which gendered physical space is only one aspect), I refer the reader to the recent and thorough studies on the issue by, in particular, Liz Herbert McAvoy (2002, 2005).

Julian, Rolle, and the *Cloud* author all consider the body to be of importance in the contemplative life, stressing that it is neither to be abused nor overzealously mortified. Of the three, the *Cloud* author most minimizes the role of the body. His approach to mystical experience, the apophatic mode, makes such minimizing appropriate. That is, if the contemplative is "to forȝete alle þe creat[u]res þat euer God maad & þe werkes of hem" (Cl. 3.16: 6–7),[47] then the body must also be forgotten. Obviously, the body cannot be completely ignored, so what the author seems to mean is that the contemplative should redirect his focus from bodily to spiritual concerns. The dangers of paying too much attention to the body include the possibility that certain bodily reactions may be mistaken for true mystical experience when the *Cloud* author stresses that contemplation is always spiritual work. Thus he urges his reader that "for godes loue gouerne þee

47. "to forget all the creatures that God ever made and all their works/actions"

discreetly in body & in soule, & gete þee þin hele as mochel as þou mayst" (Cl. 41.80: 17–19).[48] At the same time, he acknowledges the body as God's creation and sees the interrelatedness of the body and the soul and their dual role in serving God. Additionally, the author expresses the belief that the body, as well as the soul, will share in the heavenly reward. He acknowledges the body's role both in the service of God in the physical space and its reward in soul-space when he says,

> I sey not þis for I wil þat þou leue any tyme, ȝif þou be stirid for to preie wiþ þi mouþ, or for to brest oute, for habundaunce of deuocion in þi spirit, for to speke vnto God as vnto man, & sey som good worde as þou felist þee sterid. . . . Nay, God forbede þat I schuld departe þat god haþ couplid, þe body & þe spirit, for god wil be seruid wiþ body & soule, boþe togeders, as seemly is, & rewarde man his mede in blis boþe in body & in soule. (Cl. 48.90: 11–19)[49]

The *Cloud* author, however, primarily instructs his reader to

> put a cloude of forȝetyng bineþ þee, bitwix þee & alle þe cretures þat euer ben maad. . . . As ofte as I sey "alle þe creatures þat euer ben maad," as ofte I mene, not only þe self creatures, bot also alle þe werkes & þe condicions of þe same creatures. (Cl. 5.24: 3–11)[50]

Though, on the surface, this instruction seems to suggest the putting aside of all material associations, the direction is not really a dismiss-

---

48. "for God's love, look after yourself carefully, in body and in soul, and keep as well as you can"

49. "I am not saying that I never want you to pray vocally if you are so stirred, nor to break out, because of the abundance of devotion in your spirit, and to speak about God to others and to say the words you feel stirred to say. . . . No . . . God forbid that I should divide what God has joined, the body and the spirit, for God wants to be served with body and soul, both together, as is right, and to reward man in heavenly bliss, both in body and in soul."

50. "put a cloud of forgetting beneath you, between you and all creatures that have ever been made. . . . Whenever I say 'all creatures that have ever been made' I always mean not only those creatures, but also all the actions and conditions of those same creatures."

al of the physical when it is remembered that the successful putting aside of material needs by the contemplative can only be accomplished with a level of assistance from others, as the *Cloud* author advises his reader:

For trist stedfastly þou, what-so-euer þat þou be þat trewly tornest þee fro þe woreld vnto God, þat one of þe two God schal sende þee, wiþ-outen besines of þi-self: & þat is, ouþer habundaunce of nessessaries, or strengþe in body & pacience in spirite to bere nede. (Cl. 23.57: 11–15)[51]

Here he is suggesting that others are somehow modeled in charity to help those already practicing the contemplative life. This therefore partly obviates the need for bodily attention by the contemplative him- or herself. The approach reemphasizes the mystic's place within a society and shows that, when others provide the necessities of life for the recluse, they are expressing confidence and claiming a share in the work of his or her enterprise. As I will discuss in Chapter Two, this sharing has implications in the social space.

Rolle's approach to the body is more straightforward. He stresses moderation in eating and drinking, warning particularly against excessive abstinence, stating that

with-outyn comparison treuly more mede sall he be worthy with songfull ioy prayand, behaldand, redeand & þinkand well bot discretely etand, þen if he with-outen þis euermore suld fast, brede allone or herbys if he suld ete & besily suld pray & rede. (*Fire*, 1.12.25: 38–26: 2)[52]

Rolle is more emphatic, however, about the need for sexual continence. He warns the reader to "Behald, þou wrechyd lityll man, how in lykynge off fleschly lust of endles dampnacion cruelte slepis" (*Fire*,

51. "For you can trust absolutely that because you have has truly turned from the world to God, that God will send you one of two things, without any effort on your part: and that is, either an abundance of [life's] necessities, or the strength in body and patience in spirit to bear the need."

52. "Truly, without comparison, he will be more worthy of reward who prays with joyful song and contemplates, reads, and thinks with discretion, than if he was constantly fasting on bread alone, or eating only herbs and busily praying and reading."

1.29.61: 15–16),[53] having already cautioned that "No þing sothely is more perlius, fowler, more stynkard to man, þan to put hys mynde in womans lufe & hir desyr als blistfull rest. After þe deed soyn no meruayll it waxis foull, þat before he desird so grete blys with mikyll angwys" (*Fire*, 1.25.53: 19–21).[54] In this formulation, Rolle expresses an inversion of material and spiritual aspiration and the consequences of searching for "blistfull rest" in something physical that is, ultimately, transitory.

Nevertheless, in *The Commandment* Rolle tells the reader to

ordane þi prayng and þi wakyng and þi fastyng þat it be in discrecion, noght over mykel na over litel. . . . seke mare to lufe hym þan do any penance. (Com. 75: 79–76: 83)[55]

The recommendation to bodily discretion in preference to any form of extreme bodily stringencies is echoed in *The Fire of Love* when Rolle states

Hym þerfore it behoues þat in godis lufe will synge & syngandly lufe & byrne, in wildernes to be, & in to mykill abstinence not to lyfe, nor to be gifyn on any wyse to superfluite or waste. Neuer-þe-les bettyr it wer to hym in lityll þing vnknawyng mesure to passe, whils he with gude ententt dose it to sustene kynde, þen if he for to mikyll fastynge began to fayll & for febilnes of body he myght not synge. (*Fire*, 1.12.25: 28–34)[56]

53. "Behold, you wretched little man, how delighting in fleshly lust puts to sleep [thoughts of] the cruelty of damnation."

54. "Nothing is more dangerous, more foul, more putrid to man, than to put his whole mind toward a woman's love and to desire her as his blissful rest. After the deed is over, it soon seems foul, that which he earlier had desired as his supreme bliss with so much anguish."

55. "Organize your praying and your waking and fasting with discretion, not too much, not too little . . . seek more to love him than to do any penance."

56. "It therefore behoves him who in God's love wants to sing and burn and rejoice in love, to be in the wilderness/(solitude), and not to give into too much abstinence, nor to be given in any way to excess or waste. Nevertheless, it is better for him to exceed his measure a little out of ignorance, if he does so with the good intent of sustaining his life, than if he were to begin to falter because of too much fasting and, [as a result] of feebleness of body, to be unable to sing."

That is, it is preferable to treat the body kindly so that it can do that which it entered solitude to do: love God and work toward the experience of the heavenly heat and song.

Julian, approaching the writing of her text from an experiential rather than a didactic stance, makes no suggestions as to how her readers should deal with their own bodies and, in fact, makes no reference to her own bodily approach to God beyond describing the progress of her illness.[57] In view of this, it could be suggested that Julian felt, as is the case in the *Cloud* author's approach, that specific reference to the body, either in the text or by "writing" the body through visible mortification, focuses undue attention on the body. Instead, Julian diverts the focus from her body onto the suffering body of Christ. That is, as her own body "dies" in strata, first the lower, then the upper, she becomes attuned to particular aspects of Christ's suffering. Her body, in fact, is dying in the ultimate *imitatio Christi,* reflected across the small space between her and the crucifix on which she gazes. Simultaneously, though, she becomes "alive" to spiritual understanding. Her body here exemplifies the edifice of mystical encounter, in a prefigurement of her anchoritic life, enclosed, dead to the world, but alive to Christ. Julian's body here is part of the creation she has witnessed previously as being as small as a hazelnut and, in diminishing her awareness of herself and her body, she seems to be honoring her expressed conviction that "yf I looke syngulery to my selfe I am ry3t nought; but in generall I am, I hope, in onehede of cheryte with alle my evyn cristen. For in thys oned stondyth the lyfe of alle mankynd that shalle be savyd" (LT. 9.322: 9–11).[58] Therefore, Julian remains, and we with her, a careful observer. Certainly, though,

---

57. My view here seems to be supported by Denise Baker's opinion that "Julian herself does not . . . allude to this 'outer rule' governing behaviour in either version of A Book of Showings, perhaps because she is reporting her own experience rather than composing a guide for other anchorites" (1993, 150).

58. "If I look individually at myself I am nothing; but in general, I am, I hope, in charitable union with all my fellow Christians. For in this unity resides the life of all mankind who shall be saved."

it is the body—more precisely, a bodily illness—that provides the entry into her mystical experiences. As I have said, Julian does give details of the effects that illness has on her body as it takes her to the very point of death. And, in reflection, it is the revelations of Christ's own sufferings that effect a return to health for Julian. While Julian's illness and its relation to her revelations are considered in detail in Chapter Six, it is appropriate to note here that Julian, in requesting a bodily illness some years before her revelations, can be regarded as having possessed, from a young age, a deep understanding of the role of the body as a conduit to God and mystical experience. Thus she foregrounds the detailing of her revelations with the declaration that "[I] desyred before thre gyftes by the grace of god. The fyrst was mynd of the passion. The secund was bodilie sicknes. The thurde was to haue of godes gyfte thre woundys" (LT. 2.285: 4–6).[59] Julian further explains that it was the realization that her request for a sickness had been granted that prompted her to reiterate her former request for a "mynd of the passion." This request is duly granted, precipitating the complete series of revelations. Julian's body can be considered, spatially, as a *site* of mystical experience, that is, as a site of suffering in reflection of Jesus' own suffering. In Wertheim's schema, Julian could be viewed as representing a true fusion of body-space and soul-space.

The conception of the body as site is corroborated, perhaps surprisingly so, in Bakhtin's discussion of the Rabelaisian world, in which he draws attention to the *grotesque body,* a body divided into strata.[60] The word *grotesque* derives from the word *grotto,* meaning a natural covered opening in the earth. Bakhtin states that, in his for-

59. "[I] had desired before three gifts by the grace of God. The first was thoughts of the Passion. The second was bodily sickness. The third was to have, as God's gift, three wounds."

60. Laurie A. Finke's (1992) discussion of the "grotesque mystical body" is concerned particularly with a consideration of the relationship of the "grotesque body" and "the discourse of late medieval mysticism as it exhibits at least some women's ability to speak and be heard within a patriarchal and forthrightly misogynistic society" (77). As such it is not of direct relevance to my interest here.

mulation, "[d]egradation digs a bodily grave for a new birth. . . . Grotesque realism is the fruitful earth and womb. It is always conceiving" (1984/1968, 21). Further, "the grotesque body is not separated from the rest of the world. It is not a closed, completed unit; it is unfinished, outgrows itself, transgresses its own limits. The stress is laid on those parts of the body that are open to the outside world . . . the open mouth, the genital organs, the breasts, the phallus, the pot belly, the nose" (26). Ironically, the private space of mystical experience came to imitate the natural grotto—frequently a dark, dank, small cell, partially hidden from public gaze. But, I contend, entry into this space was for the purpose of reversing the grotesque: those apertures that are open to a relationship with the world become narrowed, if not completely closed, in the mystical life. The mouth takes in less food, the nose breathes the air of a circumscribed abode, and copulation, childbirth, and subsequently breastfeeding are curtailed.[61] In so doing the mystics simultaneously deny the body and embody the mystical experience. That is, in closing the apertures, the lower stratum, and its grotesque representation, they were exhibiting a life lived in an upward direction. They were indeed closed to the world but only in order to be open to spiritual possibilities. They redirected their fruitfulness and the growth inherent in the grotesque body into a spiritual growth and rebirth. Their fecundity translated into the exemplary form that the mystics were able to eventually present to the public world for the public's own edification.

Julian, in fact, makes specific reference to the bodily function of elimination, explaining that

A man goyth vppe ryght and the soule[62] of his body is sparyde as a purse fulle feyer. And whan it is tyme of his nescessery it is openyde and sparyde

61. The descriptions of some of these activities, particularly breastfeeding, in the works of (generally female) continental medieval mystics, can be understood, in terms of the reversal I am suggesting, as a transference of these bodily activities to an entirely spiritual space.

62. In an editorial note about Julian's use of *soule* here Colledge and Walsh point

ayen fulle honestly. And that it is he that doyth this, it is schewed ther wher he seyth he comyth downe to vs to the lowest parte of oure nede. For he hath no dispite of that he made. (LT. 6.306: 35–307: 39)[63]

While, on the one hand, this seems a surprising inclusion in a mystical and didactic text, on the other hand, it can be viewed also as a subtle reversal of the grotesque in that a spiritual lesson is implicit. That is, by emphasizing the idea that God is with us always, even in the "lowest part of oure nede," that "lowest nede" is raised in status from an expression of a basic function of the physical world to a function that God has made.[64]

Mysticism, therefore, perhaps can be regarded not as a rejection of the society and the culture that produced it but, more, as a symbolic reversal of the inherently grotesque within the culture and a conscious or unconscious exchange of body-space for soul-space during the lifetime. Ironically, however, the means to eternal life for Christians, in general, is via the Incarnation, death, and Resurrection of Jesus Christ and this, too, can be viewed as sharing some of the characteristics of grotesque realism. The difference for the medieval mystics and their readers, of course, is that death for them did not mean a return to the earth and the reabsorption into the natural cycle, but a liberation from the physical space to the final soul-space of heaven. Ultimately, then, just as Bakhtin stresses that "the image of death in medieval and Renaissance grotesque is a more or less funny monstrosity" (51), so mystics, like religion as a whole, were also able to

---

out that it derives from "<OE sufol, '(cooked, digested) food' [and that] NED, MED show that this word was rare, doubtless in Julian's time obsolescent, perhaps because of conflict with its homophone, <OE sawol, 'soul' (as most translators of the text have erroneously rendered it)" (306 n. 35).

63. "A man walks upright and the food of his body is stored as in a well-made purse. And when it is the time of his necessity it is opened and then stored again simply. And that it is God who does this is shown when he says that he comes down to us in the lowest of our needs. For he has no distaste for what he has made."

64. See Liz Herbert McAvoy (2002) for a discussion of the particular feminine imagery and implications of Julian's statement here.

laugh at death, putting their trust in eternal life, subsuming the grotesque body's dictate that death, and the return to the earth, are the only means for renewal.

Ancrene Wisse, an early thirteenth-century text that offers advice to three sisters embarking on the contemplative life, prefigures something of this inversion of light and dark, of life and death. The *Ancrene Wisse* author was at particular pains to make the connection between the anchoresses' choice to follow Christ and their own cramped living conditions. He points out that "twa þing limpeð to ancre. nearowðe & bitterness. For wombe is nearow wununge. þer ure lauerd wes reclus" (f.102a.25–27).[65] In this, the author is drawing an analogy between the lifestyle and living space of the anchoresses and Christ's willing acceptance of humanity with the concomitant assurance of death. Thus the narrowness and confinement of the womb, the tomb, and the anchorhold are all invoked and linked. Catherine Innes-Parker enlarges the link by noting that "[t]he Virgin's womb is an image for the heart and soul of the reader, who prays that she might feel Christ stir in her by divine grace, as Mary felt him stir when he took flesh and blood in her womb" (2005, 175).

It is a juxtaposition of life and death that is a clear reflection of the women's own situation—ostensibly dead to the world but "alive" to spiritual possibilities just as Christ was alive after death. The author takes the analogy further, adding, "Tis word marie as ich of te ofte iseid spealeð bitternesse. ȝef ȝe þenne i nearow stude þolieð bitternesse. ȝe beoð his feolahes reclus as he wes i Marie wombe" (f.102a27–b2).[66] The analogy here is circular: Jesus had to be first confined in Mary's

---

65. "two things belong to an anchorite: narrowness and bitterness. For a womb is a narrow dwelling and there our Lord was a recluse." This and subsequent quotations from *Ancrene Wisse* are from MS. Corpus Christi, Cambridge 402, ed. J. R. R. Tolkien, EETS o.s. 249 (Oxford: Oxford University Press, 1962). The translations are mine.

66. "This word 'Mary,' as I have often said, means 'bitterness.' If you then, in a narrow place, suffer bitterness, you are his fellow recluses, just as he was in Mary's womb."

womb to attest to, and define, his humanity. The anchoresses, too, are similarly confined in their anchorhold and their human existence is thus redefined. But in their anchorhold their humanity is, in a way, given up for a spiritual goal whereas Jesus' humanity was taken on in the womb for the purpose of bestowing a spiritual reward on humanity: ultimate redemption. Certainly Mary conceived in bitterness insofar as Jesus was born only to die. But through his death, spiritual rebirth was made possible, just as the anchoresses' "death" to the world contains the possibility of spiritual rebirth. Renevey finds a spatial parallel in several of the anchoritic works, referring to the authors' strategy of drawing attention to "the geography of the reclusorium" (1997, 55) and pointing to the way in which "[t]he *reclusorium* imagery is recalled in several instances to maintain this identification with the most important episodes of the humanity of Jesus. The audience is made to feel the comfort of the *reclusorium* in comparison with the coming of Christ on earth, in a house without walls" (57). A reflection of Renevey's idea is found in the texts of Rolle, the *Cloud* author, and Julian. Their use of architectural imagery frequently draws attention to the connection between their own physical situation and the spiritual enclosure of God within their souls and their souls within God. Just as in the anchoritic literature, "Jesus becomes the symbol of the anchoritic life, devoid of any earthly comfort" (ibid.), so God in the soul and Jesus in his humanity are presented as symbols for the physical solitude of the mystics and their specific readers.

For the three mystics, like the anchoresses, the human body is thus both necessary and unnecessary and mystical experience is both embodied and disembodied: embodied in that it requires a body as initiator and conduit but disembodied in that the experience is spiritual, not physical. The simultaneous embodiment and disembodiment of mystical experience points to a conception of space that is both reflective of the Aristotelian view of space as a receptacle, in that the body is the receptacle and site of mystical experience, and its negative image in that it is not contained within a definable space. In this way the mystics' experiences can be considered to be encompassing of multiple spatial possibilities.

In their mystical space Richard Rolle, the *Cloud* author, and Julian of Norwich remained a visible part of their society. In the writing and disseminating of their mystical experiences for others' edification, they also retained an active role in society. An awareness of the necessity of their participation in the social world was an essential principle that informed their mystical space. A consideration of the interconnection between the social and the mystical space is the focus of the next chapter.

Chapter Two

SOCIAL SPACE

> *While analyzing past ages we are too often obliged to "take each epoch at its word," that is, to believe its official ideologists. We do not hear the voice of the people and cannot find and decipher its pure unmixed expression. All the acts of world history were performed before a chorus of laughing people. Without hearing the chorus we cannot understand the drama as a whole.*
>
> *(Mikhail Bakhtin)*

MEDIEVAL SOCIETY AND MYSTICISM FROM A CONTEMPORARY PERSPECTIVE

Richard Rolle, Julian of Norwich, and the *Cloud* author did not live and die in a vacuum. Their extant texts bear witness to lives lived in dedication to God, but these lives were firmly rooted in medieval society.[1] Like the medieval physical space, the space of that society exhibited, at least on the surface, a pattern of order and conformity. Within that overarching order, however, we can assume that, as in all societies, past and present, a great variety of ideas and actions found

---

1. Some reference will also be made to contemporaneous biographical material on Rolle contained in the *Officium* written shortly after his death by his followers who were hoping for his canonization. As such, the material is strongly hagiographical in mode and is treated therefore with some reservations.

expression. Social space refers to that space in which social ideas develop and social actions and interactions take place. It is the space where, individually and collectively, people "develop, give expression to themselves, and encounter prohibitions [and in which] they perish" (Lefebvre 1991/1974, 34).

Social space is vitally replicated in all strata of the conceptual *mise en abîme* of mystical space, providing a context in which Rolle's, the *Cloud* author's, and Julian's religious beliefs were shaped, in which their mystical insights were gained, and in which their texts were produced, disseminated, and received. The acceptance of the social space as influential in the formation and expression of mystical experience does not negate the possibility of that experience being authentic. Peter Moore pertinently observes, for instance, that

[w]hile it is undoubtedly the case that a mystic's beliefs and expectations are likely to affect the nature both of his experience and his report of his experience, this influence constitutes no more of a problem in the case of mysticism than it does in the case of any other form of experience. The mystic's doctrinal background should, therefore, be seen as a key to his experience rather than a door which shuts us off from it. (Quoted in Baker 1994, 7)

Moore's summation points to a way of viewing medieval mysticism that admits of both its posited transcendent aspects and the possibility of social influence on the expression of mysticism. Equally, Lefebvre's theory of space as a social production is enlightening when applied to medieval mysticism despite it obvious prohibition against the possibility of "real" spiritual experience. The theory becomes useful when its basic premise is inverted rather than dismissed. Such inversion is possible because the concept of space is malleable, and therefore it is equally valid to claim that social space is an aspect of mystical space as it is for Lefebvre to claim, for example, that spiritual experience is a product of social space.

Lefebvre bases his theory on a stated awareness that, currently, space is divided conceptually into three separately apprehended "fields": the physical, the mental, and the social.[2] His aim has been to redefine space so that those separate fields are all regarded as components of a socially produced space.[3] I do not agree with this formulation in its entirety, preferring to regard space as multifaceted and accepting, in line with the mystics (and many physicists), that there is a space beyond discernible space, a space that cannot be "produced" in practice but only intimated in theory or spiritually experienced. Furthermore, the positing of spiritual space as a social production is an already biased view as it admits of God as an idea only and effaces any possibility of God as an actuality. However, by inverting the conception and placing social space "within" physical space, God as an idea and God as an actuality can be equally accommodated. Therefore, my view is the inverse of Lefebvre's when he considers that

following the physical model [of the physicists, and the theological model] would prevent a theory of societies from using a number of useful procedures, notably the separation of levels, domains, and regions. Physical theory's search for unity puts all the emphasis on the bringing together of disparate elements. It might therefore serve as a guardrail but never as a paradigm. (13)

That is, I believe that Lefebvre's theory of space as a social production offers a useful "guardrail" for containing and providing access to the everyday lived space of the mystics but that it could not act as a paradigm if applied to a concept like spiritual or mystical space. Certainly

2. Lefebvre makes no attempt to engage with the theories of contemporary physics or cosmology except to comment that he regards the physical theories of astronomer Fred Hoyle as being of some relevance to his project since they take the production of energy into account. While it may be appropriate that Lefebvre's work is avowedly socially driven, such an approach assumes that social space "produces" (concepts of) physical space whereas physicists and cosmologists may easily argue the reverse.

3. Stephen Hawking and other prominent physicists have been working on the development of a "unified theory" of space. However, their project is concerned with a theoretical synthesis of the theory of relativity and of quantum theory, and therefore, in Lefebvre's formulation, would represent a limited theory in that they have confined their research to the physical field of space. For an elaboration of the search for a unified theory, see Hawking (1988).

Lefebvre's theory can be applied at the level of allowing that the expression of mysticism might be a social production but such allowance need not invalidate the content of the experience.

Similarly, Pierre Bourdieu's notion of *habitus* seems to me to offer an insight into the way that mystics were "products" of Christian society and, equally, unique contributors to that society. Bourdieu defines *habitus* as

> systems of durable, transposable dispositions, structured structures predisposed to function as structuring structures, that is, as principles which generate and organize practices and representations that can be objectively adapted to their outcomes without presupposing a conscious aiming at ends. (1990, 53)[4]

Expressed more simply, *habitus* is "an embodiment of structure," which Bourdieu believes enables the transcendence of "the dichotomy of objectivism and subjectivism" (Nash 1999, 176).[5] Even more

---

4. Bourdieu did not "invent" the concept of *habitus*. It was first suggested by Aristotle and thoroughly applied by the medieval Schoolmen, most notably Thomas Aquinas, who used it in reference to certain dispositions and tendencies, particularly in regard to the choosing of sin or goodness. (See *Summa Theologiae*, ed. Timothy McDermott [London: Methuen, 1989], 102–3.) John B. Thompson (1991), in his introduction to Bourdieu's *Language and Symbolic Power*, remarks that "Bourdieu uses [*habitus*] in a distinctive and quite specific way . . . [as a] set of *dispositions* which incline agents to act and react in certain ways" (12).

5. Thompson (1991) explains that "[b]y 'subjectivism' Bourdieu means an intellectual orientation to the social world which seeks to grasp the way the world appears to the individuals who are situated within it. Subjectivism presupposes the possibility of some kind of immediate apprehension of the lived experience of others and it assumes that this apprehension is by itself a more or less adequate form of knowledge about the social world. . . . By 'objectivism' Bourdieu means an intellectual orientation to the social word which seeks to construct the objective relations which structure practices and representations. Objectivism presupposes a break with immediate experience; it places the primary experiences of the social world in brackets and attempts to elucidate the structures and principles upon which primary experience depends but which it cannot directly grasp. . . . Bourdieu's view is that both subjectivism and objectivism are inadequate intellectual orientations but that the latter is less inadequate than the former" (11).

simply, Bourdieu's *habitus* is now frequently expressed as "a feel for the rules of the game" (see, e.g., Jenkins 1992), an unconscious understanding of the way in which societal structures predispose societal members, individually and collectively, toward certain social practices. *Habitus* therefore operates at an unconscious level but the results of its operation are often apparent.

When Bourdieu's formulation is applied, medieval Christian mysticism can be understood as having its formation and expression in deeply ingrained Christian ideas and practices. And though the personal experience of God may be unique, its communication back to society (in the form of texts) contributes to the continuance and enlargement of Christian *habitus*.

Likewise, Caroline Bynum's (1982) case for regarding medieval society as one based on groups rather than individuality, on conformity not opposition, is one way in which the social space of mysticism can be regarded as being linked to social production. For example, the explosion in the numbers of religious houses and vocations to the religious life in England in the twelfth century, and to the anchoritic life during the thirteenth and fourteenth centuries, all seem to lend support to Bynum's proposition. Clay (1914) gives evidence of the existence of about one thousand hermits and anchorites in England between 1125 and 1531. Similarly, Pelphrey (1982) offers evidence for numerous occupied anchorholds in Norwich around the time of Julian's enclosure. Elkins (1988) notes a period of expansion in the numbers of female religious houses in twelfth-century England, while Lawrence (1989) gives details of increased monastery populations. No doubt a variety of social factors contributed to the burgeoning of religious vocations but principal among these must be the high level of monetary and social support extended to religious houses, not just by the wealthy, but by all levels of society. Ann Warren's study of English anchorites and their patrons gives ample evidence of the range and conditions of support given to those pursuing an anchoritic lifestyle. More generally, however, Warren points out that "anchorites [existed] within a framework that [bound] them to other individuals and entities found worthy of medieval charity" (1985, 127–28).

Of course, religious, especially conventual, life had always had an appeal. The establishment, by St. Benedict, of a rule for coenobitic life in the early sixth century was really the codification of the increasing practice of ascetic communal living among early Christian groups (Herrin 1987).

The idea of Christian society continued to exert its influence in the Middle Ages with religious life considered to be of benefit not just to the individual undertaking it but to all Christians. Bynum's suggestion that monks were "the vicarious worshippers for all society" (1982, 9) finds an echo, I suggest, in the mystics' relationship with their social world. This relationship will be shown to be one of reciprocation insofar as society "makes room" for mystical experience while mystics "give back" something of the experience to society. The three mystics' texts stand as the clearest testimony to this reciprocity. However, this reciprocity did not obviate the mystics' unique place in medieval society, poised, as it were, between the material and the spiritual worlds. I will suggest that they inhabited the medieval equivalent of a Foucauldian *heterotopia,* a term that Michel Foucault uses to refer to places that "are outside of all place, even though it might be possible to indicate their location in reality . . . [and which are] a sort of simultaneously mythic and real contestation of space in which we live" (1986/1967, 24).[6]

Within the heterotopic space, the mystics may well have been visible to the public, though their mystical endeavors remained pri-

6. The idea of *heterotopias* was first presented in a lecture given by Foucault in 1967. The lecture was neither published nor otherwise released into the public domain until after Foucault's death. This translation (1986) of the lecture represents the first public textual release of the concept. Foucault does not apply the concept of *heterotopias* to any medieval phenomena. However, he does apply the term broadly to include both "primitive" and "modern" societies, including such diverse places as cemeteries, boarding schools, brothels, trains, and vacation villages as examples of *heterotopias.*

vate until they were revealed via the text. In their visibility the mystics were exemplars for society in the same way that Peter Brown suggests that the early saints were both imitable and inimitable (1999).[7] The mystics, however, though exemplary in their capacity as vicarious worshippers for society, occupied a spatial position that was liminal. Arnold van Gennep's theory of *rites of passage* will be employed, in part, to elucidate the mystics' negotiation of private and public space. Van Gennep identifies three stages in the *rites of passage:* separation, liminality, and reaggregation. All three stages will be shown to be identifiable in the mystics' approaches, as presented in their texts.[8]

THE SPACE OF CHRISTIAN SOCIETY

There has always been a social component in the elaborative writings of Christianity. St. Augustine stressed the social dimension of Christian life as early as the fourth century (Louth 1981, 136), though his emphasis on it had as much to do with a consideration of the mystical body of Christ, the Church, and final beatitude as it did with earthly socialization. Jeffrey Burton Russell points out that an informing metaphor in St. Augustine's *City of God* is that "the communion of saints is the bond between the free citizens of the polis, civitas, respublica, congregatio of heaven. And it is as this society, this communion, rather than as individuals, that we are saved" (1997, 86).

This understanding of the connection between the earthly and the heavenly society persisted to inform the medieval social space. In Margaret Wertheim's schema, this represents the ultimate connection of body-space and soul-space in which the "community" of the saints

7. This suggestion was made by historian Peter Brown in his keynote address at the International Medieval Conference at the University of Leeds, July 1999.

8. I am applying these theoretical stages in an effort to elaborate the social space of the *Cloud* author, Richard Rolle, and Julian of Norwich; they are not intended to have any relationship with the frequently posited stages of mystical life: illumination, purgation, and union.

in heaven are the spiritual component of the community of the faithful on earth. Victor Turner notes a parallel between Christian society
and the proposed hierarchical structure of heaven. He comments that

> [there was] a perfect synthesis of communitas and hierarchical structure. It
> was not only Dante and Thomas Aquinas who pictured heaven as a hierar-
> chical structure with many levels of sanctity and, at the same time, as a lumi-
> nous unity or communitas in which no lesser saint felt envy of a greater saint
> nor any pride of position. Equality and hierarchy were there mysteriously
> one. (1989/1969, 182)

Rolle exemplifies Turner's point when he reproduces in his texts the
angelic hierarchies most prominently expounded by the pseudo-Dionysius. In his elaboration Rolle expresses the conviction that just as
the angels are designated places in relation to God according to their
service, so God's followers can expect a similar ordering in heaven.
That is, Rolle indicates that individuals can affect their future heavenly positions by their earthly behavior, explaining that

> For al þat er gude and haly, when þai passe owt of þis worlde, sal be taken
> intil þies orders: some intil þe lawest, þat hase lufed mykel; some intil þe
> mydelmest, þat hase lufed mare; oþer intil þe heest, þat maste lufed God and
> byrnandest es in hys lufe. (E.D. 62: 29–34)[9]

Julian acknowledges this "social" connection between earth and heav-
en when she explains that "all the helpe that we haue of speciall sainctes
and of all the blessed companie of heauen, the dere worthie loue and
the holie endles frinshipe that we haue of them, it is of his goodnes"
(LT. 6.305: 20–22).[10]

In addition, Julian finds this social component is manifested in

---

9. "All those who are good and holy, when they pass out of this world, shall be
taken into these orders: some, who have loved much, into the lowest; some who have
loved more, into the middle; others into the highest, [that is] those who have most
loved God and have burned for his love."

10. "all the help that we have from special saints and from all the blessed company
of heaven, the devoted love and the holy endless friendship that we have with them,
it is of [God's] goodness."

the interconnectedness of Christians on earth in the form of a metaphorical corporate of the Church and of all Christians. Thus, Glasscoe's consideration that "what might be impossible for individuals
was possible within the larger body of society" (1993, 20) finds particular expression in Julian's statement that "one singular person may
oftyn tymes be broken, as it semyth to þe selfe, but the hole body
of holy chyrch was nevyr broken, nor nevyr shall be with out ende.
And therfore a suer thyng it is, a good and a gracious to wylle mekly
and myghtly be fastenyd and onyd to oure moder holy church, that is
Crist Jhesu" (LT. 61.607: 59–63).[11]

Here Julian juxtaposes the potentially "broken" individual with
the unbreakable alliance between the mystical "body," "holy chyrch,"
and "Crist Jhesu." In this alliance all three components are analogous,
with each one able to stand for the other. That is, "Crist Jhesu" *is* the
"holy chyrch" and the mystical body that incorporates all the faithful.
Julian's suggestion, then, that she is "the one standing for all" Christians and that all Christians are united as one can be understood as
another representation of the interconnectedness of Christian society. For example, after reiterating that her revelations have general application, when she says that "though oure lorde shewyd me that I
shuld synne, by me aloone is vnderstonde alle" (LT. 37.442: 8–9),[12]
Julian asks rhetorically, "What may make me more to love myn evyn
cristen than to see in god that he louyth alle that shalle be savyd as it
were alle one soule?" (LT. 37.443: 13–15).[13]

That is, if all Christians are joined in "holy chyrch," then an individual can stand for the faithful in general and the spiritual achieve-

11. "one individual person may often be broken, as it seems to him, but the whole
body of holy Church was never broken, nor ever shall be without end. And therefore
it is a sure thing, good and gracious, to will meekly and powerfully to be fastened and
united to our mother holy Church, that is Christ Jesus."

12. "though our Lord showed me that I would sin, by me is understood everyone."

13. "What could make me love my fellow Christian more than to see in God that
he loves all who shall be saved as if they were all one soul."

ments of that individual can have benefits for all the faithful. The *Cloud* author foregrounds the notion that the contemplative is acting on behalf of all other Christians in undertaking a contemplative life when he advises that

[I]t suffisiþ now vnto þee to do hole worschip vnto God wiþ þi substaunce & for to offre up þi nakid beyng, þe whiche is þe first of þi frutes, in contynowel sacrifiȝe of preising of God, boþe for þi-self & for alle oþer as charite askiþ, vncloþid with eny qualite or special beholdyng þat on eny maner falliþ or may falle vnto þe beyng of þi-self or of any oþer, as þou woldest by þat beholding help þe nede, forþer þe spede, or encrese þe profite to perfeccion of þi-self or of eny oþer. (P.C. 142: 1–8)[14]

In *The Cloud of Unknowing* he assures his reader that "Alle men leuyng in erþe ben wonderfuli holpen of þis werk, þou wost not how. ȝe, þe soules in purgatori ben esed of þeire peine by vertewe of þis werk. Þi-self arte clensid & maad vertewos by no werk so mochel" (Cl. 3.16: 13–16).[15]

That is, the contemplative life is not a life assumed in the pursuit of individual spiritual achievement and ultimate personal salvation only but is seen as an undertaking in which the individual acts on behalf of all Christians, living and dead. Thus the *Cloud* author endorses the view that not only can the saints in heaven intervene for the faithful on earth but that the body-space and the soul-space interconnection works in the opposite direction as well, with contemplative life being capable of effecting liberation of the "soules in purgatori."

14. "It is sufficient now for you to worship God with your whole substance and to offer up your naked being, which is the first of your fruits, in a continual sacrifice of praise for God, both for yourself and for all others as charity demands. [Do this] unadorned, without any special quality or consideration that in any manner occurs or may occur to your own being or to any other, as if you would by that consideration help the needy, or further the well-being or increase the profit of perfection of yourself or anyone else."

15. "You cannot know how wonderfully helpful this work is to all men living on earth. Yes, the souls in purgatory are eased of their pain by virtue of this work. You, yourself, are cleansed and made virtuous by no other work as much as this."

The encompassing nature of medieval Christian society also extended to the "saintly" departed who were frequently invoked as exemplary models for the (living) community members who were striving toward greater devotion to God. Julian of Norwich, for example, can be viewed as having modeled herself toward a life dedicated to God by requesting, at a young age, "thre gyftes by the grace of god. The first was to have mynd of the passion. The secund was bodilie sicknes. The thurde was to haue of gides gyfte three woundys" (LT. 2.285: 4–6).[16]

While on one level this suggests that, in part, Julian's revelations can be understood to have been the result of the early direction of her will toward God, on another level such desires are indicative of some degree of social modeling as her particular request for the "thre wonndys" are mapped onto St. Cecelia's reported wounds in response to an earlier experience in which Julian states that she "harde a man telle of halye kyrke of the storye of saynte Cecylle" (ST. 1.204: 46–47).[17] Denise Baker, in fact, finds that the request for the three wounds in general "discloses [Julian's] familiarity with the typical sequence of spiritual progress articulated in popular treatises and handbooks about meditation" (1994, 25) and, further, that "[h]er desire to envision and imitate Christ's passion in order to enhance her compassion, contrition, and longing for God reveals her comprehension of the literature of affective spirituality prior to her visionary experience in May 1373" (ibid.).

Richard Rolle invokes the early Church eremites as a precedent when he is criticized for apparently not maintaining a fixed abode.[18] In his defense Rolle argues:

16. "three gifts by the grace of God. The first was thoughts of the Passion. The second was bodily sickness. The third was to have, as God's gift, three wounds."

17. "heard a man of holy Church tell the story of St. Cecilia." The reference to St. Cecelia, and the man telling the story, are unique to the Short Text.

18. Clay (1914) gives details of differences between hermits and anchorites, the major one being that hermits were not required necessarily to be of fixed abode for life. In addition, they were largely self-supporting. Rolle's stated difficulties with

Cellis forsoth to leue for cause resonable, to harmetis is not ill, & eft, if it accorde, to þe same to turn agayn. Some treuly of holy fadyrs þus ha done, þof all þa suffyrd þerfor mans grochynge, neuer-þeþless not of goyd. (*Fire,* 1.16.35: 22–25)[19]

Both Rolle and the *Cloud* author devote several chapters of their texts to defending and praising the contemplative life. While Rolle treats of the praiseworthiness of the solitary over the common life,[20] the *Cloud* author introduces Martha and Mary as the types for active and contemplative life, respectively.[21] In doing so, he positions them as exemplars. Mary, in her concentrated love and devotion for Jesus, is presented as the ideal model for contemplatives. The author explains that

[s]weet was þat loue bitwix oure Lorde & Marye. Moche loue had sche to hym; moche more had he to hir. For who-so wolde utterly beholde alle þe contynaunce þat was bitwix hym & hir . . . he schulde fynde þat sche was so hertly set for to loue hym, þat no þing beneþe hym miȝt counforte hir, ne ȝit holde hir herte fro hym. (Cl. 22.55: 7–13)[22]

The *Cloud* author recommends the use of Gospel models in general when he continues:

Sekirly who-so wil loke verrely in þe story of þe Gospel, he schal fynde many wonderful poynte of parfite loue wreten of hir to oure ensaumple, & as euen

<hr/>

change of abode therefore seems to imply that there were other (unnamed) problems that prompted his move.

19. "Cells can be left for a reasonable cause, as it is not harmful to hermits, and after, if it is desirable, the same cell returned to again. Truly, some of the holy [desert] fathers have done so, though they suffered men's complaining, though not from good men."

20. See *Fire of Love,* Chapters 14–16 inclusive.

21. See *The Cloud of Unknowing,* Chapter 18ff.

22. "Sweet was that love between our Lord and Mary. Great love had she for him; much more had he for her. For anyone who wants to understand completely what passed between them . . . he would find that she was so wholeheartedly set in her love for him, that nothing less than he could comfort her, [and nothing] could take her heart from him."

acordyng to þe werke of þis writyng, as þei had ben set & wretyn þerfore. (Cl. 22.55: 21–56: 1)[23]

The conforming to models encompassed both a physical and a spiritual dimension in that the mystics exhibit a conviction that the physical appearance is important as a reflection of the spiritual and that the two modes should enhance each other. This not only links with the medieval interest in a body-space/soul-space nexus but contains a social implication as the *Cloud* author exemplifies when he considers that

Who-so had þis werk, it schuld gouerne him ful semely, as wele in body as in soule, & make hym ful fauorable vnto iche man or womman þat lokyd apon hym; in so moche, þat þe worst fauored man or womman þat leueð in þis liif, & þei miȝte come to by grace to worche in þis werk, þeire fauour schuld sodenly & gracyously be chaunged, þat iche good man þat hem sawe schulde be fayne & ioiful to haue hem in companye, & ful mochil þei schuld þink þat þei were plesid in spirit & holpen by grace vnto God in þeire presence. (Cl. 54.100: 5–13)[24]

Here the author presents an interesting juxtaposition of seclusion and society. That is, the word "werk" refers to the contemplative life, practiced in seclusion, but the suggestion that the same contemplative should be "ful fauorable vnto iche man or womman þat loky[s] apon hym" and that anyone who sees the contemplative should be "ioiful to haue hem in companye," weakens the literal and metaphori-

23. "Surely anyone who looks carefully into the stories of the Gospel will find many wonderful points about her perfect love, written for our example, and so closely in accordance with the work of this writing, it is as if they had been set down and written for the purpose."

24. "Anyone who has this work will find that it has a very good effect on the body as well as the soul, making him very favorable to every man and woman who looks upon him; so much so that the least attractive man or woman who lives this life, and who, by grace, has come to work in contemplation, will find their appearance suddenly and graciously changed, so that every good man who saw them would be glad and joyful to have them in their company, and would very much think that they were raised in spirit and helped by God's grace in their presence."

cal barrier between contemplative seclusion and society and points
to a unique position for contemplatives in medieval England, a position in both the public and the private space. In Lefebvre's formulation, the mystics' *spatial practice* can be therefore viewed as a negotiation between the private space of their contemplative abode and
the public space in which the abode is visible. That is, their *spatial
practice* incorporates a duality of spatial occupation and strengthens
the likelihood that the mystics were both modeled by society in the
particular way in which they pursued their vocation and, simultaneously, became models of sanctity for others in society to follow.[25] Bynum refers to the twelfth-century concept of "reform by model" and
proposes that it was

> applied to groups as well as to individuals ... [and that] all the basic con-
> cerns of early twelfth-century spirituality—poverty and preaching, with-
> drawal and community, love of neighbor and love of God—were expressed
> in terms of models. ... Furthermore, the groups not only aspired to conform
> to models. They saw themselves as *being* models. In their own terms, they
> taught by example. (1982, 103)

She further proposes that "a saint is one in whom extraordinary
life (without) reflects extraordinary virtue and grace (within) ...
[and] sanctity is finally reformation of the total man and it can be
gained by imitation of the sanctity of others which is accessible to us
exactly because it is outer as well as inner" (1982, 101–2).[26]

An application and extrapolation of Bynum's propositions yields
a view of the mystics as persons who exhibited an "outer" dedication to God by their mode of life that was reflective of their inward
dedication. This complementarity of the "inner" and the "outer" per-

---

25. "Guigo II (Carthusian) reminds us that 'Follow me' means 'imitate me' as far
as Christ is concerned" (Bynum 1982, 100).

26. Coincidentally, the "re-formation" of the soul is the essential subject and message of Walter Hilton's *Scale of Perfection,* Book 2, and "both Hilton and Julian regard contemplative union as the culmination of a process of self-examination which
leads the mystic to see the *image Dei* within" (Baker 1998, 40).

son points to the possibility that mystics functioned as living icons (of sanctity, or of the possibility of sanctity) in the midst of society. Mulder-Bakker makes a similar point in specific reference to continental anchoresses when she explains that, to their contemporaries, "[t]hese [women] were their 'living saints.' For them saintliness was incarnated sanctity" (2005, 197). In Lefebvre's formulation, the mystics would be considered to be, in the social space, a type of living *representational space* in the way that they stand as symbols and signs for a personal experience of God.

The modes of expression of mysticism in the Middle Ages showed considerable variation and not all those modes were sanctioned by the Church. Indeed, some modes evoked deep suspicion, if not outright condemnation.[27] However, the types of expression that were tolerated, if not actively encouraged, by the prevailing power structure were not a subversion of authority but, more fairly, can be regarded as a societally sanctioned undertaking that enabled all community members vicariously to partake of God's transcendence. This understanding of the mystics offers a possible reason for the *Cloud* author's strident condemnation of false contemplatives. That is, he may well have seen them as subverting or misrepresenting the signs of sanctity and dedication that society expected that they should uphold.[28] Thus he decries the way in which

Som sette þeire iȝen in þeire hedes as þei were sturdy scheep betyn in þe heed & as þei schulde diȝe anone. Som hangen here hedes on syde, as a worme were in þeire eres. Som pipyn when þei schuld speke. . . . Som crien & whinen in þeire þrote, so ben þei gredy & hasty to sey þat þei þink. (Cl. 53.97: 21–98: 5)[29]

27. E.g., Margery Kempe, by her own admission, attracted equal portions of support and condemnation from her contemporaries and continues to divide the opinions of modern scholars. For an investigation into approaches to Kempe scholarship, see Mitchell (2005).

28. Langland, too, gives an account of false hermits; see *Piers Plowman C-Text,* ed. Derek Pearsall (London: Edward Arnold, 1978), 9: 203–18.

29. "Some fix their eyes in their heads as if they were silly sheep bitten/wounded

He also makes specific allusion to the experience of a false fire of love following a beginner's overexertion in contemplation and an incorrect approach: "& ȝit, parauenture, þei wene it be þe fiir of loue, getyn & kyndelid by þe grace & þe goodnes of þe Holy Goost. Treuly of þis disceite, & of þe braunches þer-of, spryngyn many mescheues: moche ypocrisis, moche heresye, & moche errour" (Cl. 45.86: 13–15).[30] The author's reports of such physical shows of purported sanctity indicate that there must have been some societal value attached to publicly displayed sanctity if individuals attempted to gain recognition for it by false demonstrations. In falsely exhibiting the signs without the underlying spiritual transformation the individual might have been considered to be breaking the "unwritten" social rule that demanded, in medieval society, that outward appearance and inner intention be somehow aligned.

SPACE AND *HABITUS*

The conformity to models and the apparent expectation of alignment of inner and outer sanctity find particular expression in the medieval Church and its representations. In fact, the Church commanded the medieval physical space at all levels, from the awe-inspiring magnificence of its cathedrals to the professed power of the smallest icon.

Lefebvre comments in relation to the Church's pervasiveness:

What a narrow, indeed mistaken, view it is which pictures the Church as an entity having its main "seat" in Rome and maintaining its presence by means of clerics in individual "churches" or villages and towns, in convents, monas-

---

on the head and about to die. Some hang their heads to one side, as if there were a worm in their ears. Some squeak when they should speak. . . . Some cry and whine in their throat, as they are so anxious and hasty to say what they think."

30. "And, yet, perhaps, they believe that it is the fire of love, given and kindled by the grace and goodness of the Holy Spirit. In truth, from this deceit springs many problems: great hypocrisy, great heresy and great error."

teries, basilicas, and so forth. The fact is that the "world"—that imaginary-real space of shadows—was inhabited, haunted by the Church. (255)

That is, as a *representational space* the Church incorporated the physical features of its edifices, the social features of its extensive organization, and the spiritual features of God's "chosen" place on earth. And such pervasiveness on multiple levels had already been in continuing evidence for centuries before the time of the mystics. The Church's persistent influence can be understood in terms of Bourdieu's notion of *habitus*. That is, Christianity in the medieval West informed individual and collective social, as well as religious, action and practices and pervaded the culture to the extent that the "dispositions" of the people were recognizably Christian and any religious practice or representation was firmly within the Christian framework. In addition, further "religious" productions, in the form of texts and architecture, for example, reproduced the Christian *habitus*.

Julian's elaboration of the way in which great sinners become great saints, obtaining their forgiveness of sins and their elevation to exemplary position though the intermediary action of the Church, on God's behalf, is an example of the acknowledged power of the Church in the Middle Ages. Julian explains that "what synners they are that so shalbe rewarded is made knowen in holy church in erth and also in heaven by over passyng worshypes" (LT. 38.445: 10–12).[31]

She reinforces her point by providing examples of sinners who became saints, from both the Old and the New Testament, and even a local example, John of Beverly, thereby invoking the implicit historical element that *habitus* embodies. Julian, too, holds herself within the Christian *habitus* of established canons and emphasizes that "in all thing I beleue as holy chyrch prechyth and techyth" (LT. 9.323: 21–22).[32] While she acknowledges that some things will not be known in

---

31. "what sinners are to be so rewarded is made known in holy Church on earth and also in heaven by surpassing honors."

32. "in all things I believe as holy Church preaches and teaches."

life or until such time as "god of hys goodnes hath made vs wurthy to se it" (LT. 46.494: 48),[33] she considers that it is the Church that holds and presents the truth until then. In this regard, Julian has been enabled to see that there are two judgments, an earthly and a heavenly, the former taught by the Church, the latter taught in revelation. In acceptance of her "earthly" position at the time of the revelations Julian declares that, "now I ӡelde me to my modyr holy chyrch, as a sympyll chylde owyth" (LT. 46.494: 50).[34] Julian posits the Church as necessary in effecting reconciliation between God and humanity after sin in that "the holy gost ledyth [us] to confession" (LT. 39.450: 9).[35]

Rolle, too, advises his reader in *Ego Dormio* to "seke [Christ] inwardly, in trouth and hope and charite of haly kyrk" (77: 120–21),[36] foregrounding the Church's role as the keeper of truth, hope, and love.

The *Cloud* author recommends the Church as the way to cleanse one's conscience as a preparation for entry into the contemplative life when he advises that "ӡif þei wil proue whens þis steryng comeþ, þei mowe proue þus, þif hem likyþ. First lat hem loke ӡif þei haue done þat in hem is before, ablyng hem þerto in clensyng of þeire concyence, at þe dome of Holi Chirche, þeire counseil acordyng" (Cl. 75.131: 6–9).[37]

The *Cloud* author, however, puts something ahead of the Church's influence on the mystical life. He indicates that, first of all, what might be termed a "spiritual *habitus*" is in operation, in the form of God's grace. Thus he states that "ӡit he ӡeuiþ not þis grace, ne worcheþ not þis werk, in ani soule þat is vnable þerto. & ӡit þer is no soul wiþouten þis grace, abil to haue þis grace" (Cl. 34.69: 12–13).[38]

33. "God of his goodness has made us worthy to see it."
34. "now I yield myself to my mother holy Church, as a simple child should."
35. "the Holy Spirit leads [us] to confession."
36. "seek [Christ] inwardly, in the faith and hope and charity of holy Church."
37. "if they want to test from where the stirring comes, they may test it thus, if they like. First let them be sure that they have prepared before, by cleansing their conscience, in holy Church, according to their counsel."
38. "yet he does not give this grace, nor work this work, in any soul that is unable

That is, he believes that the capacity for contemplation and the act of contemplation are the same thing, explaining that "þe abilnes to þis werk is onyd to þe selue werk" (Cl. 34.70: 3)[39] and that it is God who enables it. The author proceeds to describe the melding of desire and enactment in terms of unfinished timber that is wrought by a carpenter, and a house and its householder: "Be þou bot þe tre, & lat it be þe wriзt; be þou bot þe hous, & lat it be þe hosbonde wonyng þerin" (Cl. 34.70: 15–16).[40] Thus the work of contemplation is wrought by God in those who are called to the work by God's grace. Apart from this necessity of a prevenient grace, however, the *Cloud* author disavows the action of any sort of social *habitus* with the statement that "in þis werk men schul use no mene, ne зit men mowe not com þerto wiþ menes. Alle good menes hangen upon it, & it on no mene; ne no mene may lede þerto" (Cl. 34.71: 7–10).[41]

The disavowal is paradoxical, for while God's grace is proposed as the only necessary "menes" initially, the *Cloud* author recommends that "a contemplatiif prentys schuld be ocupyed, þe whiche ben þeese: Lesson, Meditacion, & Oryson. Or elles to þin vnderstondyng þei mowe be clepid: Redyng, þinkyng & Preiing" (Cl. 35.71: 11–13).[42]

If the reading, thinking, and praying are to center on "Goddes worde" then the contemplative apprentice can be considered to be informed by Christian *habitus* insofar as the recommended books, thoughts, and prayers are products of that *habitus*. In fact, even when

---

to do so. And yet there is no soul without this grace, who is able to have this grace [without God]."

39. "the ability to do this work is one with the same work"

40. "You be the tree, and let it be the carpenter; you be the house, and let it be the husband/householder living therein."

41. "in this work, men should use no means/practices, nor may men come to it by practices. All good practices depend upon it, but it depends on no practices; nor will practices lead you to it."

42. "a beginner in contemplation should be occupied with these: Lesson, Meditation, and Orison. Or as they are more usually called: Reading, Thinking and Praying."

the author goes on to reposition reading, thinking, and praying by declaring that "it is not so wiþ hem þat contynuely worchen in þe werk of þis book" (Cl. 36.72: 25–73: 1),[43] such a tactic might be considered as part of the prerequisite general destabilizing and detachment of a contemplative aspirant from the material world. That is, destabilization can be regarded as a part of the *habitus* of the mystical life. Equally, the suggestion that "þe werk of þis book" somehow places contemplatives beyond the need for "menes" is paradoxical in that the possession and reading of the book is plainly a "menes" in itself.

Demonstrably, too, though God's grace may have been the initiator of the work of contemplation, the mystics followed overtly and covertly prescribed forms of behavior in the pursuit of their vocation. In their commitment to God they exchanged worldly for spiritual interests. They denied themselves certain material comforts in the hope of attracting spiritual gains for themselves and others. They remained *in* the world but not *of* it. The mystics differed from other religious, however, in that they retired from the social world but, at some point, returned to that society bringing some testimony of their experiences for the edification of others who had remained in secular life. They may be considered, therefore, to be particular examples of Bourdieu's *habitus,* especially with regard to how he applies the concept to the interrelationship between the individual and the social world. That is, Bourdieu posits that "[t]he habitus is the product of the work of inculcation and appropriation necessary in order for those products of collective history, the objectives structures (e.g. of language, economy, etc.) to succeed in reproducing themselves more or less completely, in the form of durable dispositions, in the organisms (which one can, if one wishes, call individuals) lastingly subjected to the same conditionings" (1977, 85).

An extrapolation of Bourdieu's formulation into the mystics' social world yields an interpretation that positions the *Cloud* author,

---

43. "it is not so with those who continually work in the work of this book"

Julian, and Rolle as fully participatory members of society. That is, they may be considered to have entered into contemplation, the outward form of which was grounded and framed in Christianity, and which in turn represented a direct reflection of the practices of religion in the social world. They then either spoke or wrote about their resultant experiences and in this way contributed toward, if not exactly a "reproduction" of themselves, then certainly an understanding and furtherance of participation in contemplation and/or dedication to God within the society. Medieval society, then, can be seen to be literally "making room" for mysticism and providing supportive social structures for solitariness with the aim of benefiting not just the solitary individual but Christian society in general.[44] In turn, mystics can be viewed as undertaking the mystical enterprise both for themselves and on behalf of their fellow Christians in a simultaneously personal and public act directed toward greater spiritual benefit for all concerned. In this way, mystics can also be understood to be participants, on behalf of their society, in what Arnold van Gennep has described as *rites of passage* (1908). *Rites of passage* are

[t]ransitional rituals accompanying changes of place, state, social position, and age in a culture. They have a basically tripartite processual structure, consisting of three phases: separation, margin or limen, and reagreggation. (Turner 1978, 249)

Though mystics remain largely visible within the social space at the same time as they are occupying mystical space, they can still be

44. It should here be remarked that Bourdieu, when discussing and theorizing about social space, is primarily envisaging his theory in neocapitalist parameters and imbuing it with his own gloss on "capital." I have applied parts of his theory retrospectively, however, as they seem to have particular relevance in facilitating an understanding of the social space of the mystics. Here I am following Bourdieu's lead when he opines that "[s]ociology presents itself as a social topology. . . . [T]he social world can be represented in the form of a (multi-dimensional) space constructed on the basis of principles of differentiation or distribution constituted by the set of properties active in the social universe under consideration; that is, able to confer force or power on their possessor in that universe" (1991, 229).

charted as following the "basically tripartite processual structure" and, in the enacting of that rite, to be making the transition from body-space to soul-space on behalf of their fellows.

SEPARATION

In the England of the Middle Ages, private and personal union with God called for a retirement, a separation, from the distractions of the day-to-day world. This separation is the first and most obvious sign given by the *Cloud* author, Rolle, and Julian to convey, to their community, that they were intent on a life dedicated to God.

Van Gennep has designated *separation* as the first stage in his conception of the processual *rites de passage*. The separation phase "detaches the ritual subjects from their old places in society, and installs them, inwardly transformed and outwardly changed, in a new place in society" (Turner 1978, 249).

That is, this stage visibly severs the individual's existing attachments to, and status in, the society and allows the candidate to establish a new and changed relationship to that society.

As has been illustrated, Richard Rolle, Julian of Norwich, and the *Cloud* author all give evidence of having retired to solitude at some stage in their lives. I now want to consider some other ways in which the mystics suggest, in their texts, that they effected a separation from society.

Rolle, in particular, overtly signals this separation from general society and an alteration to life state, by a change in clothing.

The idea of reclothing oneself to signal a change in lifestyle is well expressed in the use of the word *habit* to apply to the clothing of religious. In Middle English, *habit* had a threefold connotation: clothing, particularly religious attire; outward form or appearance; and bodily constitution, mental habit, or customary practice. Here, too, then, is implied the idea of *habitus,* of the assumption of a long-established way of life. In adopting a particular clothing habit, the religious or mystic could be expected to be also adopting the inner habit of holiness, thereby keeping within the medieval expectation of inner and outer compliance. This multiplicity of meaning of *habit* persists to the present day though now the behavior-related meaning is far more common than either the clothing or outward appearance connotation.

Rolle cautions his reader in *The Form of Living* "þan es it schame til þe, bot if þou be als gode, or better, within þi sawle, als þou ert semand at þe syght of men. Turne forþi þi thoghtes perfitely till God, als it semes þat þou hase done þi body. For I will not þat þou wene þat all er hali þat hase þe abet of halynes and er noght ocupyed with þe worlde" (F.L. 93: 2–8).[45]

His use of the word "abet" could have all three meanings: clothes, outward appearance, and behavior related to mental habit. The multiplicity of meaning is reflected in other uses of clothing imagery in the mystical texts. The idea that Christ was clothed in humanity pertains particularly to His assumption of the outward form and is reflected in the mystics' acknowledgment that they are clothed in Christ. In assuming human form, Christ stands as the ultimate example of humility. In imitation of Christ's humility and of His humble approach to clothing (and material possessions in general) and in response to His exhortation to His followers to be "poor in spirit," Rolle warns his reader in *Ego Dormio* that

Þow will noght covayte þan to be riche, to have many mantels and fayre, many kyrtels and drewryse; bot al þou wil sett at noght, and despise it als noght it ware, and take na mare þan þe nedes. Þe wil thynk twa mantels or ane inogh; þow þat hase fyve or sex, gyf some til Criste, þat gase naked in a pore wede. (E.D. 67: 204–10)[46]

45. "it is to your shame if you are not as good or better in your soul than you seem to be in the sight of men. Therefore, turn your thoughts perfectly to God, as it seems that you have done with your body. For I do not want you to think that all are holy who have the habit of holiness and are not occupied with the world."

46. "You will not desire to be rich, to have many pretty cloaks and many tunics and lovers' gifts/jewelry; but all these you will count as nothing, and despise it all as if it were nothing, and take no more than you need. You will think that one or two

In *The Commandment* Rolle is more explicit about clothing, pointing out that, as Christ at His birth, was "swedeld in clowtes sympely, as a pore barne" (Com. 77: 128–29),[47] his readers should question their own covetousness with regard to clothes. He asks them, "How may þou for schame, þat es bot servand, with many clathes and riche folow þi spowse and þi Lorde, þat yhede in a kyrtel, and þou trayles als mykel behynd þe as al þat he had on?" (Com. 77: 131–34).[48]

Here Rolle implies the necessity of ensuring that the outward appearance of humility and holiness is truly reflected in spiritual dedication and practice and vice versa. It seems that Rolle, personally, practiced what he preached in this regard. The first lesson in his *Officium* details that

[a]fter he had returned from Oxford to his father's house, he said one day to his sister, who loved him with tender affection: "My beloved sister, thou hast two tunics, which I greatly covet, one white and the other grey. Therefore I ask thee if thou wilt kindly give them to me, and bring them [to] me tomorrow to the wood near by, together with my father's rain-hood." She agreed willingly. . . . And when he had received them he straightway cut off the sleeves from the grey tunic and the buttons from the white, and as best he could he fitted the sleeves to the white tunic, so that they might in some manner be suited to his purpose. Then he took off his own clothes with which he was clad and put on his sister's white tunic next his skin, but

cloaks are enough; you now have five or six; give some to Christ, who walks [almost] naked in poor clothes."

47. "wrapped in simple clothes, like a poor child."

48. "How shameful are you, who are but a servant, to have so many clothes and riches as you follow your husband and Lord, who wears only a tunic while you trail behind you as much as he has on?" These reprimands delivered by Rolle to his initial readers of both *Ego Dormio* and *The Commandment* on their unsuitably extravagant clothing is informative in additional ways. For example, as the recipient of *The Commandment* is known to have been a nun, the reprimand suggests that conventual enclosure of women may have formed the alternate *habitus* to the clothing habits of the male religious who, presumably had more contact with the public. Allen notes, too, that "the evidence of the bishops' registers show that the gay clothing of nuns was a constant cause of censure at the contemporary visitations of nunneries" (1963/1931, 60).

the grey, with the sleeves cut out, he put on over it, and put his arms through the holes which had been cut; then he covered his head with the rainhood. ("A translation of *The Legenda* in the Office prepared for the blessed hermit Richard," from the *York Breviary,* Vol. 2, Appendix 5, quoted in Comper, 1969/1928, 301)

In this dramatic change of clothing before assuming his eremitic lifestyle, Rolle is presented as signifying his inner spiritual transformation by the purposeful change in his outward appearance. The changed outward appearance alerts his society to his new status or life state. It also provides Rolle with a means of effecting a clear separation between his former life and his (intended) new life, and between himself and society. Thus, his transformed "habit" is exemplified by the donning of a habit. Watson, following Noetinger and Arnould's view that the *Officium* presents Rolle in terms of exemplary norms, finds biblical precedents for Rolle's reclothing. He notes that "[i]n ordination and baptism rites a change of garments always symbolizes a changed life: putting off the old, putting on the new (Ephesians 4.22–24); being clothed with the longed-for garments of heaven (2 Corinthians 5.1–4)" (1991, 41).

Watson further offers hagiographical and hermitic precedents, finding a particular parallel in Bonaventure's account of the life of St. Francis in which it is described that "Francis strips naked in Assisi's main piazza" (ibid.), and in the details of profession of hermits in such accounts as the fourteenth-century *Regula Heremitarum.* Though Watson rightly cautions, especially in regard to Rolle, that "to present oneself as exemplary is not necessarily to be perceived as such" (39), the assuming of a habit by those taking religious orders has a social significance. That is, a habit represented not only the adoption of a certain way of life but it also defined an individual in society's eyes and made public his or her private life of dedication to God with its attendant expectations of avoidance of sin and eschewal of material pleasures. If the individual's behavior did not coincide with society's expectations of vocational sanctity, then the professed person was obvious in his deviation because the clothes distinguished him at a glance. In addition, it is probable that the presence of readily distinguishable religious persons may have had a regulatory effect on society as, in their habits, they served as exemplary reminders of that toward which all should be striving. In Bourdieu's definition, they would be contributing toward a furtherance of the *habitus*. In Lefebvrian terms, the religious (clothing) habit can be interpreted as a particular *representational space* that symbolized far more than a fixation on fashion.

In view of this, it is perhaps not surprising that the numerous allusions to clothing in writings *about* Rolle find an interesting parallel in writings *by* Rolle. In addition to the previously quoted reprimands about covetousness with regard to clothing, Rolle is contemptuous of women's fashion in general. For example, he finds it appropriate to criticize women's clothes and hairstyles at the denouement to his chapter on friendship, in which he states that friendship between a man and a woman is generally to be shunned as "perlius" (*Fire*, 1.9.92: 22).[49] Rolle's detailing of the aspects of women's fashion that he particularly dislikes provides a good window, for modern readers, onto the most popular types of adornment in the north of England in the first half of the fourteenth century. He complains that

Not onely agayns þe sentens of þe aostyll [*sic*] in golde & dressynge of here to pryde & wantonhede þa go sarifand, bot also agayns mans honeste & kynde be god ordand brode horns & in gretnes horribyll of here wroyght þat grw not þer, on þer hedis þa sett, of qwhome sum þer fowles to hyde or þer bewte þa study to increse with payntynge of begillynge avotre þer faces þa color & qwhittyn. Clethyng also newly korvin both men & wymmen ful fondly vsis, not seand kynde qwhat besemys, bot qwhat newe nysed of tithandis & vayne nwelte þe feynd stirande he may vp brynge. (*Fire*, 2.9.94: 35–95: 6)[50]

49. "dangerous"

50. "Not only are they going against the words of the apostle with their gold and dressed hair, slavishly following their pride and wantonness, but also against honest men and the nature which God ordained [when they] wear broad and very horrible horns on their heads, made of hair not their own; while some of them hide their ugli-

The *Cloud* author, on the other hand, makes no reference to material clothing though he does allude to a spiritual reclothing in the contemplative process. He advises his reader that a union with God is approached "in þis blinde beholdyng of þi nakid beyng" (P.C. 147: 17)[51] and, playing on the figure of the "nakid beyng," he goes on to advise that

In þis tyme it is þat þou boþe seest þi God & þi loue, & nakidly felist hym also bi goostly onyng to his loue in þe souereyn poynte of þi spirit, as he is in hymself, bot blyndely, as it may be here, vtterly spoylid of þi-self & nakidly cloþed in hymself as he is, vncloþed & not lappid in any of þees sensible felynges (be þei neuer so sweet ne so holy) þat mowen falle in þis liif. (P.C. 169: 17–26)[52]

Here, in the elaboration of the figure of the "nakid beyng" the author reinscribes the physical and social habitus that seems to encourage a change in outward appearance in line with inward change, with a spiritual reclothing in Christ.

Likewise, Julian effects an inversion of the clothing image when she says of Christ that "He is oure clothing, that for loue wrappeth vs and wyndeth vs, halseth vs and all becloseth vs, hangeth about vs for tender loue, þat he may never leeue vs" (LT. 5.299: 4–6).[53] Here the clothing metaphor is devoid of any allusions to vanity or covetousness and serves the function of pointing to the protective purpose of clothing as a metaphor for Christ's enfolding care of humanity.

---

ness or increase their beauty by deceitfully painting their faces with color and whitening. Clothing also in the newest cut is foolishly worn by both men and women, without regard for what is seemly in nature but for what is new according to gossip and to what fashion brings up."

51. "in this blind beholding of your naked being"

52. "It is at this time that you both see your God and your love, and also nakedly feel him by way of spiritual unity to his love in the deepest point of your spirit. [In this] you feel him as he is in himself, though blindly, as it must be here. Utterly stripped of yourself and naked, clothed in him as he is, unclothed and not wrapped in any of the sensual feelings (that are never so sweet or so holy) that might occur in life."

53. "He is our clothing, who for love wraps and enfolds us, holds and encloses us, covers us with tender love, that he may never leave us."

Julian makes no mention of her own clothing, but the separation from her former life is signaled by her entrance to mystical experience via illness. I am not suggesting that Julian in any way engineered or falsely exhibited an illness, merely that an illness happened to provide a means of signaling a separation from the social world prior to the full assumption of a mystical life.[54] Whilst an illness is isolating for the individual in pain, causing that individual to be able to focus on little else but herself during the time of the pain, such illness also attracts a contingent of others, in the form of caregivers, concerned relatives, and friends. Like the enclosed mystic, therefore, who alone can experience the mystical insights but who simultaneously may be the center of some attention from the public because of his or her solitariness and socially accepted sanctity, so the individual suffering a severe illness is both solitary and yet in the public view.

Bourdieu, offering the point of view of comparative anthropology from his study of the Kabyle culture, considers that "to be ill and dying was a social status, with its attendant rights and duties" (1994, 161). Bourdieu elaborates that, in the preindustrial cultures, to be ill was to be in the process of preparing for death, and therefore relatives and friends gathered at the bedside (162). As such, then, severe illness

54. Margery Kempe had her first mystical experience after the birth of her first child and a subsequent illness that had both physical and mental components. During her deepest anguish, she relates, Jesus appeared to her. It was to be the first of many visions and experiences for Margery. This initial experience within illness, however, set Margery on a course of seeking a means of outward expression for her inner transformation. Her subsequent insistence on wearing white clothing, fasting, and weeping loudly and copiously can be considered to be her outward show of sanctity, but Margery was by no means unanimously believed in her endeavors. Nevertheless, the process of illness had effected a transformation, not only in a physical and spiritual sense, but in Margery's life state—she moved from the private to the public sphere. Margery, who constantly desired "solitude" in the form of sexual continence within marriage, also imposed a form of solitariness on herself by her frequently bizarre behavior. If she were not solitary and reclusive in the usual "religious" sense, she was certainly socially ostracized, separated from society as a consequence of the bizarre behavior.

represents a particular type of *spatial practice* that involves not only the ill individual but his family and friends in a new approach to spatial negotiation. Similarly, from a religious point of view, it could be argued that God brought about Julian's illness in order to allow her to effect a degree of separation from her usual social space in order to prepare for the reception of her mystical knowledge. Even Julian, in requesting her illness from God many years before she was inflicted with it, could be seen as having been inspired by God's grace in those early years to request the illness when the time for mystical illumination was right. The illness may have served, then, at some level, as a manifestation of the sacred, and of divine action and intervention in the world. This is especially the case if Julian's subsequent recovery from the seemingly fatal illness was regarded as miraculous by her social circle.

LIMINALITY

In Van Gennep's formulation, *liminality* is the central phase of the *rite of passage.* It is during this phase that "the characteristics of the *liminars* (the ritual subjects in this phase) are ambiguous, for they pass through a cultural realm that has few or none of the attributes of the past or coming state. Liminars are betwixt and between. The liminal state has been frequently likened to death; to being in the womb" (Turner 1978, 249). The notion of liminars as "betwixt and between" finds resonance in the mystics' situation. The "past state" that is their life in the material world is discarded in the hope of spiritual attainment. In the assuming of solitude, the contemplative enters a state that is "dead" to the world but alive to spiritual possibilities. The exact nature of this spiritual "coming state," however, is not fully realizable in life but finds its total expression after death. In undertaking such a life, the mystics may be viewed as individuals standing for all Christians whose ultimate aim is to attain everlasting union with God. My argument here is that the mystics represented the possibility of the human attainment of the divine, assuming a dedicated and difficult life that few in general society would embrace. In this way the mystics become comparable to Brown's (1999) proposition that the saints of the early Church can be regarded as simultaneously imitable and inimitable. That is, the mystics are models of sanctity for others but others cannot attain the same level of spiritual experience that the mystics report. Like van Gennep's "liminars," the mystics can be considered to be "making the journey" on behalf of all society.

Victor Turner (1978) takes up van Gennep's theory of *rites of passage* and applies it to the idea of pilgrimage in the Middle Ages.[55] He refers to the idea that "pilgrimage can be thought of as extroverted mysticism, just as mysticism is introverted pilgrimage" (33). This is valid on the personal, individual level, as both the pilgrim and the mystic have, as their first goal, a meeting with the sacred. An earthly pilgrimage implies a traversing of space but a mystical pilgrimage is an inward journey. That is, for the mystic, the "sacred" is not just an earthly representation of the Divine, however transforming that representation may prove to be, but the *most* sacred God, experienced not concretely nor in a group, as the pilgrim experiences, but inwardly and singularly.

The actual metaphor of pilgrimage, however, is used in various mystical texts. Rolle, in particular, uses the metaphor to encapsulate the dual notions of life as a difficult journey and of God as the destination of that journey when he states that "Emonge truly in labore and stryff of my pilgremage, with swetnes of his lufe I beseke he me make glad" (*Fire,* 1.27.56: 34–36).[56] The *Cloud* author inscribes the idea covertly, emphasizing spiritual progression and the final destination of heaven. For example, the author relays his hope for his reader that "In þe whiche solitari forme & maner of leuyng þou maist le-

---

55. The notion of liminality is frequently and incorrectly attributed to Victor Turner, though Turner clearly acknowledges his debt to van Gennep.

56. "In the midst of the labor and strife of my pilgrimage, I beseech him to make me glad with the sweetness of his love."

rne to lift up þe fote of þi loue, & step towardes þat state & degre of leuyng þat is parfite" (Cl. 1.14: 11–15).[57]

The images of spiritual versus actual destinations mark the difference in motivation and attainment between mysticism and pilgrimage. That is, the mystics travel inward, away from the world, while the pilgrims travel far and wide, exposing themselves to worldly peril. It seems that while mysticism begins as a private and personal approach to God, it results in a return of benefits to society as a whole. Conversely, pilgrimage begins as a communal journey to God and results in a personal experience of the sacred that is not necessarily shared with others on return to one's point of origin. The central phase of the processual form of ritual, which van Gennep expounds as the liminal phase, also differs markedly for mystic and pilgrim. Pilgrims, because of the nature of their undertaking, are away from their usual community (albeit frequently in the company of some of its members), whereas the mystics are within their own communities, experiencing their mystical journey. In this way, they are more easily and obviously exemplars of the sacred for their community, situated so as to be visible to the members of their society, living icons who provided a service for their communities by their example. Thus, though a mystic might have sought inwardly to find his or her "true self," this cannot be viewed in the same way as our twenty-first century idea of "finding oneself." Our present approach has much to do with the assertion of individuality whereas, as Bynum has stressed, in the Middle Ages a person "did not find himself by casting off inhibiting patterns but by adopting appropriate ones" (1982, 101). Moreover, because to convert was to find a stricter pattern and because Christians learned what it was to be Christian from models, an individual who put off the "old man" for "the new" became himself a model available to others (ibid., 90).

---

57. "In the solitary form and manner of living you may learn to lift up the feet of your love, and step toward that state and degree of living that is perfect."

Underlying this concept of becoming a model for others was the medieval emphasis on *imitatio Christi*.[58] Jesus Christ prompted such widespread and diverse imitation—from poverty and preaching by mendicants, to actual physical imitations as exemplified by the bodily mortifications of some followers and the stigmata experienced by saints such as Francis of Assisi—that he is positioned as the ultimate model in an age of "sacred" models. Additionally, Christ's duality as man and God places him in the most liminal position possible. In coincidental imitation, the mystics place themselves in a societally liminal position. Turner's description of the liminal state as "ambiguous" and one that has "frequently been likened to death; to being in the womb; to invisibility, darkness, bisexuality and the wilderness" (249) all find resonance in the mystical state and in the duality of Jesus Christ.[59] It is the "in between" state just as the coexistence of death and life find ultimate expression in Jesus Christ.

The original meaning of *liminal,* from the Latin *limen,* is "threshold." Biblically and theologically, Christ is described as both a door and a doorkeeper (John 10: 9). Thus Christ stands at the limen as both door and doorkeeper. In *The Book of Privy Counselling* the *Cloud* author refers to the "housholde [of] gostlines"[60] in which "þe Lorde is not only portour hym-self, bot also he is þe dore: þe porter he is bi his Godheed, & þe dore he is by his manheed" (P.C. 159: 5–7).[61] In reference to the *Cloud* author's use of the biblical metaphor, Whitehead comments that

58. I have chosen not to discuss either the precipitating reasons or the various ways in which this imitation of Christ was effected across wide sectors of medieval society, as it is too enormous a subject to introduce here. Instead I refer the reader to the thorough consideration of this topic undertaken by Sarah Beckwith (1993).

59. The resonance with bisexuality here I see as referring not to sexual orientation but to a life state in which gender is not relevant and that is absorbent of male and female qualities equally.

60. "spiritual household"

61. "the Lord himself is not only the porter but also the door: he is the porter by his Godhead, and the door by his humanity."

[t]he reutilization of the building as an apt sign for contemplation places a new pressure of importance upon the threshold, since, according to the criteria of *The Book of Privy Counselling,* it is here that the vast majority of Christians are likely to remain. This pressure of attention entails a break with allegorical tradition, more particularly with patristic hermeneutic thought, since in all such writings, the threshold was never more than a nameless area to be crossed and discarded. (1998, 199)

In fact, the *Cloud* author does not suggest that most Christians remain on the threshold but that all those who seek entrance without humility will always remain standing outside. He advises that "many weneþ þat þei ben wiþ-inne þe goostly dore, & zit stonden þei þer-oute, & scholen do vnto þe tyme þat þey sechen meekly þe dore" (P.C. 158: 27–159: 2).[62]

The degree of access achieved via humility, however, does not necessarily remain constant nor does it facilitate a continual experience of God for the contemplative. Of course, here the *Cloud* author's threshold is a spiritual one and his readers are also positioned in a spiritually liminal space when he writes that "þis cloude of vnknow-yng is abouen þee, bitwix þee & þi God" and there is "a cloude of forzetyng bineþ þee, bitwix þee & alle þe cretures þat euer ben maad" (Cl. 5.24: 2–4).[63]

Turner notes, in applying the concept of liminality to both tribal cultures and cultures based on historical religions that

one obvious difference was seen in the spatial location of liminality . . . [such that] in many tribal societies, initiands [those in the process of the *rite de passage*] are secluded in a sacralized enclosure . . . clearly set apart from villages, markets, pastures, and gardens of everyday usage and trafficking. . . . But in the "historical" religions, comparable seclusion has been exemplified only in the total lifestyle of the specialized religious orders. (1978, 4)

62. "many want to go inside the spiritual door, and yet they stand outside, and will do until the time that they humbly seek the door."
63. "this cloud of unknowing is above you, between you and God [and there is] a cloud of forgetting beneath you, between you and all creatures that were ever made."

Here, though, Turner is not entirely correct for, in addition to the religious orders, the Middle Ages incorporated persons who assumed a contemplative lifestyle. As I have argued, the "sacralized enclosure" of mystical experience in medieval England was not necessarily set apart from "everyday usage and trafficking," but often, as in Julian's and other anchorites' cases, in the center of social interaction: the precincts of the local church. In addition, as Lefebvre has observed, the church, as a *representational space,* was one of the key foci of medieval social space. While Turner considers that the best representation of liminality for medieval laity was "the pilgrimage to a sacred site or holy shrine located at some distance away from the pilgrim's place of residence and daily labor" (1978, 4), I suggest that mystics, together with hermits and anchorites, represented a local, *in situ,* "sacred site" for the laity and a visible example of liminality.

HETEROTOPIA: THE LIMINAL SPACE MADE VISIBLE

In the general practice of a retirement to seclusion, the mystics' models were the early eremites of the Church. Those early hermits sought solitude in isolated places in order to concentrate on their relationship with God without the distractions of the material world. It seems, though, that they were often observed in this *flight* to isolation and consequently gathered a following of faithful for whom eremitic solitude signified sanctity. For example, Athanasius tells us that St. Antony retired to desert solitude after being unable to have complete privacy while living in an enclosed cell when "very many sufferers simply slept outside his cell, since he would not open the door to them" (1950, 61).

Even after retiring there, his recognized sanctity continued to draw a following, as Athanasius demonstrates when he relates that "after some days he returned to his mountain [and] from then on many came to him, and there were those, too, who had an affliction and risked the journey to him" (66).

Likewise, the medieval mystics lived away from society and within the view of it simultaneously. And just as the "between" state that they inhabited can be understood as liminal, so the site of their experiences may be understood in terms of that which Michel Foucault has termed a *heterotopia*. As I pointed out earlier in this chapter, Foucault uses the term *heterotopia[s]* to refer to places which "are outside of all place, even though it might be possible to indicate their location in reality ... [and which are] a sort of simultaneously mythic and real contestation of space in which we live" (1986/1967, 24). In this respect, *heterotopias* are real sites, existing visibly within a society, but often acting as a "countersite," a space that is *within* the society and yet representing something that is *beyond* that society.

Rolle, Julian, and the *Cloud* author, in their general practice of a degree of retirement from the material world, occupied a type of *heterotopia*—a space that they entered physically and spiritually in order to pursue their mystical longings but that, though existing in reality, in a real location, and physically obvious to observers, was closed to all except the contemplatives as far as its true purpose—that of personal communion with God—was concerned.

In the same way, the mystics' bodies, at the time of mystical experience, may have been observable but the exact nature of their experience could neither be known nor adequately expressed to any onlookers. As Susannah Mary Chewning comments, "[T]he mystic ... exist[s], paradoxically, in a type of *figurative* exile even from within a community; alone, though not solitary, by means of her extraordinary experience of God, she is separated spiritually and emotionally from those people with whom she may have physical contact" (2005, 104).

As Rolle explains in *The Form of Living*, "þai se oure body; bot þai se noght oure hert" (89: 15).[64] Likewise, the exact nature of the space, unknowable to present-day readers of the mystical texts, was a real

---

64. "they see our body; but they do not see our heart."

place where mystical experience was lived. In the language of paradox so intrinsic to Christianity's tenets, the diminishing of the outer
physical space (in the assuming of a contemplative or solitary abode)
offered the possibility of an inexhaustibly expansive internal space in
which an individual's relationship with God could be explored and
secured. Like Foucault's elaboration of the heterotopic space, the
space of mystical experience was visible and mythic simultaneously.

In addition, Foucault endows *heterotopias* with several "principles,"
two of which are particularly applicable to the study at hand.[65] Firstly, Foucault considers that "the heterotopia is capable of juxtaposing
in a single real place several spaces, several sites that are in themselves
incompatible" (1986/1967, 25).

This juxtaposing of several spaces in one single real place is attested to implicitly by the initial audience for Rolle's epistles and by
Julian's anchoritic lifestyle. That is, anchoritic life, in its definition
and practice, juxtaposed life and death. Recent archaeological exca-
vations of anchoritic cells of medieval England provide physical evidence of a literal as well as a metaphorical alignment. That is, life
and death were juxtaposed not only metaphorically for recluses but
in daily actuality to the extent that anchorholds frequently incorporated predug graves within their interiors, positioned so that the anchorite would have had to kneel in the grave to have a view through
the squint during offerings of the mass.

Julian's situation as an anchoress enclosed in a cell within church

---

65. Foucault (1986 [1967]) proposes five principles altogether in relation to *heterotopias*. Above I have chosen to elaborate the third and fifth principles. The other
three are, first, that "there is probably not a single culture in the world that fails to
constitute heterotopias" (24); second, that "a society, as its history unfolds, can make
an existing heterotopia function in a very different fashion" (25); and lastly that "heterotopias are most often linked to slices in time. . . . The heterotopia begins to function at full capacity when men arrive at a sort of absolute break with their traditional
time" (26). A case could be made for the applicability of all five principles to the mystics' sites but the third and fifth principles seem to me to be the most useful in contributing to an understanding of the space of mysticism.

precincts would have been a powerful symbol for the faithful. Mulder-Bakker summarizes the impact effectively when she says that "[f]or [the faithful] heaven and earth met in the sacred space of the church building and on the sacred spot of the anchorhold" (2005, 197). In addition to the church representing, for the populace, the sacred space of encounter with God, it was decorated with icons of the incarnation of God and of revered saints. Julian, as a living example of unmediated communion with the sacred, would have multiplied the iconography of the Norwich church. She thus existed in a "real" site but the site had a view to a space that was beyond the access of most people.

The second of Foucault's principles that finds resonance in the mystics' experiences is that

[*heterotopias*] always presuppose a system of opening and closing that both isolates them and makes them penetrable. In general, the heterotopic site is not freely accessible like a public place. Either the entry is compulsory, as in the case of entering a barracks or prison, or else the individual has to submit to rites and purifications. To get in, one must have a certain permission and make certain gestures. (24)

The medieval mystical space was not accessible to all. In fact, in order to gain access, an individual generally had to be first admitted to the formal religious life with all the rites that such admittance entailed or else had to manifest some other sign ("make certain gestures") of the desire to lead a life dedicated to God. This leads back to van Gennep's idea of the separation phase in the *rite of passage* and to the way in which the mystics signaled the beginning of their mystical undertakings.

RETURN, REAGGREGATION, AND RECIPROCITY IN THE SOCIAL SPACE

The mystics, like all religiously professed, inhabited a unique place in society. In their commitment to God they exchanged worldly for

spiritual interests. They denied themselves transitory material comforts in the hope of attracting eternal reward. They remained in the
world but experienced things that were not always *of* it. The mystics
differ from other religious, however, in that they retire from the social world but at some point return to that society bringing some
testimony of their experiences for the edification of others. Julian of
Norwich is adamant that her revelations were not given only to her
but that she was God's instrument, compelled to share her insights
with other "evyn Christians."[66] The *Cloud* author and Rolle exempli-
fy this same "return to society," too, in the writing of their didactic
works for others embarking on the contemplative life.

By doing so, they can be considered to be enacting van Gennep's
proposed final stage of the *rite of passage*. This third stage is termed
reaggregation and refers to the return of the liminar into society as
one who is "inwardly transformed and outwardly changed, [and to] a
new place in society" (Turner, 249). Inwardly, of course, the mystics
have been spiritually transformed by their experience of God. Outwardly, they assume a life of dedication and service. The writing and
dissemination of their didactic texts is another outward and visible
sign of their inner love of God.

Julian makes several allusions to her recognition of responsibility
to her fellow Christians and to her conviction that she is only the conduit of God's message for all Christians. For example, she stresses,

Alle that I say of me I mene in person of alle my evyn cristen, for I am lernyd
in the gostely shewyng of our lord god that he meneth so. And therfore I pray
yow alle for gods sake, and counceyle yow for yowre awne pro(f)yght, þat ye
leue the beholdyng of a wrech that it was schewde to, and myghtely, wysely
and mekely behold in god, that of hys curteyse loue and endlesse goodnesse
wolld shew it generally in comfort of vs alle. (LT. 8.319: 33–320: 39)[67]

66. "fellow Christians"
67. "All that I say about me I mean [to apply] to all my fellow Christians for I am
taught in the spiritual showing of our Lord God that he meant it so. And therefore I
pray you all for God's sake, and counsel you for your own profit, that you leave aside

The *Cloud* author tells his reader that the reason for his writing is that "for trewly I wolde haue profitid vnto þee [in þis writyng] at my simple kunnyng, & þat was myn entent" (Cl. 74.129: 16–18).[68]

Rolle, in his Prologue to *The Fire of Love,* records a similar intention, recommending a simple love of God in his readers: "Qwharefore þis boke I offyr to be sene, noȝt to philosophyrs nor wyes men of þis warld, ne to grete, devyens lappyd in questions infenyte, bot vnto boystus & vntaght, more besy to con lufe god þen many þinges to knawe" (*Fire,* 1.1.3: 23–25).[69]

In some ways, it is a curious inversion to understand mystics as teachers when, simultaneously, it has been ultimate privacy and solitude that have provided the environment that produced the material of their texts. There emerges a peculiar effacement of the private world in the act of writing about it. However, if it is not written about, it cannot be known. Thus, many mystics who did not write of their experiences are known to us through the writings of others. Underhill reminds us that true mysticism encompasses an active element, a giving back to others something of the mystical experience. She explains,

[A]ll records of mysticism in the west . . . are also the records of supreme human activity. . . . It is true that in nearly every case such "great actives" have first left the world, as a necessary condition of establishing communion with that Absolute life which reinforced their own: for a mind distracted by the many cannot apprehend the One. Hence something equivalent to the solitude of the wilderness is an essential part of mystical education. But, hav-

---

the consideration of the wretch to whom it was shown, and powerfully, wisely and meekly behold God, who of his courteous love and endless goodness willed to show it generally for the comfort of us all."

68. "for truly, I want you to profit by this writing, as far as my own simple knowledge, and that was my intention."

69. "Therefore I offer this book to be seen, not by philosophers nor wise men of this world, nor by the scholars heavily concerned with infinite questions, but to the simple and unlearned who are more concerned with loving God than with the knowledge of many things."

ing established that communion, re-ordered their lives upon transcendent levels, being united with their source not merely in temporary ecstasies but in virtue of a permanent condition of the soul, they were impelled to abandon their solitude; and resumed in some way, their contact with the world in order to become the medium whereby that Life flowed out to other men.... [T]his systole—and—diastole motion of retreat as the preliminary to a return remains the true ideal of Christian Mysticism in its highest development. Those in whom it is not found, however great in other respects they may be, must be considered as having stopped short of the final stage. (1995/1911, 174)

The Middle English mystics all reached this final stage, as defined by Underhill, in their fervent attempts to disseminate their experiences by the writing of them for others. Yet they make no claims to be speaking independently; the concepts they present are credited to God, and the mystics consider themselves to be mere channels for the message. Each expresses an unavoidable responsibility to disseminate the knowledge and experience that has been gained. In view of this, the mystical experience may be considered incomplete until the reaggregation of the mystic is effected and the texts are offered for others' edification.

An extrapolation of this edification, in terms of a link between mystical space and contemporary social space, between the spatial and the social connotations of "site," is interestingly exemplified by the current interest in Julian's reconstructed cell in St. Julian's church in Norwich. In her own lifetime, Julian's reputation for holiness had spread far enough beyond her anchorhold to make her a "site of visitation" for many pilgrims, including Margery Kempe. Rolle's hagiographer, too, gives details of miraculous healings at his burial site in the decades after his death though this site is not preserved. Julian's reputation, however, continues and enlarges, assuring her of continued *exemplum* status.[70]

70. Cynthia Hahn, in an article on the construction of sanctity in early-medieval saints' shrines, observes that "as a group, saints through their community, construct-

In their production of texts, Rolle, Julian, and the *Cloud* author can be considered to be still contributing to a form of Christian *habitus*. Their texts have entered the social space of the twenty-first century, to be "sites" of study and discussion. Their reaggregation is therefore ongoing and, in entering into the educative offerings of the texts, members of current society are enabled to participate vicariously in the mystical *rite of passage* in a similar way to the mystics' own contemporaries. An examination of the textual space and the particular "language of space" in the texts of Richard Rolle, Julian of Norwich, and the *Cloud* author are the interest of the next chapter.

---

ed not only a city of God but also a sacred geography of localities on earth" (1997, 1079–1105). Such a notion can be usefully applied to sites that are associated with mystics, such as Julian of Norwich.

Chapter Three

THE SPACE OF THE TEXT AND
THE LANGUAGE OF SPACE

Words move, music moves

Only in time; but that which is only living

Can only die. Words, after speech, reach

Into the silence. Only by the form, the pattern,

Can words or music reach

The stillness, as a Chinese jar still

Moves perpetually in its stillness.

(*T. S. Eliot,* Four Quartets 5)

THE SPACE OF THE MEDIEVAL BOOK

Texts are central to our knowledge and understanding of the mystics. The extant texts of Richard Rolle, Julian of Norwich, and the *Cloud* author who lived and wrote over six hundred years ago serve as witnesses to their authors' lives, endeavors, mystical experiences, and teachings, and are therefore the principal frames through which we now view them. In the *mise en abîme* of mystical space, texts and language can be seen to be represented in all strata. Texts existed as material objects in the day-to-day physical space of the mystics' lives.[1]

---

1. On the importance and relevance of the materiality of texts, see Mitchell (2005, 97–98).

They were the foci of examination and discussion in the social space, a space that was already heavily steeped in a long tradition of textual *habitus*. Language mediated between these strata and, in addition, textual and spatial metaphors were called into service in the expression of the mystics' encounters with God and, in turn, were employed in relaying details and insights from those experiences back into the social and physical space. Texts and the language of those texts provide a spatial interface in which the mystics and their readers meet.

The translation of mystical experience into word is partially contained by Lefebvre's concept of *spatial practice* in that the text is representative of a "dialectical interaction . . . [which results in society's] deciphering of its space" (1991/1974, 38). Such a dialectic is implicit in the manner in which, for the mystics themselves, texts formed an integral part of their lives, providing links to, and sources for, the framework of their experience and their writing. That is, though the mystics may have personally experienced God, the interpretation and conveyance of that experience to others finds expression within an existing framework of texts. The majority of texts considered in this present study are written in the vernacular but a long history of (predominantly) Latin textual culture underpins them. That is, as Irvine points out,

For over 1,200 years, the textual culture of Western Europe was governed by *grammatica,* the first of the liberal arts, which was known as "the art [or science] of interpreting the poets and other writers and the principles for speaking and writing correctly . . . [and] *grammatica* was foundational, a social practice that provided the exclusive access to literacy, the understanding of Scripture, the knowledge of a literary canon, and membership in an international Latin textual community. (1994, 1)

Thus, Rolle, Julian, and the *Cloud* author lived in a culture that valued the book and drew authority from the long-established practices of reading and writing.

The centrality of the book to medieval culture found its expression in many ways, one of the most prominent being the metaphorical connection between God, the conception of space, and the idea of textuality. This connection had been made at least as early as St Augustine who, in his *Confessions,* says of God: "You have extended like a skin the firmament of your Book."[2] Similarly, creation was often depicted as a book in which God's works could be read. The principal work of God within creation was his own son, Jesus Christ. This reinforces the idea that God is both inside and outside created space.

In the textual culture of the Middle Ages, not only was God and his creation likened to a book, but texts from past writers were copied and reproduced for dissemination, and consulted and quoted in order to imbue new texts with the authority needed for their own dissemination. Though it is sometimes suggested that creativity and originality in writing were anathema to the authors of the Middle Ages, this is to misunderstand the medieval ideas of *auctor* and *auctoritas.* Indeed, no advances could be made in any field of endeavor without the addition of new ideas and theories. However, in the Middle Ages, new ideas and advances were expected to give due recognition to the foundation of knowledge and to advance only on the firm base of that which had preceded them. Most especially, this foundation was God.

Rolle, Julian of Norwich, and the *Cloud* author all secure their writings with scriptural authority, the authority of the Church, and the writings and examples of the Church Fathers and saints, the ultimate authority for all of these being God. In addition, of course, the mystics experienced their own private revelations. However, the public nature of textual culture and the private sphere of personal experience were not mutually exclusive. As Umberto Eco points out, "When the medieval mystic turned away from earthly beauty he took refuge in the Scriptures and in the contemplative enjoyment of the inner rhythms of a soul in the state of grace" (1986, 9).

This dual concentration can be likened, spatially, to the apprehen-

2. Quoted in Jesse Gellrich, *The Idea of the Book in the Middle Ages: Language, Theory, Mythology and Fiction* (Ithaca: Cornell University Press, 1985), 29.

sion of the "outward" Word (in scriptural form) and the "inward" Word of God in their souls. After the mystical experience, the Word reemerges in the form of a mystic's own book, which then enters the culture to contribute to its textual *habitus,* thus subtly enlarging and redefining it, just as Jesus Christ as the Word made flesh had entered and redefined culture, particularly textual culture. However, Christ was not only written about but his body was sometimes analogized as a text. The *Fasciculum Morum,* for example, presents the idea that Christ's birth and death are artfully written into creation:

Just such a charter did God write for us on the cross when he who was beautiful above the sons of men stretched out his blessed body, as a parchment maker can be seen to spread a hide in the sun. In this way Christ, when his hands and feet were nailed to the cross, offered his body like a charter to be written on. The nails in his hands were used as a quill and his precious blood as ink. (in Bauerschmidt 1997, 208)

Richard Rolle uses this simile when he writes the following:

More yit, swet Jhesu, þy body is lyke a boke written al with rede ynke; so is þy body al written with rede woundes. Now, swete Jhesu, graunt me to rede upon þy boke, and somwhate to understond þe swetnes of þat writynge, and to have likynge in studious abydynge of þat redynge . . . and let me upon þis boke study at my matyns and hours and evynsonge and complyne, and evyre to be my meditacion, my speche, and my dalyaunce. (Med. 36:285–297)[3]

For Rolle, the wounded body of Christ is a focus of study, a meditative "book" to be held in the mind and not in the hand, to be read with the heart and not the physical eye. Thus the idea of the book in the Middle Ages encompasses both general notions of space in that it was represented both as the container and that which is contained—

3. "Moreover, sweet Jesus, your body is like a book written all in red ink; because your body is all written with red wounds. Now, sweet Jesus, allow me to read in this book, and to somewhat understand the sweetness of that writing, and to have the desire to studiously abide in that reading . . . and let me study this book at my matins and hours and evensong and compline, and ever to be my meditation, my speech and my occupation."

that is, the book, as container, contained words and ideas; and the book, indeed all books, are contained within creation. More specifically, a book represented both form and content. This idea, when applied to the medieval understanding of God, space, and the book, yields the conclusion that God was both the "container" in the person of God the Father as creator and the "contained" in the person of Jesus Christ who came into creation. That is, Christ was the Word made flesh and as such was able to be read within the book of creation and was Himself a created book.[4]

I discussed the notion of mystics as exemplars in the previous chapter. In effect, this means that they, too, could be "read" by society as an example to be followed. In the same way that iconography in a church, for example, offered a "literary" opportunity for the illiterate, so the mystics' lives of contemplation offered a living model of a pathway to God. In this way, the notion of Christ's body as a text, and a text as Christ's body, is expanded to include bodies of Christ's followers as examples. There is a scriptural precedent for this. Reference to "the book written within and without" occurs in Apocalypse 5:1 and Ezekial 2:9. More pointedly, St. Paul's second letter to the Corinthians explains that the then-standard letters of recommendation associated with traveling were not required because

You yourselves are the letter we carry about with us, written in our hearts, for all to recognise and to read. You are an open letter from Christ, promulgated through us; a message written in ink, but in the spirit of the living God, with human hearts instead of stone to carry it. Such, through Christ, is the confidence in which we make our appeal to God. Not that, left to ourselves, we are able to frame any thought as coming from ourselves; all our

---

4. See also Gellrich (1985) who offers the following analogy of Christ as a book from Pierre Bersuire: "For Christ is a sort of book written into the skin of the virgin. . . . That book was spoken in the disposition of the Father, written in the conception of the mother, exposited in the clarification of the nativity, corrected in the passion, erased in the flagellation, punctuated in the imprint of the wounds, adorned in the crucifixion above the pulpit, illuminated in the outpouring of blood, bound in the resurrection, and examined in the ascension" (17).

ability comes from God since it is he who has enabled us to promulgate his new law to men. It is a spiritual, not a written law; the written law inflicts death, whereas the spiritual law brings life. (2 Cor. 3: 2–7)

This passage highlights a central concern that the mystics, in writing of their experiences, also faced. Like St. Paul, they express the belief that the authority for, and the initiator of, their writing is God. Thus, while the body may be likened to a text, the mystics would not regard themselves as the writers of their bodies, but would see that God was writing them, fashioning them as a text for the rest of society to read. Thus, like their texts, they "contained" the word of God and simultaneously were contained *by* God, acting only under His instigation and direction.

POSITIVE AND NEGATIVE SPACES

The notion of the text and the body as container and that which is contained is parallel to the two broad conceptions of medieval space and potentially to the two approaches to the practice and understanding of medieval mysticism. These approaches are termed *via negativa* (or *apophatic*) and *via affirmativa* (or *cataphatic* or *affective*). It is generally considered that the former is Eastern in origin, its main source for the West being the writings of the pseudo-Dionysius, while the latter is more closely associated with Origen and Augustine (Louth 1981). In mystical theology, the *via negativa* is an approach that posits the notion that God is beyond the scope of human reason and therefore "may wel be loued, bot not þouȝt" (Cl. 6.26: 4).[5] That is, the "knowledge" of God is accessed by negation and by "successively abstracting God from images of Him" (Hart 1989, 190). In contrast, the *via affirmativa* proposes that God can be understood by his effects and by an application of the "language of gesture" (Gillespie and Ross 1992, 54) in a cumulative addition of images. The *via affirmativa*

5. "may well be loved but not thought"

regards everything as like God whereas the *via negativa* posits the opposite: that nothing is like God (Medcalf and Reeves 1981, 161).

The informing notion of the *via negativa* proved to have much in common with the later theory of the operation of reason and of cosmology as expounded by Ockham.[6] That is, that God cannot be reached by an application of human reason; faith and reason are ultimately separate. In contrast, affective mysticism, with its approach to God grounded in the successive application of images, seems to have some affinity with Scholasticism which, according to Erwin Panofsky, posited that "the existence of God was . . . demonstrable from His creation rather than *a priori*" (1967/1951, 7). The association between affective mysticism and Scholasticism is my own interpretive extrapolation of part of Panofsky's thesis. In fact, Panofsky does not elaborate any association between the two, although he does discuss mysticism and nominalism together, asserting that "these two extremes, mysticism and nominalism, are, in a sense, nothing but opposite aspects of the same thing. Both mysticism and nominalism cut the tie between reason and faith" (1967/1951, 14). His views are contentious and are not of direct interest to the present project. However, it has been suggested, for example, that nominalism, "in emphasising the indeterminism of the supernatural order [and] the impossiblity of knowing God at the natural level [opened] the door . . . to mystical, non-rational approaches" (Medcalf and Reeves, 1981, 70–71). Of course, this view can be challenged. Affective mysticism, in fact, operated very much within the natural world, certainly insofar as it drew its images from that world and inasmuch as Christ's body was a focus of adoration. I would argue, then, that the mystics acknowledged the embodiment of God in the person of Jesus Christ, and were therefore able to ascend to the Godhead by an immersion

6. Generally, William Ockham is described as a "nominalist" but, as Ruud cautions, "'nominalism' was never a 'school' in any strict sense, and . . . although Ockham was the outstanding thinker of the fourteenth century, even his closest followers disagree with aspects of his thought" (1995, 33).

in the humanity of Jesus. That is, "the Word made flesh" allowed the mystics to assimilate the Word as part of their fleshly experience and to translate that experience back into the words of their texts. Thus, the Word, their words, and their experiences all can be considered to be contained in mystical space. Even when a specific emphasis on Jesus Christ is absent from the texts, as is the case in *The Cloud of Unknowing,* the Christian underpinning of the text implies Christ's presence throughout, lending credence to Jacques Derrida's opinion that "the negative movement of the discourse on God is only a phase of positive ontotheology" (quoted in Hart 1989, 189). Hart is of a similar opinion, reasoning from Thomas Aquinas's view that "the transcendental properties of being belong eminently to God [and] if this is so, negative theology and positive theology work together in a dialectic; moreover this dialectic has a positive accent for it affirms that God is the highest value" (190).[7]

With regard to a consideration of space, the notion of a dialectic between positive and negative mysticism is apt, especially when considering the approaches to mysticism of Richard Rolle, the *Cloud* author, and Julian of Norwich. The implications of such a dialectic are too vast to be considered adequately here, so the following brief observations will have to suffice. The *Cloud* author broadly takes the apophatic approach by insisting that as God cannot be known but only loved, then the approach to God should be likewise. He therefore recommends that his reader divest himself of all thoughts "so þat nouȝt worche in þi witte ne in þi wille bot only [God] him-self" (Cl. 3.16: 5–6).[8] The author is unequivocal in his recommendation to obliterate all thought when he goes on to point out that "bot of God him-self can no man þinke" (Cl. 6.26: 1–2).[9] Rolle's approach is

7. Ninian Smart holds a similar opinion, declaring that "bare being differs not a whit from bare nonbeing save that it signals the commitment to a certain style of ontology" (1992, 19).
8. "so that nothing works in the intellect or the will but only [God] himself"
9. "but of God himself no-one can think"

more ambiguous for, while he is adamant that "He treuly knawes god parfitly, þat hym felys incomprehensibyll & vnabyl to be knawen" (*Fire*, 1.7,14: 24–26),[10] he makes liberal reference to hierarchically ascending angelic orders that progressively get closer to God, and his lyrics are replete with graphic images of his love for Christ and, in turn, the suffering Christ in his humanity. Rolle's approach, then, is variously considered both apophatic and affective or, perhaps more correctly, Rolle stresses the ineffability of God but at the same time approaches him from a cataphatic base. Julian's approach is broadly affective: she declares that "God will be knowen" (LT. 5.301: 29)[11] and, in the elaboration of her showings, she offers complex images that indicate God's accessibility.

Of the two approaches it seems that a text based on affective mysticism can more possibly "contain" God while the negatively orientated text seeks to show God's "absence." Thus, if affective mysticism is envisaged as a filling of the distance between God and the self, and negative mysticism as the emptying of the distance between God and the self, then the filled and the emptied space become the same thing because both enable access to God. Just as in medieval cosmology the area outside the *primum mobile* was considered to be a void "full of God" (Lewis 1964, 97), so the two opposite approaches to mysticism can be understood, in the metaphorical spatial sense, as two halves of a whole or as the positive and the negative images of the same thing. That is, the two aspects encompass the wholeness of God in His immanence and transcendence. Textually, affective approaches revolve around God's immanence as expressed in the second person of God, Jesus Christ, and He, like the text, is the solid embodiment of the Word. Texts of negative mysticism, in contrast, focus on the transcendence of God and therefore emphasise the ineffability of God by use of words that frequently indicate absence and negation.

10. "He truly knows God perfectly, who feels him to be incomprehensible and unknowable."
11. "God will be known"

The ineffability of God, however, does not necessarily mean that the language of the mystical texts is inadequate to the task.

THE LANGUAGE OF SPACE: PRESENCE, REPRESENTATION, AND INEXPRESSIBILITY

The carefully crafted language of the vernacular texts of Richard Rolle, the *Cloud* author, and Julian of Norwich has been shown by several scholars to be a vital component of the realization of the authors' stated aim of strengthening their readers' relationship with God. Stephen Katz, for example, has demonstrated that language in mystical texts serves several functions in addition to signification, "an essential one being the transformation of consciousness" (1992, 6). Considerable attention has also been drawn to the prominence of "ineffability topoi" in the texts that seem to suggest, at first, that language is inadequate to the mystics' task of writing of their own mystical experiences for the edification of others. It is possible, however, that ineffability has been overstated in regard to these texts and that far from being inadequate to the task of expressing mystical experience, the language the mystics use not only establishes clear meaning but also works in other ways to accomplish a metaphorical and spiritual diminution of space between the reader and God. Furthermore, in the process of assisting the "ascent" of the reader, the language of the mystical texts also "ascends" to the extent that the gap between presence and representation is diminished and often completely erased. In this regard, the common medieval practice of reading texts exegetically (and the world as an analogous representation of divine order) cannot be disregarded in a study of the "language of space" of the mystical texts. By that I mean that though exegetical levels of themselves are not evocative of spatiality, the shifting signification between each level, and particularly between the literal and anogogical levels, implies a recuperation of the fallen language to the extent that, by the anogogical level, language has delivered meaning to its highest possible earthly signification: God. In Lefebvrian terms, then, here I am positing the interplay between literal and (the highest) metaphorical signification as a *representation of space* in that it conceptualizes an ascent of language.

In medieval times, the notional "gap" between presence and representation in both spoken and written language was conceived of, philosophically, as a consequence of the Fall. That is, though originally Adam may have possessed "hermeneutic mastery . . . [as] he deftly distinguished between *signum* and *res significata,*"[12] the consequence of his trespass is that "signs [became] the indispensable and imperfect vehicle for knowledge, religious or otherwise" (Katz 8). While Christ, as the Word made flesh, was considered to be the perfect mediator between presence and representation, the translation of Christ to the written and spoken word was not a straightforward matter. Thomas Aquinas insisted, for example, that in speaking of God, "we must distinguish what [the words] express—goodness, life and the like—from their manner of expressing it."[13]

In these terms, God could be talked about in certain ways, literally and metaphorically, but could neither be known nor expressed in his own *esse.* That is, in the medieval conception, there was a difference between talking *about* God and *defining* God and many, like Aquinas, believed that the former was possible while the latter was impossible.

Neither of the two main modes of medieval mystical practice, the *via negativa* and the *via affirmativa,* sought to "define" God but merely to describe and facilitate for others an experience of God, the

12. Kevin Hart, *The Trespass of the Sign: Deconstruction, Theology and Philosophy* (Cambridge: Cambridge University Press, 1989), 3.

13. Thomas Aquinas, *Summa Theologiae,* trans. and ed. Timothy McDermott (London: Methuen, 1989), 31.3. McDermott retains the original sequence of St. Thomas's work (incorporating *sequence of articles, question articles, objections, sed contra, etc.*) but uses a modern paragraph format. Therefore, my method of citation of the work consists only of page and paragraph numbers as featured in this edition.

former approach by its use of a language of negation and absence, the latter by its utilization of metaphor and analogy.

In reality, however, in attempting to convey something of their experience of the Divine to others, it may appear that the mystical writers were constrained in their attempts by an earthly, "fallen" language. That is, language mediates between the experience of the divine presence and the representation of that experience and, once the experience is mediated, the exactness of the description of that experience is called into contention. Generally, this has meant that ineffability topoi have featured strongly in mystical literature. Paradoxically, however, the notion that it is difficult, even impossible, to define such experience is at least partially effaced in the very act of writing of it. Thus Richard Rolle, the *Cloud* author, and Julian of Norwich give tangible form to the view that meaning is not only possible in their texts but assured because they assert that they are operating under the influence of a "divine direction" by which they acknowledge God as the initiator of both their mystical experiences and the written accounts of them. Ineffability, then, may have troubled the mystics in theory but it had minimal effect on them in practice and, I contend, had more to do with their acknowledgment of God's inexpressible "essence" than with any limits that language may have seemed to impose on their ability to explain the human experience of God.

In Julian's case, this "divine direction" is doubly potent as it overrides the long-held theological and social objections to preaching (and teaching) by women. Thus, when Julian asks, "Botte for I am a womann schulde I therfore leve that I schulde nouȝt telle ȝowe the goodenes of god, syne that I sawe in that same tyme that is his will, that it be knawenn?" (ST. 6.222: 46–48),[14] she is clearly posing a rhetorical question because, in the very act of asking it she is challenging (or dismissing) "earthly" authority on the subject. Furthermore, Ju-

---

14. "But because I am a woman should I therefore believe that I should not tell you of the goodness of God, since I saw at that same time that it is his will that it be known?"

lian addresses possible concerns about inexpressibility when she explains that she received her revelations in three manners: "by bodyly syght and by worde formyde in my vnderstondyng, and by goostely syght" (LT. 9.323: 29–30).[15] Though she acknowledges that, in regard to "the goostely sight" that "I can nott ne may shew it as openly ne as fully as I would"[16] (LT. 9.323: 31–32), the very statement implies that the first two modes of reception *are* able to be presented to readers without impediment. Julian suggests that "bodyly syght" operates on a literal level of signification, and thus it is amenable to straightforward description. Likewise, the "worde formyde in my vnderstondynge," being already in language form, is a matter of mere transcription. Any lack of clarity implicit in the third mode is also resolved because Julian trusts "in our lord god almightie that he shall of his godnes and for iour loue make yow to take it more ghostely and more sweetly then I can or may tell it" (LT. 9.323: 32–34).[17]

Here Julian intimates that a reader's attention to the text's signifiers is sufficient because any gap between presence and representation will be resolved by *the* Word, Jesus Christ; any necessary interpretive mediation required by the reader will be effected by Christ.

Theologically, hesitation about the appropriateness and effectiveness of writing about mystical experience is reassessed in the recognition of Jesus Christ as "the Word made Flesh" who is the perfect mediator between God and humanity. That is, Christ as the embodied Word *is* the perfect intermediary who can elaborate himself unequivocally. Julian exemplifies this notion when she explains, in the beginning of her revelations, that "Right so, both god and man, the

15. "by physical sight and by words formed in my understanding, and by spiritual sight." Julian's explication here of the three modes of mystical apprehension shows some parallel with Hugh of St. Victor's elaboration of *letter, sense,* and *sentence* in discourse.

16. "I cannot and may not show it as openly nor as fully as I wish"

17. "in our Lord God Almighty that he shall out of his goodness and love for you make you receive it more spiritually and sweetly than I can or may tell it."

same that sufferd for me, I conceived truly and mightly that it was him selfe that shewed it me without anie meane" (LT. 4.294: 6–8).[18]

When Rolle proclaims himself Christ's messenger in *Ego Dormio,* he, too, is immersed in the duty he believes he has been called to accomplish and he demonstrates absolute assurance in the success of his undertaking. Similarly, the *Cloud* author offers *The Cloud of Unknowing* to aspiring contemplatives in the firm conviction that "ȝif soche men miȝt se it, þei schuld by þe grace of God be greetly counforted þer-by" (Cl. Pro.3: 7–8).[19]

Once confidence in the clear communication of their message is achieved, the mystics put their language to other uses far beyond straightforward signification. As I have said, language in mysticism has many functions, one in particular being to "mak[e] one self an appropriate subject for mystical ascent" (Katz 13). Implicit even in the notion of ascent is a change, a movement, in metaphorical and spiritual space toward God. Often in the texts, however, this ascent is translated into a shift in focus for the reader/contemplative from exterior to interior space. One way in which it was recommended that the shift be achieved was through the recitation of the Holy Name of "Jesus." Denis Renevey explains, in regard to Rolle's concentration on the Holy Name, for example, that this is a

moving of the attention from signified to signifier [which] results in the ability on the part of the contemplative to perceive and decode the meaning couched in spiritually charged words. Such sophisticated literary competence is developed in part within the commentary tradition, with the historical, allegorical, tropological and anagogical readings of the text. (1999, 110)[20]

18. "Just so, I perceived truly and powerfully that it was he, both God and man, the same who suffered for me, that showed me [the revelation] without any intermediary."

19. "If such men could see it, they would by the grace of God be greatly comforted."

20. Renevey points to the practice of the short so-called Jesus prayer in the Orthodox tradition and the more general use of the name of Jesus in that tradition as

Like the mantra of many present-day meditative practices, the repetition of the name was aimed at centering the concentration to such an extent that thought did not intrude. Rolle seems to be advocating something similar to this when he recommends "[I]f þou wil be wele with God, and have grace to rewle þi lyf, and com til þe joy of luf, þis name Jhesu, fest it swa fast in þi hert, þat it com never owt of þi thoght. And when þou spekes til hym, and says "Jhesu," thurgh custom, it sal be in þi ere joy, in þi mouth hony, and in þi hert melody" (F.L. 108: 1–6).[21] An important interspersion here is the phrase "thurgh custom" which suggests that the frequent repetition of the name acts as a type of transforming mechanism into a God-centered state. The Holy Name elicits in Rolle a response that is akin to his three modalities of mystical apprehension. That is, the "joy," "hony," and "melody" are virtually synonymous with *fervor, dulcor,* and *canor* and the elevation of the discourse to its highest mystical level works to effect a transfer of desire from the physical to the spiritual domain. Thus, Rolle's language is not just an expression of his mystical experience but is an aspect of the experience itself, not only facilitating his transportation from the physical to the spiritual space but also providing him with a physical rapture that registers in several of the sensory modalities.

Similarly, a translocation of focus is implicit in the *Cloud* author's formulation and language becomes the means of accomplishing it. Thus, he recommends a concentration on little words such as "god"

---

an efficient and complete devotion. However, he clearly demonstrated a similar devotion to the name of Jesus in Rolle's time. He points out that "[i]n 1274, the second council of Lyon adopted the Pope Gregory X constitution, *Decet Donum Dei Sanctitudo,* which encouraged kneeling and bowing of the head at the mention of the Name, especially during mass" (1999, 103).

21. "[I]f you want to be well with God, and have his grace to rule your life, and to come to the joy of his love, then this name Jesus, fasten it so firmly in your heart, that it never leaves your thoughts. And when you speak to him, and say 'Jhesu' through custom/habit, it shall be joy to your ears, honey to your mouth, and melody to your heart."

or "love" without any accompanying concentration on the words'
meanings. However, he is nearer to Julian in approach than he is to
Rolle when he presents "litil worde[s] of o silable" (Cl. 7.28: 11–12)[22]
as particularly powerful, not in their connotations, but as signifiers
alone. Any word of one syllable is suitable in the *Cloud* author's opinion, as long as the word is "best accordyng vnto þe propirte of preier"
(Cl. 39.76: 23).[23] He recommends that the contemplative

Cheese þee wheþer þou wilt, or anoþer as þe list: whiche þat þee likeþ best
of o silable. & fasten þis worde to þin herte, so þat it neuer go þens for þing
þat bifalleþ. Þis worde schal be þi scheeld & þi spere, wheþer þou ridest on
pees or on werre. Wiþ þis worde þou schalt bete on þis cloude & þis derknes
abouen þee. Wiþ þis worde þou schalt smite doun al maner þouȝt vnder þe
cloude of forȝeting; inso-mochel þat ȝif any þouȝt prees apon þee to aske
þee what þou woldest haue, answere him wiþ no mo wordes bot wiþ þis o
worde. & ȝif he profre þee of his grete clergie to expoune þee þat worde &
to telle þee þe condicions of þat worde, sey him þat þou wilt haue it al hole,
& not broken ne vndon. & ȝif þow wilt holde þee fast on þis purpose, sekir
be þou he wil no while abide. & whi? For þou wilt not late him fede him on
soche swete meditacions touchid before. (Cl. 7.28: 14–29:6)[24]

The little word here is posited as serving a multiplicity of functions,
none of which is signification. First, the word is to be fixed in the
heart and to remain there, immovably. As such, it is internalized and

---

22. "little word[s] of one syllable"
23. "well suited to the property of prayer"
24. "Choose whatever you will, or another [word] as you please: whatever you
like best of one syllable. And fasten this word to your heart, so that it never goes from
there, no matter what happens. This word will be your shield and your spear, whether
you ride in peace or war. With this word you will beat on this cloud and this darkness
above you. With this word you will push down all thought under the cloud of forgetting; so much so that if any thought presses upon you to ask what you want, answer it
with no other word except this one word. And if you are prompted, because of much
learning, to expound on the word and to consider the conditions of that word, say
that you will keep the word whole, and will not break or undo it. And if you will hold
fast to this purpose, you can be sure that the thought will not stay. And why? Because
you will not let it be fed on such sweet meditations that we touched on before."

enclosed by the heart so that its previous (and usual) function as a signifier is erased. That is, the word no longer acts as a means of communication in the outside world but, like the contemplative himself, is enclosed and directed toward a wholly spiritual intention. Second, as both "þi scheeld & þi spere," the word is to provide protection and a means of attack against life's vicissitudes. That is, the word becomes an effective means of keeping the world at a distance. Third, it is to act as a "key" to the contemplative state, the mere thought or uttering of it precipitating a translation of the individual from the earthly state to the liminal state between the cloud of forgetting and the cloud of unknowing. Fourth, the word is to stand for all words. Like the divine Word made flesh, this little word contains all words and meanings within it. Last, the word is impenetrable and indivisible, closed to interpretation. That is, the word *is*, just as God *is*. In literal spatial terms, this little word—spoken or written—takes up minimal space on the page, yet, in the *Cloud* author's view of it, it is able to encompass all meaning. The *Cloud* author makes use of this idea of a small word full of meaning when he specifically considers that God is best described by the word "is." He states that

Þer is no name, ne felyng ne beholdyng more, ne so moche, acordyng vnto euer-lastyngnes, þe whiche is God, as is þat þe whiche may be had, seen & felt in þe blinde & þe louely beholding of þis worde IS. For ȝif þou sey "Good" or "Faire Lorde," "Swete," "Merciful" or "Riȝtwise," "Wise," or "Alwitty," "Miȝti" or "Almiȝti," "Witte" or "Wisdome," "Miȝte" or "Strengþe," "Loue" or "Charite" or what oþer soche þing þat þou sey of God: al it is hid & enstorid in þis litil worde IS. For þat same is to him only to be, þat is alle þees for to be. (PC. 143: 19–27)[25]

25. "There is no name, no feeling, no experience of God that is more, so much more in terms of eternity, as that which may be had, seen and felt in the blind and lovely beholding of the word IS. For if you say 'Good' or 'Fair Lord' or 'Sweet,' 'Merciful' or 'Righteous,' 'Wise,' 'All-knowing,' 'Mighty' or 'Almighty,' 'Knowledge' or 'Wisdom,' 'Might' or 'Strength,' 'Love' or 'Charity' or any other such thing that you say of God: all of it is hidden and contained in this little word IS. For it [belongs] to him only to be, and to be all."

More recently, in an echo of the *Cloud* author's consideration that God is encompassed in the word "is," Northrop Frye has suggested that God can be regarded more appropriately as a "verb" than a "noun," as a process rather than a thing.[26] The "noun" proceeds from the "process" into the earthly, descriptive realm and God becomes the trace of the idea behind the ideas. Frye explains that he is concerned not with "the question of whether God is dead or obsolete, but with the question of what resources of language may be dead or obsolete" (1982, 6). Frye further explains that

God always gives himself a name, defin[ing] himself ... as "I am that I am" which scholars say is more accurately rendered "I will be what I will be." That is, we might come closer to what is meant in the Bible by the word 'God' if we understood it as a verb and not a verb of simple asserted existence but a verb implying a process accomplishing itself. This would involve trying to think our way back to a conception of language in which words were words of power, conveying primarily the sense of forces and energies rather than analogues of physical bodies. To some extent this would be a reversion to the metaphorical language of primitive communities.... But it would also be oddly contemporary with post-Einsteinian physics, where atoms and electrons are no longer thought of as things but rather as traces of processes. God may have lost his function as the subject or object of a predicate, but may not be so much dead as entombed in a dead language. (Ibid.)

The emphasis in the mystical texts on the role of the will in approaching God is related to Frye's proposition. Potentially, the area of influence of a process, as opposed to a thing, is vast. The emphasis on the alignment of the will of the mystics with the will of God captures, in part, this notion of the "process." Love becomes a way of being rather than an objectification. Rolle stresses that "lufe es a wilful stiryng of owre thoght intil God" (Com. 73: 8–9),[27] though

26. St. Thomas Aquinas says that "St. John Damascene variously derives the Greek name for God—*theos*—from Greek words for running, burning and gazing at, all of them activities. Nevertheless the word expresses not what God does but what God is" (*Summa* 33: 8).
27. "love is a willful stirring of our thoughts toward God"

here Rolle is only partly in agreement with the *Cloud* author who, while equally stressing the "stirring of will," does not regard that the will should propel our thoughts toward God. Instead, the *Cloud* author recommends the putting aside of thought in order that "noþing leue in þi worching mynde bot a nakid entent streching into God, not cloþid in any specyal þouȝt of God in hym-self, how he is in him-self or in any of his werkes, bot only þat he is as he is" (P.C. 135: 20–22).[28] Thus, in the *Cloud* author's formulation, God is not a "thing" to which attributes can be attached. The author's insistence that God "may wel be loued, bot not þouȝt" (Cl. 6.26: 4)[29] also works toward the deobjectification of God. That is, God can be loved by the act of the will but cannot be "known" by the application of thought or descriptors.

Julian also finds God explained in five particular words or phrases, all verbs of volition without objects with the exception of the final "schalle se." She states that "in this fyve wordes [I wille, I schalle, I maye, I can, and þowe schalle se] god wille be closed in ryste and in pees" (ST. 15.249: 12).[30] In the Long Text Julian expands the scope of the volitional verbs, aligning them directly with God in the persons of the Trinity:

There he seyth: I may, I vnderstonde for the father; and there he seyth: I can, I vnderstond for the sonne; and there he seyth: I wylle, I vnderstonde for the holy gost; and there he seyth: I shalle, I vnderstonde for the vnyte of the blessyd trinite, thre persons and oon truth; and there he seyth: Thou shalt se thy selfe, I vnderstond the (onyng) of alle man kynde that shalle be sauyd in to the blyssedfulle trynite. (LT. 31.417: 6–12)[31]

28. "nothing [is] left in the working mind except a naked intent stretching to God, not clothed in any special thought of God himself, how he is in himself or in any of his works, but only that he is as he is."

29. "may well be loved, but not thought"

30. "in these five words [I will, I shall, I may, I can, and you shall see] God wants to be enclosed in rest and peace." Here, of course, Julian is using "wordes" to refer to phrases and not individual words.

31. "Where he says: I may, I understand this as the father; and where he says: I

The final reflexive verb of the processual series aligns the self with God in the Trinity and thereby effects a deobjectification of both self and God. This suggested subsuming of the self in God appears to be the consequential outcome of Julian's earlier vision of the glorified Christ. In that vision Christ says, "I it am," elaborating the statement only, in repetition, with the addition of one superlative and then a series of related clauses that are predicated, almost exclusively, on Julian:

I it am, I it am. I it am that is the hyghest. I it am that thou lovyst. I it am that thou lykyst. I it am that thou servyst. I it am that thou longest. I it am that thou desyryst. I it am that thou menyste. I it am that holy church prechyth the and techeyth thee. I it am that shewde me before to the. (LT. 26.402: 7–11)[32]

Thus, Christ is shown to be both beyond description and the ultimate description of the most basic statement of being. This statement of being places Christ both outside and inside the sign system simultaneously and is comparable, spatially, with God as container and as that which is contained.

Initially, this vision greatly puzzles Julian, but she trusts God will provide understanding. She admits that

The nomber of the words passyth my wyttes and my vnderstandyng and alle my myghtes for they were in þe hyghest as to my syght, for ther in is com-

---

can, I understand the son; and where he says: I will, I understand the Holy Spirit; and where he says: I shall, I understand the unity of the blessed Trinity, three persons and one truth; and where he says: You shall see yourself, I understand the [onyng] of all man kind who shall be saved with the blessed Trinity."

32. Note that here, in my modern rendering of the quote, I do not invert the word order of the leading, and repeated, clause as I consider that, in its original form, it more nearly represents the collapse of distance between subject, verb, and object that Julian is describing more broadly as applying to the relationship between God and herself, God and humanity: "I it am, I it am. I it am that is the highest. I it am that you love; I it am that you like; I it am that you serve. I it am that you long for; I it am that you desire. I it am that you speak of. I it am that holy Church preaches and teaches you. I it am that showed me before to you."

prehendyd I can nott telle what; but the joy that I saw in the shewyng of them passyth alle that hart can thynk or soule desyr. And therfore theyse wordes be nott declaryd here; but evyry man, aftyr the grace that god gevyth hym in vnder standyng and lovyng, receyve them in our lordes menyng. (LT. 26.403: 11–18)[33]

Thus, Julian, like the *Cloud* author and Rolle, finds that God contains all meaning and that issues of inexpressibility, presence, and representation are all resolved in God. In the *via affirmativa* approach to mystical practice, of course, Christ specifically functions as the ultimate Word in which signifier and signified are flawlessly combined, thereby offering an opening of language in which signification can expand endlessly. While such expansion and multiplication of signification is a feature of the *via affirmativa,* the *Cloud* author's *via negativa* approach works toward reducing signification possibilities. Despite this, he warns against too literal an interpretation of words in general and of prepositions in particular. For example, he advises the reader to, "Beware þat þou conceyue not bodely þat þat is mente goostely, þof al it be spokyn in bodely wordes, as ben þees: UP or DOUN, IN or OUTE, BEHINDE or BEFORE, ON O SIDE or ON OÞER" (Cl. 61.114: 3–5).[34]

While *the Cloud* author is thus prepared to disavow the literal power of earthly prepositions, it is interesting to note that the prepositions that he uses, metaphorical or otherwise, are always "upward" in their literal connotation. That is, in describing the longing for God he uses the image of the "dart of love piercing the cloud," not a dart

33. "The interpretation of the words surpasses my intelligence and my understanding and all my powers for they were the highest, as I see it, for what is to be comprehended in them I cannot tell; but the joy that I saw when they were shown passes all that the heart can think or the soul desire. And therefore these words are not explained here; but every man, according to the grace that God gives him in understanding and love, should receive them as our Lord intends."

34. "Beware that you do not interpret physically that which is meant spiritually, although it is spoken in physical words, such as these: UP or DOWN, IN or OUT, BEHIND or IN FRONT OF, ON ONE SIDE or the OTHER."

penetrating the soil, thus seeming to direct the spiritual attention upward and not downward. However, the author asserts that no direction can be inferred from any spiritual occurrence. Thus, in answer
to the rhetorical question (prompted by acknowledgment of Christ's
ascension upward to heaven and the sending of the Holy Ghost from
above), "whi schalt þou not directe þi mynde upward bodely in þe
tyme of þi preier?" (Cl. 60.112: 2–3),[35] the author simply states that
"it was more semely þat it was upwardes & fro abouen, þan ouþer
donwardes & fro byneþen, byhinde or before, on o side or on oþer"
(Cl. 60.112: 6–8).[36]

Marion Glasscoe considers that "the only reason for upwards being appropriate lies in the metaphorical connotations of 'up' [and]
for the *Cloud*-author there is an iconographic quality in the nature of
things which enables them to point beyond themselves" (1993, 178).
The *Cloud* author, however, is equally suspicious of both the physical and the spiritual applications of prepositions when he emphasizes
that "heuen goostly is as neiȝ doun as up" (Cl. 60.112: 10).[37] The ve-
hemence of his denunciation of prepositions, though, is somewhat
weakened when, in the following chapter, he proceeds to reinscribe
such prepositions bodily, reading an allegorical and metaphorical significance into the upright stance of humans as opposed to the bowed
aspect of animals. He writes that

a man, þe whiche is þe seemliest creature in body þat euer God maad, is not
maad crokid to þe erþewardes as ben alle oþer beestes, bot upriȝte to heu-
enwardes; for whi þat it schulde figure in licnis bodely þe werke of þe soule
goostly, þe whiche falleþ to be upriȝt goostly & not crokid goostly. Take kepe
þat I sey upriȝt goostly, & not bodely. For how schulde a soule, þe whiche in
his kynde haþ no maner þing of bodelines, be streinid upriȝt bodily? Nay, it
may not be. (Cl. 61.113: 20–114: 2)[38]

35. "why should you not direct your mind upward physically in time of prayer?"
36. "it was more seemly that it was upward and from above, than either downward and from beneath, behind or in front of, from one side or the other."
37. "heaven, spiritually, is as near down as up."
38. "a man, who, in body, is the seemliest creature God ever made, is not made

The *Cloud* author's explanation does little to clarify his point because it still contains the kernel of the idea of uprightness. However, he is persistent in his efforts to disengage other words from their conventional attachments. In order to do this he often juxtaposes a word with its negative opposite. For example, he explains that "noȝwhere bodely is eueriwhere goostly" (Cl. 68.121: 14–15)[39] and advises the reader to "lete nouȝt þerfore, bot trauayle besily in þat nouȝt with a wakyng desire to wilne to haue God, þat no man may knowe" (Cl. 68.121: 21–122: 2).[40] Further, he recommends that the contemplative "lat be þis eueriwhere & þis ouȝt, in comparison of þis [noȝwhere & þis] nouȝt" (Cl. 68.122: 6–7).[41] The recommendations represent the exchange of slippery positive signifiers for their slippery negative reflections. In fact, "everywhere" can be no more quantified than "nowhere" and yet, because the latter term points to an absence, it orientates the contemplative more directly toward his chosen life, reflecting his own chosen absence from the world. Moreover, in general, the *Cloud* author's method of detaching signifiers from their earthly signification may be seen as analogous to the author's endeavor to detach the contemplative from his attachment to all earthly things, one of which might be considered to be language.

In contrast, Rolle shows little deprecation of literalism. In fact, as I have already pointed out, in *Ego Dormio* he expresses a view of the hierarchies of angels that stretch right to the throne of God.[42]

Though Rolle is not necessarily suggesting that God's place is in

---

crooked/bent over to the earth, as are all the other beasts, but upright toward heaven; for why should it not reflect in bodily likeness, the work of the soul spiritually, which happens to be upright spiritually and not crooked spiritually. Take heed that I say upright spiritually and not physically. For how could a soul, which by its nature has no body, be strained upright physically? No, it cannot be."

39. "nowhere physically is everywhere spiritually"

40. "leave nothing therefore, and work busily in that nothing with a waking desire and will to have God, whom no man may know."

41. "leave this everywhere and this everything, in preference for this [nowhere and this] nothing."

42. See E.D. 61: 18–23.

the Empyrean, the detailing of hierarchies is evocative of concepts of ascent. Rolle has no hesitation in designating heaven as "up," nor in using a language that continually posits an upward direction. For example, he combines the notion of an upward movement and an "upward" heaven when he says that "Thoghtis truly of cristis lufars in goynge vp ar swyft & in cours acordynge, with þingis passynge þa wil not be bowde nor with fleschly fylthis tyde, bot to ascend þa cese not to þa heuyns come" (*Fire,* 1.29.63: 14–16).[43] The contemplation, therefore, of such a lover of God, is seen to be "goynge vp" in the opposite direction to earthly preoccupations. In fact, everything about contemplation is posited as metaphorically altering the focus from down to up. Thus, for example, Rolle considers that

Sothely when lufe of euerlastynge in owr saules is treuly kyndyld, with-out doute all vanite of þis warld, and all fleschly lufe, bot als foulyst fylth is haldyn; And whils þe saule to besy deuocyon gyfyn no þinge bot plesance of þe makar desyrs, meruelusly in þe self with fyer of lufe it byrns, þat soyftly in gostly godis profetand & growan hens-forth in to þe sliper way & broid þat to dede ledis it fallis not, bot raþer with a heuenly fyer vp raysid in to contemplatyue lyfe it gose & ascendis. (*Fire,* 1.20.45: 11–18)[44]

Rolle even nominates Jesus as a direction in space, a preposition of place, when he describes the directing of all love and service toward God as "clymbande tyll Jhesu-warde" (F.L. 96: 1).[45] The "clymbande" represents a combined notion of willful movement and metaphori-

---

43. "Truly, the thoughts of Christ's lovers in their ascent are swift and on course; they will not be bound by passing things nor tied up by fleshly filth, but they ascend to heaven without ceasing."

44. "In fact, when the love of eternity is truly kindled in our souls, without doubt all the vanity of this world, and all fleshly lust, is held to be the foulest filth. And while the soul is busily given to devotion, desiring nothing but the pleasure of its creator, it burns marvelously with the fire of love, and gradually in spiritual good it profits and grows and henceforth it no longer follows the broad and slippery way that leads to death, but rather, with a heavenly fire, it is raised up into the contemplative life and there it ascends."

45. "climbing Jesus-ward"

cal ascent while "Jhesu-warde" denotes God as the destination of the climb.

Julian effects a similar diverting of all attention, and of language itself, toward God in her presentation of the "lord and servant" allegory. At the same time, Julian's careful elaboration of the multiple levels of signification in this vision, I suggest, accomplishes a recuperation of language. That is, in raising the literal level of signification to the anogogical, it seems that Julian is directing her readers' attention in a metaphorical ascent to God and simultaneously offering a means by which language can be understood to ascend.

Julian first presents the story of the allegory on a literal level. The Lord sends his servant to perform the Lord's will. The servant, however, falls into a "slade" and is injured so that he cannot accomplish his task. To this point, Julian is shown the allegory "gostly in bodely lycknesse" (LT. 51.514: 6).[46] Following the vanishing of the literal presentation, however, Julian receives "another inwarde, more gostly" (41) showing "with a ledyng of [her] vnderstandyng in to the lorde" (41–42).[47] Thus Julian comes to understand that the Lord stands for God. The servant is revealed to be Adam, and Adam is to be understood as standing for all humanity for "in the syghte of god alle man is oone man, and oone man is alle man" (103–4).[48] At a deeper level, however, Julian comprehends that the servant is also "the seconde person of þe trynyte" (211).[49] The servant's fall into the ditch, Adam's "fall" in the garden "fro lyfe to deth" (221)[50] and Christ's fall "in to the slade of the meydens wombe" (222–23)[51] are revealed to be not just analogous, but one and the same thing because of "the ryght on-

46. "spiritually, in bodily form/likeness"
47. "another inner, more spiritual [showing] ... with a leading of [her] understanding to the lord."
48. "in the sight of God all humanity is one man, and one man is all humanity."
49. "the second person of the Trinity"
50. "from life to death"
51. "into the valley of the maiden's womb"

yng whych was made in hevyn" (219)[52] between Christ and humanity. The ultimate shape of the allegory, however, is circular, though such a shape can only be extrapolated from Julian's elaboration as she does not explicitly make the final connection. That is, since Christ is the second person of the Trinity, He is also God. Therefore, the ultimate level of the allegory reveals God as both Lord and servant. That is, we are turned back to God as the final meaning of the allegory, as both the signifier and the signified, literally and metaphorically.

In this allegory therefore Julian seems, in part, to have accomplished a reversal of the mutability of signs, moving the levels of signification into a sweeping circle that brings all meaning back to God. In effect, she has represented, in the completeness of her allegory, the entire fall and salvation story of Christianity.

In fact, I contend, that God remains Julian's referent not only in her allegory but throughout her text. In her final chapter she receives the answer "love" to each of her series of questions: "What, woldest thou wytt thy lordes menyng in this thyng? . . . Who shewyth it the? . . . What shewid he the? . . . Wherfore shewyth he it the ?" (LT. 86.732: 15–733: 18).[53]

When Julian concludes that "In whych love we have oure begynnyng, and alle this shalle we see in god with outyn ende" (LT. 86.734: 26–27),[54] "God" and "love" are again shown to be the same thing.

Rolle effects a similar equation but, in order to pinpoint God's location in Rolle's schema, a circuitous navigation of the metaphorical world is involved. Primarily, he locates God within, and more specifically, within the heart. Thus, from the initial rhetorical question "What is lufe?" (F.L. 108: 10), Rolle begins the answers with "Luf is a byrnand ʒernyng in God [and] God es lyght and byrnyng" (F.L. 108:

52. "the proper union which was made in heaven"
53. "What, you want to know your Lord's meaning in this thing? . . . Who revealed it to you? . . . What did he reveal to you? . . . Why does he reveal it to you?"
54. "In that love we have our beginning, and all this we shall see in God without end."

11–109: 12). To the question, "Whare es lufe?" (F.L. 110:67),[55] the answer is, "Lufe es in þe hert and in þe will of mane . . . in his sawle" (F.L. 110: 68–70).[56]

In a related explication Rolle suggests that "þe cole swa clethes it in þe fyre, þat al es fyre. . . . In þis maner sall a trewe lufar of Jhesu Criste do: his hert sal swa byrne in lufe, þat it sal be turned intil fyre of lufe, and be, als it war, al fire" (FL. 110: 59–64).[57] That is, love is a fire and yearning for God but God is also the fire and the ignition of that fire. In Rolle's allegory, the metaphor (fire of love) and the "thing" it stands for (God) are the same thing. Rolle concretizes this notion when he writes "All lufand to þer lufe treuly ar likkynd, & lufe makis hym like þat lufys to þat þat is lufyd" (*Fire*, 1.18.40: 32–34).[58] Again, God is posited as the ultimate and the complete meaning.

For Rolle, Julian, and the *Cloud* author, then, the language of their texts works toward a realization of the intention of delivering meaning to its highest possible signification: God. At the same time, the texts' readers are spiritually "delivered" to God and any concerns about ineffability, on the part of the texts' authors, are also subsumed in God as the gap between presence and representation is effectively closed. Such closure is analogous to a recuperation of language form its "fallen" state to the extent that language, the mystics, and their readers all ascend.

GOD IN A "POYNT"

The idea that God can be expressed, as the ultimate referent, in all words, functioning as the perfect amalgamation of presence and rep-

55. "Where is love?"

56. "Love is in the heart and in the will of man . . . in his soul."

57. "the coal is so clothed in fire, that it is all fire. . . . Likewise, this is what a true lover of Jesus Christ does: his heart so burns in love, that it will be turned into the fire of love, and be, as it were, all fire."

58. "All lovers to their love are truly likened, and love makes each one like the one that is he loves."

resentation, finds a somewhat surprising parallel in the mystics' explication of the word "point" which incorporates both temporal and
spatial connotations. In Middle English *poynt* (one of several spelling
variations) referred to "a small dot marked on a surface"; to "a small
amount, the smallest part, the least bit"; to "a point in space, a place,
spot, location"; and to "a brief period of time, an instant, a moment"
(M.E.D. 1087). When Julian sees God in a "point," it seems she is
referring to the concept of the smallest, indivisible part of space.
She explains that "And after this I saw god in a poynte, that is to say
in my vnderstandyng, by which syght I saw that he is in althyng"[59]
(LT. 11.336: 3–4).

Colledge and Walsh remark that "[i]t has been suggested that Julian meant that she saw God as the centre of a circle, the universe,
that the image is geometrical and the idea philosophical. This may
be so; but it seems more probable that she meant 'in an instant of
time'" (1978, 336 n. 3). However, they do not give any reason for their
privileging of the "time" over the "space" connotation, nor do they
suggest who it is that has "suggested that Julian meant she saw God
as the centre of a circle." St. Augustine, in fact, elaborates the beauty
of the point over all other geometrical concepts. In his *De Quantita-
tae Animae* St. Augustine expounds "a theory based upon geomet-

59. Note here that I do not offer a modern rendering for Julian's word "poynt" as
my contention is that she uses it very specifically with a spatial denotation: "And after this I saw God in a point, that is, as I understand it, in this vision I saw that he is
in everything."

Certainly, Julian is referring to a temporal "poynt" when she states "This is a gre-
ate profyte, for yf man knew hys tyme, he shulde nott haue pacience ovyr that tyme.
And also god wylle that whyle the soule is in the body, it seeme to it selfe þat it is evyr
at þe poynte to be takyn. For alle this lyfe and thys longyng that we haue here is but
a poynt, and when we be takyn sodeynly out of payne in to blesse, than payn shall be
nought" (LT. 64.622: 25–30). "This is a great benefit because if man knew his time,
he would not have patience over that time. And also God wishes that while the soul
is in the body, it seems to each person that he is always at the point of being taken.
For all this life and this longing that we have here is but an instant, and when we are
taken suddenly out of pain into bliss, then pain shall be nothing."

rical regularity" (Eco 1986, 43). Eco explains that, according to Augustine, certain shapes of triangles were considered more beautiful than others, a square surpassed a triangle in beauty, and, he continues, "the circle was most beautiful of all. . . . Above all these, however, is the point—indivisible, centre and beginning and end of itself, the generating point of the circle, the most beautiful of all the figures" (ibid.). If Augustine's elaboration of the point and circle is applied to Julian's declaration that she "saw god in a poynt" and, further, that she understood from this vision that "he is in althyng," then a spatial interpretation seems more apt than a temporal one. That is, God is certainly the generating point of "althyng[s]" and, as Eco has extrapolated from Augustine, God is also the highest beauty.[60] Augustine's explication of the circle as the most beautiful shape also subtly features in Julian's revelations. Her description of Jesus' crown of thorns draws attention to the shape of a circle. Julian describes vividly that as she looked at the wounded flesh and blood of Christ's scalp

it beganne to dry and stynt a parte of the weyght that was rownd about the garland and so it was enuyroned all about, as it were garland vpon garland. The garlonde of thornes was deyde with the blode; and that other garlond and the hede. All was one colowre, as cloteryd blode when it was dryed. (LT. 17. 363: 30–35)[61]

---

60. If a spatial interpretation is accepted, then Julian's reference to "God in a poynt" seems to coincide with the modern cosmological idea of a point of singularity. A singularity is theorized as being "the cusp-like edge to spacetime [which is surrounded by an] escalating curvature in [its] vicinity" (Davies 1982, 102). In addition, relativity theory predicts that "there is a point in the universe where the theory itself breaks down. Such a point is an example of what mathematicians call a singularity" (Hawking 1988, 46). Furthermore, it is hypothesized that at the big bang singularity "the curvature of space-time is infinite" (ibid.).

61. "it began to dry and lose some of the weight that was around the crown and so it was surrounded, as it were crown upon crown. The crown of thorns was dyed with the blood; and the other crown and the head. All were one color, like clotted, dried blood."

That is, Julian sees circles within circles, enclosure upon enclosure. Vincent Gillespie and Maggie Ross see, in Julian's imagery of the crown of thorns, an "[a]pophatic centre surrounded by the signs of human suffering [which] characterizes the synthetic writing of so much of the text in the way it holds in tension conflicting perspectives" (1992, 59).

Somewhat ironically, then, Julian follows this intense concentration on Christ's crowning with thorns with the statement that "we be hys crowne" (LT. 22.384: 22),[62] though of course the alignment of pain and joy and reward are prominent features of Julian's revelations.

Brant Pelphrey interprets Julian's "point" as "both dimensionless and also pan-dimensional: it is every point of space, encompassing all points of three-dimensional space equally" (1998, 306). Roland Maisonneuve goes further, seeing the "poynt" metonymically, when he states that

if I had to concretize the visionary mode of the Showings, I would choose the image of the point, one of the symbols preferred by Julian. For her the point represents the central point of a reality and all of the elements of a reality: man in his nothingness and his infinity; the created in its minuteness and immensity; god in his immanence and transcendence. All of the symbols, all of the concepts of the Showings, in their trajectories from nothingness to infinity, are contained in this point. This is why the visionary universe of Julian, woven with so many points of quasi-nothingness and divine infinity, merits continuing research and study. (1980, 93)

Rolle uses the word *point* with a spatial connotation, too, when he seeks to express the joy of his mystical experience: "Truly I may nott tell a lityll poynt of þis joy, ffor an vntold heet qwho may tell? A infenit swetnes qwho sall makyn? Certan, if I wald speke þis Ioy vnabyll to be told, me semys to my self Als and I suld teym þe see be droype and spar it all in a lityll hole of þe erth" (*Fire*, 2.4.75: 28–32).[63]

Here Rolle proceeds by way of a spatially based, inverted compari-

---

62. "we are his crown"
63. "Truly, I cannot express the littlest part of this joy, for who can tell of an untellable fervor? Who can describe an infinite sweetness? Certainly, if I would try to

son that magnifies the "lityll poynt" of spiritual joy to a vastness that makes the sea seem like a mere drop. In doing so, Rolle also accomplishes the general magnification of the joy of mystical experience and the concomitant diminution of the physical world.

It is the *Cloud* author who uses the notion of the smallest unit of (medieval) time, the "athomus."[64] He introduces it into his injunction to the reader to heed time carefully, stressing that

Þis werk askeþ no longe tyme er it be ones treulich done, as sum men wenen; For it is þe schortest werke of alle þat man may ymagyn. It is neiþer lenger ne schorter þen is an athomus; þe whiche athomus, by þe diffinicion of trewe philisophres in þe sciens of astronomye, is þe leest partie of tyme. & it is so litil þat, for þe littilnes of it, it is undepartable & neiȝhonde incomphrensible. (Cl. 4.17: 15–20)[65]

The author, in elaborating his injunction, actually recommends that time be disregarded as a sequential movement. Instead, he shifts the focus to the multiple possibilities in each moment, thus evoking a vertical rather than a horizontal/linear perspective. He advises that

Þis is þat tyme of þe whiche it is wretyn: Alle tyme þat is ȝouen to þee, it schal be askid of þee how þou haste dispendid it. & skilful þing it is þat þou ȝeue acompte of it; for it is neiþer lenger ne schorter, bot euen acording to one only steryng þat is wiþ-inne þe principal worching miȝt of þi soule, þe whiche is þi wille. (Cl. 4.17: 20–18: 5)[66]

---

speak of this ineffable joy, it seems to me that it would be like taking the sea drop by drop and squeezing it all into a little hole in the earth."

64. "According to contemporary medieval calculations there are over 20,000 atoms in an hour" (Smart 1992, 117). This means that one athomus is approximately equal to one-sixth of a second. As Smart points out, the *Cloud* author can be considered to be implying "that somehow the ultimate illuminating experience is spontaneous" (ibid.).

65. "This work does not require a long time to be well done, as some men think. In fact, it is the shortest work that man can imagine. It is no shorter or longer than one athomus; which, as defined by real philosophers in the science of astronomy, is the smallest division of time. And it is so small that it is indivisible and almost incomprehensible."

66. "This is the time of which it is written: All time that is given to you, it shall be

In fact, in highlighting that the "werk" can be accomplished virtually instantly, the *Cloud* author effaces time, bringing God, the contemplative, and contemplation itself into the present moment. Glasscoe encapsulates the *Cloud* author's point when she describes the mystics as undertaking "a spiritual journey to a goal beyond time" (1993, 4).

The *Cloud* author further stresses the importance of time in the human condition and simultaneously the infinite possibilities in the present moment when he instructs his readers that "noþing is more precious þan tyme. In oo litel tyme, as litel as it is, may heuen be wonne & lost" (Cl. 4.20: 6–7).[67] The author goes on to explain that "God . . . is ȝeuer of tyme" (8)[68] and that "tyme is maad for man, & not man for tyme" (10–11),[69] thereby suggesting an alignment between time and purpose.

The aligning of time with purpose as it is effected in space finds an interesting representation in the Christian symbol of the Cross. The Cross features a point of intersection of a vertical and a horizontal axis. The point of bisection of a two-dimensional symbolic cross has the mathematical coordinates o, o.

In Lefebvrian terms, the Cross is the ultimate symbol of Christianity and a *representational space* that makes visible on earth Christ's salvific sacrifice. On a deeper level of signification, however, the Cross, with its axial bisection, can also symbolize an intersection of temporal life, as represented by the horizontal axis, and eternity, as represented by the vertical axis, in a reflection of Christ's entry into time to enable the transcendence of humanity to eternal life. If the symbol is further extrapolated and applied to a representation of lan-

---

asked how you have spent it. And it is important that you should give an account of it; for it is neither longer nor shorter, but is in even accord to the one stirring within you, which is the principal working of the soul, and that is the will."

67. "nothing is more precious than time. In one little moment, as little as it is, heaven may be won and lost."

68. "God is the giver of time"

69. "time is made for man, and not man for time."

guage, then the horizontal axis can be understood to represent a diachronic axis replete with literal signifiers while the vertical axis can represent a synchronic axis that allows the accumulation of metaphors. That is, spatially, the Cross can also be seen to represent a combination of the literal and the metaphorical possibilities that meet at a point where transcendental possibilities intersect with time. In metaphorically entering that point, an individual would be no longer "on" the diachronic axis, nor necessarily "on" the synchronic axis, but at a point of stillness that is perfectly poised between the possibilities of ascension and descension and backward and forward movement into other possibilities. Application of this formulation to the medieval contemplatives yields the possibilities that, in entering into Christ's Cross, in all its symbolic implications, they were poised to aspire heavenward and to "descend" and "reenter" earth, as appropriate. Christ, as symbolized by the Cross, effected all possibilities by descending to the womb, living temporally and then descending further into the tomb in order to rise anew and to ascend.

Torrance elaborates the theological significance of the intersecting axes of the Cross:

The world, then, is made open to God through its intersection in the axis of Creation-Incarnation. Its space-time structures are so organized in relation to God that we who are set within them may think in and through them to their transcendent ground in God himself. Jesus Christ constitutes the actual centre in space and time where that may be done. (1969, 74)

He further explains that

[t]his relation established between God and man in Jesus Christ constitutes Him as *the place* in all space and time where God meets with man in the actualities of his human existence and man meets with God and knows Him in His own divine being. That is the place where the vertical and horizontal dimensionalities intersect, the place where human being is opened out to a transcendent ground in God and where the infinite Being of God penetrates into our existence and creates room for Himself within the horizontal dimensions of finite being in space and time. It is penetration of the horizontal

by the vertical that gives man his true place, for it relates his place in space and time to its ultimate ontological ground so that it is not submerged in the endless relativities of what is merely horizontal. . . . Unless the eternal breaks into the temporal and the boundless being of God breaks into the spatial existence of man and takes up dwelling within it, the vertical dimension vanishes out of man's life and becomes quite strange to him. (Ibid., 75–76)

The metaphorical alignment of space as represented in a vertical axis finds an echo in the way in which Julian details how a change in the direction of her visual focus precipitates her revelations. (I will deal with this subject in greater detail in Chapter Six.) Generally Julian concurs that heaven is located in an upward direction as she explains that, though close to the point of death during her illness, "My thought I was well, for my eyen was sett vpright into heauen, where I trusted to come by the mercie of god; but nevertheles I ascentyd to sett my eyen in the face of the crucyfixe, if I might, and so I dide, for my thought I might longar dure to looke even forth then right vp" (LT. 3.291: 24–28).[70] Later, Julian affirms the correctness of her altered focus by declaring that "than sawe I wele with the feyth that I felt þat ther was nothyng betwene the crosse and hevyn that myght haue dyssesyde me" (LT. 19.370: 7–9).[71]

Here, as Julian resolves to "chese Jhesu only to my hevyn" (LT. 19.371: 20),[72] she presents heaven's location as being in the here and now, its space immediately accessible in the person of Jesus Christ. For Julian, the point of intersection of the vertical and the horizontal axes of the Cross concretize the present moment that is continuously apparent in Christ.

Similarly, Julian's notion of "onyng" indicates an erasure of di-

70. "I thought I was [safe] well, for my eyes were fixed upward toward heaven, where I trusted to go by the mercy of God; but nevertheless I agreed to fix my eyes on the face of the crucifix, if I could, and so I did, for I thought I could endure longer looking forward rather than upward."

71. "then I saw well with the faith that I felt that there was nothing between the cross and heaven that could have disturbed me."

72. "choose Jesus for my heaven"

viding space. Julian elaborates this "onyng" as a necessity, declaring that "For to I am substancyallye aned to hym, I may nevere have love, reste ne varray blysse; that is to saye that I be so festenede to hym that thare be ryght nougt that is made betwyxe my god and me" (ST. 4: 18–21).[73] I have used the Short Text quotation here intentionally. The Long Text features the word "vnyted" in the place of "aned." The difference is interesting, as far as the application of the modern connotation of the word *united* is concerned.[74] That is, *united* can indicate an agreement (of wills, of intention) without implying the physicality and nondivisibility of substance that the word "aned" expresses. In the above declaration, being "aned" with Christ is aligned with the concept of the obliteration of all dividing space between Julian and God. Thus, Julian not only sees God in a point but experiences his love in the smallest, most condensed part of space to the extent that "thare be ryght nought that is made betwyxe [them]." In this, she has reached the acme of contemplative experience.

The *Cloud* author also expresses this union spatially as an "onyng." However, he advises that though the aim is to "mowe parfitely be onid vnto God in parfite charite" (Cl. 44.85: 7–8),[75] such union cannot be achieved without careful preparation in time. This preparation, in part, involves the erasure of the awareness of all earthly things, and ultimately of one's own sense of being. He explains that

For, & þou wilt besily set þee to þe preof, þou schalt fynde, when þou hast forȝeten alle oþer creatures & alle þeire werkes, ȝe, & þerto alle þin owne werkes, þat þer schal leue ȝit after, bitwix þee & þi God, a nakid weting & a felyng of þin owne beyng: þe whiche wetyng & felyng behouiþ alweis be

73. "For until I am 'oned' to him in substance, I cannot have love, rest or true bliss; that is to say, until I am so fastened to him that there is absolutely nothing in creation between my God and me."

74. Any difference in Julian's own time was apparently not as marked. (See M.E.D. under *onen*, pp. 194–95). Today, the verb "to one" is obsolete so the distinction that I am here suggesting is based on the "impression" that we gain from the idea of "being oned" compared to "being united."

75. "more perfectly united with God in perfect charity."

distroied, er þe tyme be þat þou fele soþfastly þe perfeccyon of þis werk. (Cl. 43.82: 22–83:5)[76]

Thus, for the *Cloud* author, the erasure of any dividing space between the contemplative and God is dependent upon the erasure of the awareness of the self and the notion of "God in a poynt" finds a resonance with the notion of the individual reduced to a metaphorical "point."

By expressing "God in a poynt," Rolle, Julian, and the *Cloud* author paradoxically express their confidence in God's all-encompassing greatness. That is, if He can be contained within the smallest part of space and time and yet still extend his love and influence, then he is accessible to the mystics and their readers across space and time.

GOD'S SPACIOUSNESS

Spatially, God in a "point" can be contained within the mystics. Equally, though, God can contain all within Himself. Meister Eckhart says of God that he is *spatiosissimus,* the most spacious. Rolle, Julian, and the *Cloud* author, too, elaborate the spaciousness of God, His capacity to contain all humanity within His love.

Julian finds this spaciousness in particular relation to Christ's wounds. She notes that Christ revealed the wound in His side to be a "feyer and delectable place, and large jnow for alle mankynde that shalle be savyd and rest in pees and in loue" (LT. 24.394: 6–395: 7).[77] That is, within Christ and because of His Passion and death, all humanity is encompassed and saved. His wounds represent a metaphor-

---

76. "For, if you busily set yourself to prove this, you will find, when you have forgotten all other creatures and their works, yes, and your own works, there will still remain, between you and God, a naked knowing and feeling of your own being: and this, too, must be destroyed, before the time that you can truly feel the perfection of this work."

77. "fair and delectable place, and large enough for all mankind that shall be saved and shall rest in peace and love."

ical place of healing and hiding for humanity.[78] For Julian, the "hiding place" within God is, firstly then, the space in which salvation is contained. In addition, though, it is the space in which all human feeling becomes subsumed. Paradoxically, Julian expresses this subsumption in very sensual terms. Thus, in expanding the notion of the space within Christ's wounds to refer to God, in general, as the ideal hiding place, she describes the way in which "we endlessly be alle hyd in god" (LT. 43.481: 51).[79] Julian uses a language of the senses that posits the "hiding" as "verely seyeng and fulsomly felyng and hym gostely heryng, and hym delectably smellyng, and hym swetly swelwyng" (LT. 43: 51–53).[80] Here, the sensual adverbs juxtaposed with the repetition of the present participles, without any accompanying auxiliaries, have the effect of seeming to detach the sensations from the purely earthly realm, making them evocative of the five senses without fixing them in time and space. Thus, to be "hyd" in God is presented as the ultimate sensual experience but an experience that is continual (endlessly) and outside the sensual body. The endlessness of the experience can be fully realized, therefore, only after life, as Julian highlights when she adds that "The creature that is made shall see and endlesly beholde god whych is the maker; for thus may no man se god and leue aftyr, that is to sey in this dedely lyffe" (LT. 43.481: 54–482: 56).[81]

In her own life, however, Julian experiences God's spaciousness spiritually and also experiences an inversion of it when she is shown her own soul as God's vast kingdom:

78. Colledge and Walsh note that "the notion of the wounded Sacred Heart as mankind's hiding-place reflects one of the petitions of the *Anima Christi:* In vulneribus tuis late me" (1978, 394 n. 6).

79. "we are all endlessly hidden in God."

80. "truly seeing and wholly feeling and spiritually hearing him, and delectably smelling and sweetly tasting him."

81. "The creature who is made shall see and endlessly behold God who is the Creator; for it is so that no man may see God and live afterward, that is to say, in this mortal life."

And then oure good lorde opynnyd my gostely eye and shewde me my soule in þe myddys of my harte. I saw þe soule so large as it were an endlesse warde, and also as it were a blessyd kyngdom; and by the condicions þat I saw ther in I vnderstode þat it is a wurschypfulle cytte, in myddes of that cytte (sitts) oure lorde Jhesu, very god and very man. (LT. 68.639: 2–6)[82]

Though metaphorical, the architectural terms are resonant with Lefebvre's idea of decryption. That is, in positing a large city within her soul within her heart, Julian brings to light that which is hidden within her: the capacity and willingness to house God always within her soul. The decrypting then functions as a reflection of God in His ultimate capacity and willingness to house all humanity within Himself. In terms of language and space, it might be said that the spaciousness of God allows the containment of these reflective possibilities.

In *Meditations on the Passion* Rolle, too, finds a spiritual space within Christ as a consequence of Christ's wounded physical body. Thus, Rolle lyricizes "And yit, Lord, sweet Jhesu, þy body is lyk to a nette; for as a nette is ful of holys, so is þy body ful of woundes. Here, swet Jhesu, I beseche þe, cache me into þis net of scourgynge, þat al my hert and love be to þe" (Med. 35:251–54).[83] Rolle continues building the metaphor of space within the wounds, here repeating the refrain that links the spatially evocative "holys" with the bodily wounds: "Efte, swet Jhesu, þy body is like to a dufhouse. For a dufhouse is ful of holys, so is þy body ful of woundes. And as a dove pursued of an hauk, yf she mow cache an hool of hir hous she is siker ynowe, so, swete Jhesu, in temptacion þy woundes ben best refuyt to us" (Med. 35:265–70).[84]

82. "And then our good Lord opened my spiritual eye and showed me my soul in the midst of my heart. I saw the soul as large as if it were an endless citadel, and also as it were a blessed kingdom; and by the conditions that I saw therein I understood that it is an honorable city [and] in the midst of that city (sits) our Lord Jesus, true God and true man."

83. "And yet, Lord, sweet Jesus, your body is like a net; for just as a net is full of holes, so is your body full of wounds. Here, sweet Jesus, I beseech you, catch me in this net of scourging, so that all my heart and love be for you."

84. "Also, sweet Jesus, your body is like a dovecote. For a dovecote is full of holes,

The likening of the body to a "honycombe . . . ful of cellis, and each celle ful of hony" (Med. 35:274–75)[85] also expresses the idea of spaciousness within Christ's wounds as well as the spiritual sweetness that is to be found therein. Paradoxically, Christ's wounded body provides healing to all who choose to reside within it. For example, Rolle completes his *Meditations on the Passion* by describing the body as a "medow ful of swete flours and holsome herbes; so is þy body fulle of woundes, swet savorynge to a devout soule, and holsome as herbes to euch synful man" (Med. 36:298–301).[86]

This reinforces Rolle's earlier juxtaposing of Jesus' pains and suffering against his power to heal sin: "swet Jhesu, in þe is al sovereyne medicyne, and I, Lord, am al sek in synnes; þerfor, swet Jhesu, tak me to þe, and set me undyr þy cure" (Med. 30:85–87).[87]

In *The Commandment* Rolle advises his reader to "set þi lufe on hys Jhesu, þat es 'hele'" (Com. 81:283–84).[88] The reference is to the spiritual healing that the Name effects, but it seems its benefits are not confined to soul-space. Thus, in body-space the Name "chaces devels, and destroyes temptacions, and puttes away wykked dredes and vices, and clenses þe thoght" (Com. 81:286–87).[89]

In a similar way, the *Cloud* author's allusions to God's spaciousness are related to the utterance of a prayer. He poses the rhetorical question, "& whi peersiþ it heuen, þis lityl schort preier of o silable" (Cl. 38.75: 6)[90] and answers that it is because "it is preyed wiþ a fulle spirite,

---

just as your body is full of wounds. And just as a dove pursued by a hawk is safe enough if she can hide in one hole of her house, so, sweet Jesus, in temptation your wounds are our best refuge."

85. "honeycomb . . . full of cells, and each cell full of honey"

86. "meadow full of sweet flowers and healing herbs; so your body is full of wounds, sweet nourishment to a devout soul, and healing as herbs to every sinner."

87. "sweet Jesus, in you is all supreme medicine, and I, Lord, am all sick with sin; therefore, sweet Jesus, take me to you, and cure me."

88. "set your love on Jesus, that is 'healing.'"

89. "chases away devils, and destroys temptations, and removes wicked fears and vices, and cleanses the thoughts."

90. "and why does it pierce to heaven, this little short prayer of one syllable?"

in þe heiȝt & in þe depnes, in þe lengþe & in þe breed of his spirit þat preieþ it" (Cl. 38.75: 7–8).[91] Thus, the "lityl schort preier" is representative, in body-space, of its opposite quantity in soul-space. This notion is then extrapolated and applied to God as spatial attributes: "Þe euerlastyngnes of God is his lengþe; his loue is his breed; his miȝt is his heiȝt; his wisdam is his depnes" (Cl. 38.75: 17–19).[92] Thus prayer, though literally small and seemingly ineffectual in the physical world, is posited as inversely proportional to the "fulle spirite," and both prayer and spirit find their metaphorical reflection in the vastness of God.

In addition, as discussed in Chapter Two, the *Cloud* author's metaphor of Christ as the threshold and the doorkeeper posits Him as guarding the access to a Godhead that is large enough to contain all the faithful. The concept can also be considered to be related to the mystical body of Christ, as Russell explains that "[t]he body of Christ is an ontological metaphor of the highest importance throughout Christian thought. It represents, and in the deepest sense it is, the earthly body of Jesus, the glorified body of Jesus, the consecrated Eucharist and the ecclesia (church), the community of those who love God" (1997, 41). In this sense, God's spaciousness is manifest in an earthly sense as well and is expressed symbolically in the *representational space* of a church building and in the enactment of the Eucharist. In addition, as the Church is also considered to be the "ecclesia"—the people who constitute the Church—the spaciousness of God could be understood to be represented in the participation of the faithful in the practices of the liturgy and in overt obedience to the Church hierarchy. God's spaciousness, therefore, extends far beyond the spiritual realm to reveal itself in the physical and social structures of body-space and can be understood as being notionally present in all the levels of the conceptual *mise en abîme*.

91. "it is prayed with a full spirit, in the height and the depth, in the length and the breadth of the spirit of him who prays it."
92. "The everlastingness of God is his length; his love is his breadth; his might is his height; his wisdom is his depth."

Chapter Four

THE MYSTICAL SPACE OF
RICHARD ROLLE

Alas for those who never sing,

But die with all their music in them.

(Oliver Wendall Holmes)

What are the servants of the Lord but his minstrels?

(St. Francis of Assisi)

A MAN OF HIS TIME

The mystical space of Richard Rolle is represented by a curious alternation between an apparent denigration of the material (body-space) world in favor of the embracing of the spiritual (soul-space) dimension, and a conflation of physical sensation and its spiritual source in the expression of the delight of experiencing God. In this dichotomous attitude, I consider Rolle to be representative of his time. By that I mean that, in the elucidation of his mystical experiences, Rolle demonstrates a decidedly medieval worldview in which the physical and spiritual worlds coexist in a unity of reciprocal indication and in which all the senses, not just the visual, are credited with a part to play in the apprehension and interpretation of the spiritual realm.

In his texts, Rolle reveals himself to be a man living a (predomi-

nantly) hermitic lifestyle who experiences something that is beyond
sensuality. Yet, in his writing, he describes his mystical experience in
the most sensual of terms with each of the five senses represented at
some level. Additionally, Rolle appears not only to use the sensible
world as a source of analogy for spiritual experience but also to indicate a mingling of body-space and soul-space in which bodily senses
are attuned to the spiritual world.

Rolle's sensual descriptions of spiritual apprehensions are representative of the medieval *habitus* that conceived of the ineluctable
connection of heaven and earth. At times, Rolle can be seen to be unconsciously confirming that such a connection existed by the way in
which he seeks to sever it. For example, he recommends a separation
of self from the world for his readers who desire closeness to God,
and he frequently denigrates materiality, while at the same time he
uses sensible metaphors as the primary descriptors of his mystical experience. Thus, the nexus of physical and spiritual is maintained even
in Rolle's advocating of the conscious exchange of physical sensibility
for spiritual sensibility. In Lefebvrian terms, Rolle's appropriation of
physical concepts such as heat, sweetness, and song becomes a product of *representational space* that participates in the interplay between
symbol and meaning.

The interdependence of body-space and soul-space in Rolle's schema has an impact on spatial representation and the elaboration of mystical space in his texts. That is, both the mystical experience (which,
for the purposes of this chapter, I designate as *content*) and the way
in which the experience is expressed in words *(form),* are of equal
importance to Rolle. My use of the term *form* is partly informed by
Marion Glasscoe's application of it. She notes, in referring to Rolle's
use of the word in the phrase "form of lyvyng," that 'form' refers "to
[Rolle's] writing as well as to a lifestyle" (1993, 70). In my consideration of Rolle's mystical space, therefore, I will examine both form and
content for spatial implications.

Rolle's tendency to structure the form and content of his mystical space into, very often, a tripartite arrangement is relevant to this examination. Thus Rolle's explication of three degrees of love and the reception of the threefold mystical phenomena of *calor, dulcor,* and *canor* are considered and allusion is made to the three levels of heavenly reward to be enjoyed in the company of the three hierarchies of angels which, in turn, are each divided into three subcategories. In Lefebvre's terms again, the conceptualization of experience into such a careful triadic arrangement fits into the category of *representations of space,* in which Rolle can be understood to be advancing a very definite schema for the way he wishes his readers to conceptualize the mystical experience.

The idea of *form* also refers to the textual expression of Rolle's mystical space in that language is a crucial component of Rolle's mysticism. The importance that he places on the Holy Name, for example, indicates his confidence in the power of certain words to effect a level of spiritual transformation. That is, to Rolle, the form of expression is equal in importance to the content of his mystical experiences. At the most basic level, of course, the words are the container of the message but, for Rolle, the words are also part of the message. Sara De Ford considers, in regard to Rolle's *Melos Amoris,* that "Richard is the singer and the song; his God is the singer and the song as are the angels and the blessed in heaven and they are joined in one melody both vocal and instrumental . . . the song of divine love" (1980, 189–90).

Rita Copeland expresses a similar view, though she refers to all Rolle's works in general when she notes that "Rolle's concept of stylistic procedure is bound up not only with his own pious and ecstatic mysticism but . . . with his understanding of the function of literary discourse in its highest rhetorical form as an effusion of *canor*" (1984, 65).

The interrelationship between Rolle's textual form and content can be viewed as another manifestation of an interconnected body-space and soul-space in Rolle's formulation. Interestingly, though, as several commentators have observed, Rolle frequently positions himself, in his texts, as a mediator between God and his reader and as an interpreter of mystical experience.[1] The mediative function that Rolle assigns to himself can be considered as representative of another triadic arrangement: God, Rolle, reader.

Rolle's interest in representing much of his mystical space in triadic formulations is indicative, I will argue, of a particular ordering of thought and experience that is easily transferable to his readers and that may have assisted them in committing important points to memory. More particularly, I will argue that it is an arrangement that very much reflects Rolle's worldview. For example, in the fourteenth century, the triad came to be regarded as the basis of (musical) harmony. There is an intriguing correlation between Rolle's propensity to express his ideas in triads and his complete immersion in heavenly music. I will show, in relation to Rolle's *canor* and his two other modalities of mystical apprehension, that a particular relationship to space is involved. My intention is to apply both medieval notions of cosmology and music and current theories of physical space to facilitate a new view of Rolle's work and experience. That is, I will argue that Rolle's experience of *calor, dulcor,* and *canor* are linked to medieval conceptions in which spatial considerations are implicit.

For the most part the sensually described apprehensions seem to be metaphorical representations, but, since Rolle does not always declare a distinction between the modalities of his experiences, he has sometimes been relegated to the level of a mystical beginner. In fact, he gives several pointers to the metaphorical nature of his sensual descriptions—for example, explaining that "þe flaume, whilk vndyr fygure I cald fyer" (*Fire,* 1.1.3: 2–3)[2] is used because fire "brynnes & lightis" (ibid.)[3] in the same manner as the love of God inflames and

1. See, e.g., Lisa Manter, "Rolle Playing: 'And the Word Became Flesh,'" in *The Vernacular Spirit: Essays on Medieval Religious Literature,* ed. Renate Blumenfeld-Kosinski, Duncan Robertson, and Nancy Bradley Warren (New York: Palgrave, 2002), 15–37.
2. "the flame, which I metaphorically call fire"
3. "burns and enlightens"

lights the soul. Thus, though Rolle explains that this "sensibyll fyer" (*Fire,* 1.1.2: 8)[4] has a metaphorical component to it, this initial, and many subsequent, conflations of the physical and the spiritual in his works have led to divided opinion on the value, and even the authenticity, of Rolle's mystical experience. More precisely, as Rosamund Allen points out, "Because he is silent about this 'sleep' of the senses, Rolle has been demoted by some commentators to the second grade of mystics who reach only *illuminatio* and not full union with God" (1984, 29).

Until now, critical opinion has tended to fall into either praise or condemnation of Rolle. Horstmann calls Rolle "the English Bonaventure" but tempers this claim with the opinion that Rolle "is all feeling, enthusiasm, inspiration, unrestrained by reasoning or any exterior rule; without method or discrimination" (1895, xiv).[5]

In view of such ambiguous praise it is not surprising that, from the outset, Rolle's work has incited controversy. Enthusiastic hagiographical material produced by his followers soon after his death, in addition to the production of an *Officium,* show that Rolle's contemporaries thought highly enough of him to prepare for his canonization.[6] Other fourteenth-century contemporaries were, perhaps, not quite so convinced of Rolle's holiness, with many current scholars believing that Walter Hilton's written attack on false mystical experience was implicitly directed at Rolle and his followers (see *Scale of Perfection,* 2: 30). More recently, some critics have echoed the same scepticism about Rolle's level of mystical accomplishment. Watson confesses, at the outset of his extensive study on Rolle, that he considers

4. "fire [that is real] to the senses"

5. Frances Comper disagrees with Horstmann, stating that "although [Bonaventure's] influence on Richard was great, it was rather by reason of his devout meditations upon the Passion, and his writings concerning the love of God, than for any mystical doctrine" (1969/1928, 42). Recent opinions would tend to support Horstmann's opinion insofar as Bonaventure's influence is clearly discernible, whether or not Rolle was consciously aware of Bonaventure's thought.

6. Rolle was never canonized, despite the efforts of his supporters.

that "his career as a writer, and the themes he developed throughout his career, are manifestations of an overriding concern with his own spiritual status and that the force behind most of his works is the determination to establish and exercise a form of eremitic and mystical authority" (1991, xi).

It is the opposite view to the one held by Wolfgang Riehle who regards Rolle as "a mystic with strong poetic leanings," this tendency resulting in Rolle often being misunderstood (1981, 6). Pollard, too, considers that the richness and variety of Rolle's texts "establish him as an authentic mystic with a fixed devotion to the highest order of love" (1997, 88).

Allen comments that "[f]rom regarding [Rolle] as individualistic and eccentric, and in his English writings, an innovator, criticism tends now to find him more derivative, both in content and style" (1984, 37).

The much earlier views of Frances Comper and Evelyn Underhill (1995/1911) hold Rolle in high esteem, with Comper, in the Foreword to her biography of Rolle, describing him as "a great mystic . . . a pioneer, leading the way which others were so quickly to follow: notably Walter Hilton and Dame Julian of Norwich, whose names have somewhat eclipsed Richard's since they were his disciples" (1969/1931, vii).[7] Despite the differing opinions on his authenticity Rolle does seem to have led a life that was dedicated to God. In his younger years he studied at Oxford, though perhaps did not graduate, and on his return to Yorkshire he entered enthusiastically on a life as a hermit. Within his solitude, he wrote prolifically in both Latin and the vernacular. Testimony to Richard Rolle's local popular-

---

7. Comper's biography is generally considered to be fanciful conjecture on many matters relating to Rolle. Most particularly, there is no evidence that either Julian of Norwich or Walter Hilton had anything to do with Rolle or his followers. Indeed it is most unlikely since Rolle died only six years after Julian was born and since Hilton, as mentioned above, is often considered to be criticizing Rolle directly when he writes of "false contemplatives."

ity at least is available through a consideration of the number of his surviving manuscripts. Medcalf and Reeves believe that Rolle's English works circulated widely among the nobility and gentry, and they note that "it is claimed that there are more manuscripts of his works extant than of any other medieval English writer" (1981, 81). Frances Beer elaborates that "*The Form of Living,* perhaps first copied by Margaret [Kirkeby] herself in her cell, survives in thirty eight manuscripts; forty two copies of the *Incendium Amoris* remain, while the Latin and English versions of his *Emendatio Vitae* total an astonishing one hundred and nine" (1992, 124).[8]

In addition, Rolle's didactic texts indicate that he regarded himself as having enough experience in these matters to act as adviser to others embarking on the contemplative life and to offer them a "form" in which to live that life. The more autobiographical *The Fire of Love* offers an insight into the actual "content" of the mystical experience. Together, these two types of texts provide an excellent insight into Rolle's mystical space.

FORM: SOLITUDE AND STILLNESS

For Rolle, as for many other contemplatives of fourteenth-century England, solitude was the preferred mode of life and plays an integral part in our understanding of his mystical space.

Solitude, as Rolle points out, is misunderstood and refers not to being "with-oute a fela" but to being "with-oute gode" (*Fire,* 1.14.29: 16, 17).[9] To Rolle, "a hous in wildyrnes" (*Fire,* 1.15.31: 20)[10] and "þe place of þe meruellus tabernakyll, . . . þe hous of god" (*Fire,* 1.14.30:

---

8. Though Rolle's works were widely copied in manuscript form "most of his writings were not published when printing was introduced into England" (Knowlton 1973, 10). Furthermore, of the forty extant copies of *Incendium Amoris,* none are later than the fifteenth century.

9. "without a companion . . . [not] without God"

10. "a house in the wilderness"

27–28)[11] are synonymous with both solitude and contemplation, the metaphors here evoking physical spaces that are, respectively, vast and inhospitable, and bounded and magnificent. Such physical spaces, in turn, stand for the actuality of contemplative solitude, which pairs worldly difficulty with spiritual richness. Solitude represents, then, a psychological, if not a totally physical, distance between the contemplative and his society.

Rolle illustrates the necessity for this distancing by drawing attention to the distance between the material and the spiritual worlds in both spatial and moral terms. Thus he describes earthly life as a "wrechyd dwelling place of exile" (*Fire,* 1.2.4: 8),[12] intimating that a forced separation from one's true home is in operation during life. Those who prefer the delights of the world (and, therefore, this land of exile) to the heavenly home are depicted as misguided to the extent that "ferþer þai ar fro heuenly hete þen is þe space be-twix þe hyest heuyn & lawyst place of þe erthe" (*Fire,* 1.2.4: 32–34).[13] The distance metaphor is intended on a spiritual as well as on a literal level and achieves its effect by the juxtaposing of a dual set of opposites: "hyest" with "lawyst" and "heuyn" with "erthe." Rolle repeats the idea, in almost the same words, in *The Form of Living,* commenting that they who have "delyte in any erthly thyng, . . . er als far þarfra, als es fra heven to erth" (F.L. 107: 82–83).[14]

In *Ego Dormio* Rolle again pairs concepts of literal and metaphorical distance and adds the notion of reward and punishment as being spatially separated when he advises his reader that

if þow stabil þi lufe, and be byrnande whils þou lyfes here, withowten dowte þi settel es ordande ful hegh in heven and joyful before Goddes face amang

11. "the place of the marvelous tabernacle, . . . the house of God"

12. "a wretched dwelling place of exile"

13. "they are further from the heavenly heights than is the space between the highest heaven and the lowest place on earth."

14. "delight in any earthly thing, . . . are as far from [heaven], as it is from heaven to earth."

his haly aungels. For in þe self degre þeir prowde devels fel downe fra, er meke men and wymen, Cristes dowves, sett, to have rest and joy withowten ende, for a litel schort penance and travel þat þai have sufferd for Goddes lufe. (E.D. 62: 44–51)[15]

Here, the literal distance also stands metaphorically for the gap between the material life with its "penance and travel" and the life of the spirit that leads to "joy withowten ende." In addition, in juxtaposing the "ful hegh in heven" with an indirect reference to hell in "[the] prowde devels fel downe" Rolle alludes to the medieval conception of the cosmos, which proposed that the distance between the earth and heaven was the greatest distance imaginable.

In medieval cosmological terms, as elaborated in Chapter One, the Earth is the still point around which the spheres revolve. Again, in medieval cosmology, God's place, the Empyrean, is above the fixed stars and the *primum mobile*. It is a still place in which God dwells. Thus earth and heaven are posed as two opposite still points with the former, at least in Rolle's estimation, an inferior and pale reflection of the latter. Nevertheless, Rolle advocates that the "still point" be reflected in the reader's manner of life. Thus he advises that "he þat spekes ay þe gode, and haldes ilk a man better þan hymselfe, he schewes wele þat he es stabel in godenes in hys hert and ful of charite til God and til his neghbor" (Com. 74: 27–30).[16] That is, a stability and a constancy in earthly life is encouraged by Rolle. For example, he recommends to his reader a concentration on Christ's Passion, stating that

If þou wil thynk þis ilk day, þou sal fynde swetnes þat sal draw þi hert up, þat sal gar þe ful in gretyng and in grete langyng til Jhesu & þi thoght sal al be

15. "If you are constantly burning in love while you live here, without doubt your seat is ordained in high and joyful heaven before God's face and among his angels. For in the same place where the proud devils were before they fell, are simple men and women, Christ's doves, sitting in rest and joy without end, in return for the short penance and travail that they suffered for God's love."

16. "he that speaks only good, and holds each man better than himself, he well demonstrates that he is constant in goodness in his heart and full of charity to God and to neighbor."

on Jhesu, and so be receyved abouen all erthly thyng, abouen þe firmament and þe sternes, so þat þe egh of þi hert mai loke intil heuen. (ED. 256–62)[17]

Rolle's notion of stability is held in the heart where the "egh" is also found, that "egh" with its equally constant and steady focus on heavenly things. Thus the keeping of the recommended stability of life is translated to the constant sight of God in heaven which, cosmologically, is situated by Rolle above the area of fixed stars. That is, it is a transfer of perspective to the notionally highest point in medieval spatial conception and, more importantly, in spiritual conception. However, there is no transfer of intention—the object of desire remains unchanged through life and after life. In a further reflection of this constancy and stability in love of Christ, stability and constancy of Christ's help and love are assured in return:

If þow may not dreghe to syt by þi nane, use þe stalworthly in hys lufe: and he sal sa stabyly sett þe, þat al þe solace of þis worlde sal noght remove þe, for þe will noght list þarof. (Com. 75: 74–77)[18]

As he sits in an earthly place and experiences a heavenly union, Rolle envisages a metaphorical, parallel "sitting" and union with God in an afterlife replete with song, as he expresses in the final verse of the lyric in *Ego Dormio*:

> My settel ordayne for me, and sett þou me þarin;
> For þen moun we never twyn.
> And I þi lufe sal syng throw syght of þi schynyng
> In heven withowten endyng. (72: 360–64)[19]

---

17. "If you will think of this each day, you shall find sweetness that will draw your heart upward, [and you] shall sink in weeping and great longing for Jesus and your thoughts shall all be on Jesus, and will be raised above all earthly things, above the sky and the stars, so that the eye of your heart may look into heaven."

18. "If you dislike being alone, rely on the steadiness of his love: and he will place you so stably that all the comforts of this world will not move you, for he will not leave you."

19. "My seat ordain for me, and sit me therein; / For then we may never be parted. / And I your love shall sing through sight of your shining / In heaven without ending."

In a further paralleling of body-space and soul-space, Rolle analogizes the actual physical act of sitting with the seeking of the "still-point" of spiritual life and dually develops the main connotations of standing:

Als I forsoth in scripture sekand myght fynd & knaw, þe hy lufe of criste sothely in thre þingis standis: In heet, In songe, In swetnes. And þies thre, I am expert in mynde, may not longe stand with-oute grete rest, As if I wald standand & goand in mynde behald or lygandly, me þoght my-self I wantyd full mikyll þerof & as me semyd desolate; wharfore strenyd be neyd, þat I in he deuocyon þat I myghte haue myght abyde, I chase to sytt. Caus of þis I know well: for [if] a man sum-tyme stand or walk, his body waxis wery, & so þe saule is lett And in maner yrk for charge, & he is nott in hee rest, & feloandly nor in parfytnes, for, after þe philosophir, sittynge or restynge þe saule is made wys. Knaw he þerfore þat ȝitt more standynge þen sittyng in godd is delityd, þat fro þe heght of contemplacion he is full fare. (*Fire*, 1.15.33: 9–19)[20]

Here, "standing" denotes both a state (in that it is used as a synonym of "consists") and a performative denotation (the physical activity of standing upright). The second denotation is expanded to become a metaphor for the busyness of earthly life. This metaphorical usage permits Rolle's further distinction between standing and sitting which he enlarges to include, metaphorically, the distinction between the active and the contemplative lives.[21] That is, sitting refers

20. "As far as my seeking in scripture goes I have found and know that the high love of Christ stands truly in three things: In heat, in song and in sweetness. And these three things, I know by experience, may not be sustained without rest. If I stand and walk or lie down when contemplating, I have found myself greatly wanting and desolate; therefore if I [have] strength to remain in devotion, I choose to sit. The reason for this I know well: sometimes [if] a man stands or walks, his body becomes weary, and so too does his soul. And in this state he is not at rest nor can he reach perfection for, as the philosopher says, sitting and resting makes the soul wise. Know, therefore, that he who stands more than sits when delighting in God, is very far from the full heights of contemplation."

21. The *Cloud* author also offers "standing" as a word with multiple denotations, though these differ from the denotations that Rolle assigns. The *Cloud* author ex-

to a quiet and restful attitude of contemplation as much as an actual posture, and the former "sitting" exists in soul-space while the latter is its reflection in body-space. Bernard of Clairvaux, with whose writings Rolle would have been familiar (Watson 1991), refers quite specifically to the sitting posture when he describes God as "a God of knowledge . . . who sits upon the Thrones [in the angelic hierarchy] as a judge who causes no fear among the innocent and who cannot be circumvented. . . . And sitting does not lack meaning; it is a sign of tranquility" (Cons.5. 10: 151). Likewise, Rolle, in the above example from *The Fire of Love,* is adamant that neither "standand" nor "ligand" were effective for his contemplation, and therefore he "chase to sytt."[22] In this context, sitting acts as a *representational space* that participates in an interplay between symbol and meaning as well as being a straightforward example of Lefebvre's *spatial practice* that applies to the simple negotiation of space. A similar interplay occurs in *The Commandment* when Rolle recommends a decentralization of the usual meanings of the activities of thinking, speaking, and acting:

Wharefore, þat þou may lufe hym trewly, understand þat his lufe es proved in thre thynges: in thynkyng, in spekyng, in wirkyng. Chaunge þi thoght fra þe worlde, and kast it haly on hym; and he sall norysche þe. Chaunge þi mowth fra unnayte and warldes speche, and speke of hym; and he sall comfort þe. Chaunge þi hend fra warkes of vanitese, and lyft þam in his name, and wyrke anly for hys lufe; and he sall receyve þe. (Com. 78: 177–85)[23]

---

plains that "By stondyng is vnderstonden a redynes of helping. & therfore it is seide comounly of oo frende to anoþer, whan he is in bodely bataile: 'Bere þee wel, felaw, & fiȝt fast, & ȝiue not up þe bataile ouer liȝtly; for I schal stonde by þee.' He meneþ not only bodely stondyng, for parauenture þis bataile is on hors & not on fote, & parauenture it is going & not stondyng. Bot he meneþ, whan he seiþ þat he schal stonde bi hym, þat he schal be redy to helpe him" (Cl. 58. 109:6–13).

22. Sitting, of course, is the preferred posture of many practitioners of meditation today.

23. "In order that you may love him truly, understand that your love of him is proved by three things: by thinking, by speaking and by acting. Turn your thoughts

Thus, Rolle advises that thought, word, and action be redirected from the worldly to the godly. That is, not that thought, word, and action be ceased but that they be changed in focus to be translocated into their true position in God; the space between the reader and God is thus decreased by the raising of "þar thoght aboven all erthly thyng, swa þat þai may have savoure and solace in þe swetnes of heven" (Com. 80: 235–37).[24] In a subtly juxtaposed view of earth and heaven, Rolle has presented the things of earth as mere shadows of their heavenly counterparts. By exchanging the former for the latter, in focus if not in actuality, the reader is assured of the true love of God and the true heavenly reward. The level of that heavenly reward, however, is, according to Rolle's formulation, dependent upon the degree of love that one achieves in life. That is, again, the physical and spiritual realms are simultaneously and paradoxically connected and separated.

FORM: THE THREE DEGREES OF LOVE

Rolle's three degrees of love are derived from Richard of St. Victor's *Four Steps of Passionate Love* (R. Allen, 1984; Pollard, 1997). Rolle's first degree, *insuperbabel,* refers to a love wherein "na thyng may overcome hit, þat es, nowther wele ne waa, ese ne anguys, lust of flesch ne likyng of þis worlde" (Com. 74: 35–37).[25] The second degree, *inseparabel,* is reached when "al þi thoghtes and þi willes er gederd togeder and festend haly in Jhesu Criste, swa þat þou may na

---

from this world, and fix them wholly on him; and he will nourish you. Turn your mouth from trivial and worldly conversation, and speak of him; and he will comfort you. Turn your hand from works of vanity, and raise them up in his name, and work only for his love; and he will receive you."

24. "your thoughts above all earthly things, so that [you] experience the solace and sweetness of heaven."

25. "nothing may overcome it, that is, neither well-being nor woe, contentment or anguish, fleshly lust or worldly delights."

tyme forgete hym, bot ay þou thynkes on hym" (Com. 74: 40–42).[26]
The third degree, *singuler,* is "when al þi delyte es in Jhesu Cryste, and
in nane other thyng fyndes joy and comforth" (Com. 74: 45–46).[27]

Pollard points out that Richard of St. Victor's fourth degree, that
of *insatiabilis,* though apparently missing from Rolle's schema, is actually covered by his "singular" degree, and posits that Rolle's "writings themselves are manifestations of that very 'insatiable love' which
the earlier Richard says commissions the contemplative to teach others" (1997, 91). This may be so, but Rolle does not pass on the com-
mission to his own readers. As the readers of his epistles are (initially)
women and therefore not permitted to preach, it is possible that he
has purposely suppressed the final stage. Alternatively, as I will go on
to elaborate, the tripartite arrangement is very important to Rolle and
a four-tiered system may not have blended with his overall scheme.

Each of Rolle's three English epistles depicts the three degrees of
love in a different manner. In *Ego Dormio* the stages are numbered
and described but not named as "insuperable," "inseparable," and
"singular." Hope Emily Allen posits that the lack of titles for each
grade of love seems to indicate "that these had not yet been borrowed
from Richard of St. Victor" (1963/1931, 60), but it is also possible
that Rolle is matching the level of his discourse to the requirements
of his individual readers who are at different stages of their contemplative development.

Baker proposes a link between Rolle's three degrees of love and
the three states of life: active, monastic, and solitary (1999, 92). Such
a link is generally discernible and Rolle states quite clearly in *Ego
Dormio* that entry into the third degree of love "es called contemplat-
ife lyfe" (69: 274).[28] A progression in both the states of life and the

---

26. "all your thoughts and your will are gathered together and fixed wholly on Jesus Christ, so that you can at no time forget him, but are always thinking of him."

27. "When all your delight is in Jesus Christ, and in no other thing can you find
joy or comfort."

28. "is called the contemplative life"

degrees of love are also intimated when Rolle advises his initial reader, a nun of Yedingham, that "if þou have sett al þi desyre til lufe God, here þies thre degrees of lufe, sa þat þou may rise fra ane til another, to þou be in þe heest" (E.D. 63: 81–84).[29] That is, this opening proclamation might also be read as an inducement for the nun to proceed to the solitary life. Such a view is not inconceivable particularly when Rolle's schema is considered in total. For example, the description of "insuperable" love is full of worldly associations such as "waa," "anguys," and "lust," suggestive of some of the difficulties and temptations of active life. By the "inseparable" degree, the individual may "na tyme forgete hym," indicating that even if involved in some activity, Christ should be in the fore. This need not necessarily point to monastic life, however, but could be the mixed life. By the "singular" degree, the individual finds no joy or comfort in anything else but Christ; this seems, unequivocally, to indicate the contemplative life.

Rolle describes and prescribes a progression toward the goal of God such that a progression through the degrees of love on earth equate with a particular heavenly station. Thus in *The Form of Living* he tells his reader that "Þe diversite of lufe makes þe diversite of halynes and of mede . . . men and women þat maste has of Goddes lufe, whether þai do penance or nane, þai sall be in þe heghest degre in heven; þai þat lufes hym lesse, in þe lawer order" (F.L. 103: 14–20).[30] Spatially, the direction of that progression is metaphorically upward, with a higher earthly degree of love equating to a matched, higher degree in heaven. Thus, the second degree of love is better than the first and the third degree is the best of all, but all three will earn for their exponents some share in the heavenly reward. All three degrees are thus presented with their equivalent angelic category so that pro-

---

29. "if you have set all your desire toward loving God, here [are] the three degrees of love, so that you may rise from one to another, until you are in the highest."

30. "The diversity of love results in a diversity of holiness and of reward . . . men and women who most love God, whether they do penance or not, they shall be in the highest degree of heaven; they that love him less, in a lower degree."

gression in the earthly realm is shown to have its reflection in heaven and the greater the dedication to God in body-space, the more elevated the reward in soul-space. This earthly-heavenly equating of threefold progression may have been important enough to prompt Rolle to conflate the Victorine fourfold explication of love to three degrees.[31] Thus, while the three degrees of love are emblematic of an upward spiritual direction, they also find an inverse representation in body-space in that the attainment of each successive level demands a proportionally more stringent material measure. That is, metaphorically, as the heavenly potentiality expands, the sphere of involvement in earthly matters contracts and the distance between the physical and the spiritual realms increases.

FORM: THE MYSTICAL SPACE AS TRIPARTITE

In the notional distance between Earth and the sphere of heavenly reward, Rolle indicates a space in which various intermediaries—including Rolle himself—might act. In *Ego Dormio,* for example, when he proclaims that he "will become þat messanger to bryng þe to hys bed, þat hase made þe and boght þe, Criste, þe keyng sonn of heven" (61: 8–10),[32] Rolle exemplifies what Watson refers to as the "triple set of relationships between Christ, Rolle and reader" (1991, 230). In this postulated triad, Christ is the goal and the other points in the schema are the reader and Rolle himself.[33] Whether this textual example of triadic arrangement is intentional or coincidental is not clear, but Rolle's proclamation does indicate that he considered himself to be

31. Certainly, the unitive love which, in the Victorine conception, is the fourth degree is equivalent to Rolle's third degree which he describes as the love that "hase na pere" (F.L. 105: 13) (Pollard 1997, 91).

32. "will become the messenger to bring you to the bed of he who has created you and bought you, Christ the king, the son of heaven."

33. Watson considers that ". . . *Ego Dormio* is not only a treatment of the reader's ascent to union with Christ by means of Rolle, but also a union with Rolle himself" (1991, 229).

able to act in both directions, that is, on behalf of his human charges and on God's behalf. The interest here is the way in which the assuming of a middleman position represents another example of the tripartite arrangement that is so prominent in Rolle's conception of his mystical space. The arrangement hints at a Scholastic basis but Rolle frequently sets out to disavow formal knowledge. In this way, too, then, he assumes the middle ground between knowledge and non-knowledge, between the operation of the discursive mind and the rejection of learning, between the negative theology of the pseudo-Dionysius and the rich sensuality inherent in his elaboration of his experience of *canor, calor,* and *dulcor. The Fire of Love* is offered not to wise men and theologians but "vnto boystus & vntaught, more besy to con lufe god þen many þinges to knawe" (1.1.3: 24–25).[34] Paradoxically, though, Rolle's privileging here of love over knowledge is presented in terms that are very structured and that consistently bear the stamp of the author.

Additionally, in positioning himself as messenger, Rolle becomes the third essential element for the reader's attainment of heaven. He reminds his reader of his necessary inclusion when he says, "And my dere suster in Criste, my wil þou dose if þou lufe hym" (E.D. 61: 12).[35] The quite explicit inference is that the reader will be motivated to come to God if she realizes that she is also pleasing Rolle by doing so. In effect, then, here the triad is the "suster," "Crist," and Rolle as represented by "my wil." Rolle's assumption of the intermediary position declares that he considers that he has some influence in, and knowledge of, both the material and the spiritual realms. This declaration is more than a mere reiteration of pseudo-Dionysius. It is Rolle referring to the persuasive powers of his writing skills, his claim to dual knowledge being reinforced in the way he elaborates a particular view of his mystical space. For example, he can state with confidence that

34. "to the simple and unlearned who are more concerned with loving God than with the knowledge of many things."

35. "And my dear sister in Christ, you do my will if you love him."

In heven er neyn orders of aungels, þat er contened in thre ierarchies. Þe lawest ierarchi contenes aungels, archaungels, and vertues; þe mydel ierarchi contenes principates, potestates, and dominacions; þe heest ierarchi, þat neest es to God, contenes thronos, cherubyn, and seraphyn. (E.D. 61: 18–23)[36]

His knowledge of heaven and the angelic orders extends further, however, to include insight into the manner of heavenly reward in the afterlife. Rolle writes that

For al þat er gude and haly, when þai passe owt of þis worlde, sal be taken intil þies orders: some intil þe lawest, þat hase lufed mykel; some intil þe mydelmest, þat hase lufed mare; oþer intil þe heest, þat maste lufed God and byrnandest es in hys lufe. Seraphyn es at say "brynand"; til þe whilk order þai er receyved þat leest covaytes in þis worlde, and maste swetnes feles in God, and brynandest hertes hase in his lufe. (E.D. 62: 30–38)[37]

The arrangement here clearly incorporates a triadic scheme, exemplifying the notion of a body-space and soul-space interconnection in three paired groups. Thus, the "lawest" order of reward in soul-space is reserved for those who have loved "mykel," the "mydelmest" order is for those who have loved "mare," while the "heest" order is ordained for those who have loved "maste." The apparent derogation of the "lawest" reward by Rolle may be an attempt to encourage his readers, literally, to aim higher for the "heest" place—though in Rolle's schema the highest reward, in the company of the seraphim, was reserved for hermits (Watson 1991, 130).

In offering himself as a guide, both in life and after life, for his read-

---

36. "In heaven there are nine orders of angels which are organized into three hierarchies. The lowest hierarchy contains angels, archangels and virtues; the middle hierarchy contains principalities, powers and dominations; the highest hierarchy, which is nearest to God, contains thrones, cherubim and seraphim."

37. "All those who are good and holy, when they pass out of this world, shall be taken into these orders: some, who have loved much, into the lowest; some who have loved more, into the middle; others into the highest, [that is,] those who have most loved God and have burned for his love. Seraphim means 'burning'; [and] into that order are received those who least coveted the things of this world, and who felt the most sweetness in God, and whose hearts burned most in his love."

ers, Rolle assumes the responsibility of not only encouraging the readers in their chosen pursuit but also of pointing out the potential pitfalls and difficulties along the contemplative way. In exposing these potential problems, Rolle gives a further insight into his conception of the mystical space or, more properly, the space of approach to the mystical apprehension of God. It is an "in-between" space populated not only by God's angels but by devils as well. Thus, Rolle warns *The Form of Living*'s initial reader, Margaret (Kirkeby), that physical enclosure and her commitment to complete spiritual enclosure within Christ will not make her immune to temptations and fiendish visitations. In fact, Rolle suggests that she will be even more subject to the devil's attentions because of the rarity and holiness of her vocation. Rolle cautions that "For þe devyll, þat es enmy till all mankynde, when he sees a man or a woman ymang a thousand turne haly to God, and forsake all þe vanytees and ryches þat men þat lufes þis worlde covaytise, and seke þe joy lastand, a thousand wiles he has on what maner he may desayve þam" (F.L. 85: 27–32).[38] The particular problem for solitaries is that while they are more likely to receive the "revelacion of þe Haly Gaste" (FL. 90: 24)[39] than those in the active life, they are, as a consequence, more likely to receive visions and spiritual apprehensions from a more sinister source. Thus Rolle warns that

þe fende tempes men and women, þat er solitary by þam ane, on a qwaynt maner and a sotel. He transfigurs hym in þe lyknes of an awngel of lyght, and apers till þam, and sayes þat he es ane of Goddes awngels comen to comforth þam; and swa he deceyves foles. Bot þai þat er wys, and wil not tyte trow till all spirites, bot askes cownsel of conand men, he may not begyle þam. (F.L. 90: 51–91:58)[40]

38. "For the devil, who is the enemy of all mankind, when he sees one man or woman in a thousand turn completely to God, and forsake all the vanities and riches that men who love this world covet, and seek an everlasting joy, has a thousand wiles he can use to deceive them."

39. "revelation of the Holy Spirit"

40. "The fiend tempts men and women who are solitaries, in a tricky and subtle manner. He transforms himself into the likeness of an angel of light, and appears to

Rolle goes on to offer an example of a "test" to determine the true nature of the visitor, indicating that interaction between solitaries and "other beings" within the mystical space was not unusual in Rolle's estimation and experience.

Even sleep is shown to be no foil for the fiend, with Rolle declaring that "oure enmy will noght suffer us to be in rest when we slepe" (FL. 92: 105–6).[41] Importantly, though, Rolle differentiates between actual dreaming and the waking experience of spiritual perceptions by separately detailing the "sex maners of dremes"[42] for his reader.[43] The fifth and sixth types are dreams of a positive spiritual benefit because, as Rolle explains, the fifth is prompted by "þe Hali Gast" (131)[44] and the sixth brings thoughts of "Criste or hali kyrk" (93) and both types can presage revelation. Conversely, the first two types have a physiological basis, coming about "if þair wambe be ovre tome, or ovre full" (FL. 93: 125–26).[45] The fourth is the result "of thoght before" (129).[46] The third type, however, is the one that seems to suggest the presence of the devil as it concerns "illusyons of oure enmy" (128–29),[47] which relates back to the previous statement that "oure enmy will noght suffer us to be in rest when we slepe." It is interesting, though, that Rolle positions such a potentially damaging "dream type" between dreams precipitated by an overfull stomach and those prompted by, and related to, daytime thoughts.

While Glasscoe quite rightly points out with regard to the dreams that none of it should be taken too seriously (1993, 73), the inclusion

them, and says he is one of God's angels who has come to comfort them; and so he deceives the foolish. But they who are wise, and will not trust in every spirit but rather ask advice of knowing men, he cannot beguile them."

41. "our enemy cannot bear us to be at rest when we sleep."
42. "six types of dreams"
43. Rolle's dream schema seems to have no relation to Macrobius's elaboration.
44. "the Holy Spirit"
45. "if the stomach is too empty or over full"
46. "earlier thoughts"
47. "[deceptive] illusions from our enemy"

of such a topic indicates Rolle's desire to cover a variety of contingencies in the enclosed life. And the world of dreams, as indicated in contemporaneous literature, was a subject that frequently occupied the fourteenth-century mind.[48] I suggest the interest was associated with the general interest in the status of sleep at the time. Sleep, with its dreams, was perceived, as was death, as providing a link between two worlds. Lefebvre considers that

[s]leep reproduces the womb and foreshadows death. . . . It is now that the "space of dreams" makes it paradoxical appearance. As imaginary and real, this space is different from the space of language though of the same order, and the faithful guardian of sleep rather than of social learning. . . . The space of the dream is strange and alien, yet at the same time as close to us as possible. (209)

Sleep, as a space that represents both enclosure in the womb and (inevitably) the tomb, is therefore a part of daily life that cannot be overlooked. In the modern conception, sleep allows for the unconscious to briefly surface in the symbolism of dreams. For the medieval mind, sleep gave access to other realms, represented in the form of dreams, just as enclosure in the womb presages the new world of life and as death precedes the new world of eternity. Rolle's concentration on dreams in *The Form of Living,* therefore, may not be a superfluous inclusion but a sincere attempt to address the potential dangers of entering a space over which one has little conscious control. In addition, if it is possible that "ego dormio et cor meum vigilat" (E.D. 61: 1),[49] then it is also possible that other things can be awakened during sleep. The sleeping world of dreams, then, is, like Rolle's mystical schema, alive with possibilities, and Rolle is prepared to act as intermediary there, too.

48. On the dream vision genre of the Middle Ages, see, e.g., Peter Brown (1999).
49. "I sleep and my heart is awake"

CONTENT: THE THREEFOLD MYSTICAL
APPREHENSION OF *CALOR, DULCOR, CANOR*

In many ways the experiences of *calor, dulcor,* and *canor* are not individual perceptions at all but a combined overall experience of mystical transport. Rolle tells of receiving his experiences of *calor* and *dulcor* virtually simultaneously while *canor* was achieved some months later. I will deal, therefore, with the triadic experience in general at first and then go on to consider each component separately.

In reference to Rolle's conception of mystical experience, Pollard points out that

> [w]hile it is tempting to see the three as linear—heat leading to a sweetness culminating in song—the elements of the triad frequently overlap. The normal attributes of one sensation often describe another, or the substantive form of one or two elements turns modifier to describe the second or third. Heat, sweetness and song do not line up neatly with the threefold mystical journey of purgation, illumination and union. Nor . . . do they parallel Rolle's division of love into three degrees. If anything, these three terms incorporate four of the five senses and point beyond themselves to the fifth. (1997, 90)

For example, Rolle gives all three an interdependent relationship but appears to privilege song, giving it the initiating role for heat and sweetness when he declares that "Gret longynge sothely growes qwhen þe ioy of lufe qwhen þe dyte of gostly songe is in þe sawle, & grete heytt to sweite lufe gyfis increse, & now no þinge is so lefull as to þinke dede lyfe" (*Fire,* 2.8.88: 18–21).[50] What is sometimes overlooked, however, is that all three apprehensions are part of "the fire of love." That is, they are all components of a gift of ultimate *caritas* from God, the result of mystical union, which ideally produces the "fruit" of spreading the message of God's love to others. The "fire," therefore, is meant to spread, in the form of texts, and ignite others.

---

50. "Great longing truly grows in the joy of love when the sound of spiritual song is in the soul, and great heat gives increase to the sweetness of love, and now nothing is so pleasing as to think of life after death."

Tangibly, in body-space, the *calor* component of the "fire of love" is perceived by the sense of touch and *dulcor,* sweetness, by the sense of taste. Spiritually, Rolle also situates *calor* within the sense of touch but locates the site more exactly within the heart, a deeply enclosed space. The heart is usually associated with emotion, not sensation, so Rolle's situation of *calor* there conflates the physical and the emotional into a new modality of spiritual feeling. Sweetness and its perception in the sense of taste are usually situated in the mouth, which can be considered as the boundary to another enclosed space. Deeper still, by considering the throat and lungs in the breathing process, we are at the level of the site of production for "earthly" singing. *Canor* in the physical sense also presumes not only a productive mechanism but the receptive mechanism of the human ear. *Canor,* therefore, more so than *dulcor* and, to a lesser extent, *calor,* carries with it the particular inference of spatiality in that song and sound are produced in one site and are received in another. Heat, of course, has a source but that source may well be arbitrary and nonspecific and does not carry with it the same notional intentionality that the production of song encompasses. Song implies an engagement with something quite specific in this case. That is, *calor* is general, *dulcor* is general, but *canor* alludes to notions of a site of production and of a site of reception. In addition, both heat in the heart and sweetness in the mouth are sensations that, in theory at least, are more personal than song, which can be experienced either individually or as a group.[51] Similarly Rolle moves his mystical experience from the personal and hidden space of personal warmth and taste to a space in which others—angels and saints in particular—are implicated; he moves from the most enclosed space to the dizzy heights of heaven. Rolle also aligns contemplation with the movement from physical to spiritual in an ascending progression that begins at the level of the heart, moves up to the mouth, and then moves to the ears and beyond:

51. It is appropriate to note here that liturgical song was the standard form of worship in the general and monastic communities of the Middle Ages.

þan may I say þat contemplacion es a wonderful joy of Goddes luf, þe whilk joy es lovyng of God, þat may noght be talde; and þat wonderful lovyng es in þe saule, and for abundance of joy and swettenes it ascendes intil þe mouth, swa þat þe hert and þe tonge acordes in ane, and body and sawle joyes in God lyvand. (F.L. 118: 45–51)[52]

Calor

In the medieval conception of the universe, the four elements—earth, water, air, and fire—were considered to tend naturally toward their "rightful place" (Lewis, 1964) in the order of things. Earth, being the heaviest element, took the lowest place. Next in order was water, then air, and, highest of all, somewhere near the spherical orbit of the moon, was the natural place of fire.[53] St. Augustine points out that fire is the lightest of the four elements and that a preponderance of "fire" in anything forces it to seek its natural place "on high" (O'Connell 1989/1969, 57). In addition, "the higher the element on the cosmic scale (that is, the nearer the "immovable motor") the more perfect was this element's quality" (Bakhtin 1984/1968, 363). As the highest element, then, fire is a particularly appropriate image for the expression of spiritual aspiration.

In using the metaphor of *calor* and its metonymic *fire* as both the beginning and the epitome of his mystical experience, Rolle incorporates multiple spatial connotations. For not only can fire consume an individual object, it can spread to consume other objects; its light can be seen and its heat felt from a distance; and, in addition, fire rises upward toward its true home. Rolle alludes to some of the multiple implications of fire in his prologue to *The Fire of Love* when he describes himself:

52. "Then may I say that contemplation is the wonderful joy of God's love and the joy of loving God cannot be expressed; and that wonderful loving is in the soul, and because of the abundance of joy and sweetness it ascends into the mouth, so that the heart and the tongue are in accord, and body and soul enjoy God."

53. A fifth element, aether, was believed to be above the moon and inhabited by angels (Lewis 1964).

Glad þerfore I am moltyn in-to þe desyre of grettar lufe, and namly for influence of þe moste swete likyng & gostely swetnes þe whilk with þat gostly flaume pythely my mynde has comfortyd. ffyrste treuly, or þis comfortabil heet, & in all deuocion swettyst in me wer sched, playnly I troued slyke hete to no man happyn in þis exill: ffor treuly, so it enflaumes þe saule als þe element of fyer þer wer byrnynge. (1.1.2: 14–21)[54]

Here Rolle foregrounds the emotional and spiritual effect of the heat by the use of the word "moltyn." In Middle English, "moltyn" carried the dual denotations of "molten" and "melted," both words signifying a change of state into a totally pliable condition and metaphorically encompassing the notion of a spiritual remolding into "þe desyre of grettar lufe." Additionally, Rolle acknowledges the role of heat as a physical comfort "in þis exill" and makes specific reference to its elementary status.

Like all four elements in the medieval conception, fire was essential to life. Apart from its cosmological significance, fire was seen to perform many useful and necessary tasks, not the least of which was its ability to cleanse and to fortify metals. Though never overtly expressed by Rolle, this notion of a cleansing fire seems to be part of the whole metaphor. Bernard of Clairvaux, in discussion of God's treatment of the "elect," describes the way in which "He carries them forward . . . he embraces them [and] fire consumes the youthful sins of the elect and the chaff of their ignorance, purging it and rendering it worthy of his love" (Cons. 5.10.150–51). If Rolle did indeed consider himself to be one of the elect—as Watson (1991) has argued—then the above metaphorical use of the image of fire might also be considered as implicit in Rolle's use of it. In any case, for Rolle, fire is not a static image even if the fire of love is best achieved in the stillness of

---

54. "Glad, therefore, I am [to be] melting into the desire of greater love, and especially because of the effect of the most sweet delight and spiritual sweetness which, with the spiritual flame, has so quickly comforted my mind. Truly, before this comforting flame and all this sweet devotion were showed to me, I really believed such heat could not be experienced in this [life of] exile: for truly, it enflames the soul as the real element of fire does in burning."

contemplation. However, Rolle's elaboration of it draws a surprising limit. On a physical level, heat, in the form of fire, can be seen, heard, smelt, and felt. In Rolle's elaboration of *calor* it is with the sensory modality of touch that it is most prominently paired and the modality of vision that is absent. Walter Hilton, in *The Scale of Perfection,* writes of both the understanding of spiritual fire and the "eye of the heart." He considers that when the eyes of the soul open to the knowledge of God, a reform in faith and feeling is achieved and contemplation has begun. Following St. Paul (2 Cor. 4:18), Hilton further writes that "we do not contemplate the things that are seen but those we cannot see; for the things that are seen are temporal, but those that are not seen are eternal" (2.33: 201).[55] Rolle seems to be of a similar opinion for the visual is minimized in all three of his mystical apprehensions but is most obviously absent from the discussion of *calor*.[56] In contemplation, the gaze is turned inward and upward metaphorically and simultaneously.

Lefebvre notes, in agreement with Nietzsche's postulation, that "over the course of history the visual has increasingly taken precedence over elements of thought and action deriving from the other senses. . . . So far has this trend gone that the senses of smell, taste and touch have been almost completely annexed and absorbed by sight" (139). This need not have been so during the Middle Ages, however. Even Lefebvre posits that the beginning of the dominance of visual space coincided with the time of the "decrypting" of Christianity (as I pointed out in Chapter One) with the literal rise of the gothic ca-

55. I have quoted from Sherley-Price's translation here (which I have checked against my own notes on MS. BL. Harley 6579) in the absence of a critical Middle English edition of *The Scale of Perfection (Book 2).* However, see Thomas H. Bestul, ed., *The Scale of Perfection* (Kalamazoo, Mich.: Western Michigan University for TEAMS, 2000) for an edition based on London, Lambeth Palace, MS 472 with *Scale 2* variants from Oxford, Bodleian Library, MS Bodley 100. An online version is available at *http://tigger.uic.thestul/scaleII.htm.*

56. That is, we do not expect to "see" either sweetness or song but generally associate fire with a visual representation.

thedrals. The influence of an earlier age, more attuned to the senses of touch, smell and taste, need not have been obliterated instantly but, more logically, was probably phased out in inverse proportion to the increase in the visual. For Rolle, it seems that such a reversal of the hierarchies of sensory modalities is not reflected in the mystical world. Rolle, like Hilton, takes the "visual" eye and the "visual" component of fire and relocates them both in the heart so that the inward gaze can connect with the inner fire and ascend with it to its rightful place with God.

Dulcor

Sweetness, in the modern understanding of it, was a rarity in medieval times. Sugar was unknown in fourteenth-century England and Europe. "Honey was the principle source of sweetness . . . [and] it was so precious as to be almost a currency in medieval England" (Lacey 1999, 137). Rolle does not use the idea of sweetness, however, solely in reference to honey. Wine, for example, can be sweet. This sweetness, together with wine's intoxicating effect, is the first link forged with the "kiss" of The Song of Songs.[57] The fragrances of perfume, oils, spices, incense, and flowers are also sweet. In the Middle Ages all were valued for their rarity and exoticness. Thus, though the idea of sweetness fixes on the sense of taste, it encompasses the olfactory sense as well. To some extent, the tactile sense is also implicated because, as Lefebvre points out, "tastes are hard to distinguish both from smells and from the tactile sensations of lips and tongue" (198).

An association of Rolle's *dulcor* and spatiality seems to center on the notion of the mouth and nose as boundary spaces that act as receptacles for the stimuli of the sensations of taste and smell. Of tangential relevance here is Richard Stern's theory of buccal perception primacy that argues "that the child's first notion of space is 'buccal'" (Grosz 1994, 45). "'Buccal'" refers to a space that can be contained in, or exploited by [the child's] mouth. Not only the mouth but the

57. See Songs 1:1–2.

whole respiratory apparatus gives the child a kind of experience of space. After that, other regions of the body intervene and come into prominence" (Merleau-Ponty 1965, 122, quoted in Grosz, ibid.). That is, in modern theories of psychological development of the child, the mouth is posited as the initial and primary sensory apparatus through which the early perception of spatiality is experienced and established. Rolle's mystical perception of sweetness seems to encompass the range of possibilities that I have begun to elaborate: an evocation of the earliest sensations of comfort and space and sweetness at a mother's breast, and the mixture of sensations involved in that early experience. He brings together the ideas of sweetness, nourishment, and comfort when he describes, from the point of view of the personified soul, the yearning for the kiss of the Beloved:

All erthly to me ar yrksome, my lemman lufe I feyll, moystur I taste of meruelus comforth, & þat swetnes besily I ȝerne; lufe makes me hardy hym to call þat I best lufe, þat I fro hym put far be temptacion fayll not, he me comforthand & filland myȝt kys me with kyssynge of hys mouth. þe more truly fro erthly þoghtis I am lyft, þe more I feyll swetnes desyrd; þe more fleschly desyrs ar slokynde, þe truliar euerlastynge ar kyndyld. I beseke he kys me with swetnes of his lufe refreschynge, with kissynge of his mouth me straytly halsyng, þat I fayl not, & gras in puttyng þat I may besily in lufe grow. Als childyr with mylk of pappis ar norischyd, so chosyn sawlis byrnuand in luffe with heuenly likynge is feed, be thee qwhilk to þe syght of clerenes euerlastynge þai sall be broght. (*Fire*, 1.27.58: 21–33)[58]

58. "All earthly things are burdensome to me, my beloved's love I crave, to taste his moist [lips] of marvelous comfort, for that sweetness I constantly yearn; love makes me bold to call out to him whom I love best, and temptations I put far from me so that I will not fail him, that he might comfort me and fill me with the kiss of his mouth. The further from earthly thoughts I am lifted, the more I feel the sweetness I desire; the more fleshly desires are weakened, the more truly everlasting [desires] are kindled. I beseech him to kiss me with the sweetness and refreshment of his love, and when kissing me with his mouth that he hold me tightly, so that I do not die and that I receive his grace and may actively grow in love. As children are nourished with mother's milk, so chosen souls, burning with love, are fed with heavenly delights, and are thus brought to the sight of everlasting glory."

In the medieval schema of an interconnected body-space and soul-space, these early physical experiences of sweetness link to the idea that the love of God elicits the same feelings of sweetness and comfort on the spiritual level.[59] Rosemary Drage Hale posits another view of this connection when she remarks that

whether it is sensed materially from the physical environment or immaterially in the state of ecstasy, taste emanates from inside the mouth. For the Christian mystics there is an element of inverted mimesis present in the process. In the Johannine sense the Logos was made Flesh and then eaten through reception of the Eucharist. The mystical experience reflects a theological inversion—tastes the sweetness of the divine flesh within, converts to word through written recollection the experience of divine union. Adam and Eve sought to savour the sweet fruit of knowledge and suffered exile from Paradise. The mystics seek to savour the sweet fruit of divine knowledge with the reward of divine union. (1995, 6–7)

Indeed, the "reward" may be considered to extend beyond divine union during life to the ultimate and eternal union with God after death as Rolle intimates when he says that "þa truly here in þameself þat hym feys sweett, þer doutles welcheryd þa sal hym see" (*Fire*, 2.8.89: 4–5).[60] De Ford suggests that "[Rolle] regards [*dulcor*] as a foretaste of the beatific vision . . . but the perfection of the experience is to be found only in heaven" (1980, 192–93).

I would suggest that the deepest psychological level of primary spatial buccal experience is also (unconsciously) implicated in Rolle's *dulcor*. That is, sweetness and its association with the mouth and the lips is a primary physical and spatial sensation that finds its spiritual reflection in a return to the sweetness of unity with God, such unity being understood as a return to the most primary of all spaces: enclosure within God. That is, like *calor, dulcor* points ultimately to God.

---

59. Boenig notes that in Rolle's *Commentary on the First Verses of the Canticle of Canticles,* he develops the God-as-mother theme which makes particular reference to "Christ's milk-giving breasts" (1984, 173).

60. "They who in themselves feel sweetness here, shall doubtless see him there."

Canor

Of Rolle's three mystical apprehensions, *canor* is the one with the most obvious connection to spatiality and to the conception of space in the Middle Ages. The association between music and space, particularly cosmology, was well established by Rolle's time. At the turn of the fifth century St. Augustine admitted to an inordinate love of music in his *Confessions*. In fact, as Boenig points out, Augustine had used the psalms as a "cosmological metaphor for the moral universe" (1995, 79), and that, following Augustine, "(Rolle) associates the cithara or harp with earthly things and the psaltery with celestial" (ibid., 82). Kazarow points out that Cassiodorus (ca. 485–575) regarded music as transformational and a way to deep contemplation and described it as a category in "a progression that leads from the merely physical qualities of sound, that is, from sensation to proportion and then to numbers. The Christian ascends still higher proceeding from numbers to unity" (1993, 150). Similarly, the basic text for the study of music, Boethius's *De Musica*, "was primarily concerned with mathematical relationships as a means of decoding the order of the cosmos" (Boenig 1995, 75). Likewise, Eco considers that in Boethius "we find also a very typical feature of the medieval mentality: when he speaks of 'music' he means the mathematical science of musical laws" (1986, 30).

Closer to Rolle's own time, Hugh of St Victor elaborated three kinds of music in his *Didascalicon:* "the music of the worlds, the music of humanity, the music of instruments" (quoted in Underhill 1995/1911, 77). Underhill comments on Hugh's elaboration that "[t]hus, the life of the visible and invisible universe consists in a supernal fugue" (ibid.), thereby reflecting the idea of the medieval conflation of body-space and soul-space.

It is not possible to ascertain from Rolle's description of *canor* which, if any, of Hugh's categories of music he was utilizing. However, Rolle clearly indicates that he heard heavenly music, which is evocative of the medieval cosmological notion of "the music of the spheres."[61] It was a commonplace that as the Earth was understood to be the immobile object around which all the other planets and celestial bodies revolved, it was possible to hear the movement of the spheres from the Earth. Chaucer makes mention of it in *Troilus and Criseyde* when, at the time of his death, Troilus rises up away from the Earth and hears there "[t]he erratik sterres, herkenyng armonye / With sownes ful of hevenyssh melodie" (5.1812–13).[62]

Paul Davies (1992) offers a Pythagorean source for the concept, pointing out that

[t]he Pythagoreans applied their numerology to astronomy. They devised a system of nine concentric spherical shells to convey the known heavenly bodies as they turned, and invented a mythical "counter-Earth" to make up the tetraktus number 10. This connection between musical and heavenly harmony was epitomised by the assertion that the astronomical spheres gave forth music as they turned—the music of the spheres. Pythagorean ideas were endorsed by Plato, who in his *Timaeus* developed further a musical and numerical model of the cosmos. (95)[63]

Chalcidius was a fourth-century commentator on Plato and a translator of parts of Plato's *Timaeus*.[64] To his translation Chalcidius adds a commentary that, from internal evidence, suggests he may have

61. General condemnation of music, discernible in the works of Hilton and the *Cloud* author, were most probably a response to Pope John XXII's bull that attacked affective music, which was considered to "intoxicate the ear without satisfying it" (Boenig 1995, 85).

62. "the erratic stars, harkening harmony / With sounds full of heavenly melody."

63. In 1965, two American physicists, Arno Penzias and Robert Wilson, detected what is sometimes referred to as "the background hum of the universe." It is, in fact, detectable as a noise on sensitive microwave detectors but is actually produced by radiation emanating from the edges of the observable universe. In addition, "this noise never varies by more than one part in ten thousand" (Hawking 1988, 41). Of course I am not suggesting that the medievals were able to hear this microwave sound but it is of coincidental interest that they conceived of a sound just as we, today, have detected a constant cosmic noise.

64. Chalcidius has not been dated with accuracy.

been Christian, although evidence to the contrary is also discernible. Lewis (1964) gives a short account of the evidence and decides that "Chalcidius is a Christian, writing philosphically" (51). Chalcidius's writings were known in the later Middle Ages and were particularly associated with "the twelfth-century Latin poets associated with the school of Chartres, who in their turn helped to inspire Jean de Meung and Chaucer" (ibid., 59). While I am not suggesting that Rolle had direct knowledge of Chalcidius's writings, there seems to be some similarity in the commentator's ideas and those expressed by Rolle.[65] Chalcidius's cosmic Triad is conceived "not only as a harmony but as a polity, a triad of sovereign, executive and subjects" (ibid., 57). As this chapter has suggested, the idea of a triad finds particular reflection in Rolle's elaboration of the form of his mystical space. Chalcidius, too, closely following Plato, expounds the primary values of the various senses. Sight, for example, is important because it "begets philosophy" (ibid., 55) but Chalcidius's opinion on hearing and music is of particular interest here. His view is that

hearing exists principally for the sake of music. The native operations of the soul are related to the rhythms and modes. But this relationship fades in the soul because of her union with the body, and therefore the souls of most men are out of tune. The remedy for this is music; not that sort of music which delights the vulgar . . . but that divine music which never departs from understanding and reason. (Ibid., 56)

The differentiation between "vulgar" and "divine" music has much in common with Rolle's own rejection of publicly enacted liturgical music and the embrace of his own "divine," internal music. That is, liturgical music is not to be compared with Rolle's own truly "divine," inwardly experienced music, as he points out in *The Fire of Love:*

65. Obviously Rolle (c. 1300–1349) predates Chaucer (c. 1342–c. 1400) but the possibility that Chaucer was familiar with Chalcidius's ideas suggests their circulation in England in Rolle's time.

For sweit gostly songe truly & ful speciall it is giffyn, with vtward songe acordis not þe qwhilk in kyrkis & elsqwer ar vsyd. It discordis mikyll, for all þat be mans voys vtward is formyd with bodily eris to be hard, bot emonge aungels twnys it has a acceptabyll melody & with meruale it is commendyd of þam þat has knawen it. (*Fire*, 2.3.73:16–21)[66]

The difference in the quality of the two distinct types of music represents, for Rolle, the difference between the earthly and the heavenly realm, but the cosmic triad finds a reflection in the world of material music. As I mentioned earlier in this chapter, the *triad,* since the fourteenth century, has been considered the basis of harmony. One wonders if such triadic harmony prompted Rolle to consistently represent his formulations in triads. Though Rolle is adamant that the music that he hears in church is so unlike his "heavenly music" that it puts him off his devotions, the general influence of the pervasiveness of music in the liturgy at that time cannot be disregarded. As I have also suggested in the above section on *dulcor,* Lefebvre posits a decrypting of space sometime in the twelfth century that reflected a shift from oral to visual predominance but Rolle does not exhibit any symptoms of such a shift. In fact, for Rolle, aurality dominates visuality on several levels. For example, Rolle's avowed emphasis on heavenly song may be considered to have a function of aligning his ideas with dissemination by word of mouth, leading to the (social) production of his mystical texts. Thus, he can be considered to be still "encrypting" rather than "decrypting" his space.

It is obvious from the style of Rolle's writing, with its emphasis on alliteration, rhythm, and repetition, that sound effects were important to him. In addition it seems that Rolle may have found the sense of vision attractive, perhaps very strongly attractive, considering his confession of the rebukes he received from women after he had being

66. "For sweet spiritual song truly is specially given and is unlike the outward song that is heard in churches and elsewhere. The [two songs] differ greatly because man's outward voice is formed to be heard by bodily ears but melody among angels is accepted and commended marvelously by those who have known it."

looking too closely at them.[67] In Rolle's case, then, a turning from the world logically might have involved a diminution, if not rejection, of the physical visual sense in preference for spiritual insight.[68] And this spiritual insight is expressed for Rolle in heat, sweetness, and song. Rolle verifies this view when he explains that "Hym truly none erthly þinge likys þat truly lufys criste, for be gretnes of lufe all passand semys fowle, with fflescly eyn bodily þingis ar seyn, bot with clene hert & meyk heuenly þingis rightwes behald" (*Fire* 1.29.61: 29–32).[69] In *Ego Dormio*, Rolle explicitly juxtaposes sight and song, aligning sight with the material world and song with the love of Jesus Christ:

> Alle perisches and passes þat we with eghe see
> It wanes into wrechednes, þe welth of þis worlde.
> Robes and ritches rotes in dike,
> Prowde payntyng slakes into sorow,
> Delites and drewryse stynk sal ful sone,
> Þair golde and þaire tresoure drawes þam til dede.
> Al þe wikked of þis worlde drawes til a dale,
> Þat þai may se þare sorowyng, whare waa es ever stabel.
> Bot he may syng of solace, þat lufes Jhesu Criste,
> Þe wretchesse fra wele falles into hell (E.D. 104–13)[70]

67. In the medieval conception of sin, sight was usually regarded as the way in which temptation was introduced. That is, sin entered via the eye, then coerced the heart, and finally acquired the approval of the will.

68. William F. Pollard (1997) advances a different view on the way in which the ideas of vision are treated by Rolle, finding Rolle's frequent use of the image of the *oculus cordis,* "the eye of heart," to involve a synthesis of Augustinian (and, later, Victorine) ideas on the *affectus/aspectus* dichotomy, that is, the inclination of the heart versus the rational power of the soul (92). Pollard's thesis is an interesting and well-supported one but I have chosen not to engage with it here as it is not of precise relevance, as it deals as much with the sources and influences of the image as it does with Rolle's utilization of it.

69. "Truly, he who truly loves Christ does not like earthly things, for the greatness of [his] love makes passing things seem foul. With fleshly eyes bodily things are seen but the righteous behold heavenly things with a clean and meek heart."

70. "All perishes and passes that we see with the eye / It fades into wretchedness, the wealth of this world / Robes and riches rot in the ditch / Proud adornment sinks into sorrow / Delights and tokens will soon stink / Their gold and their treasure

In this example, too, "worlde" is pejoratively associated with words suggestive of downward movement : dale and dike; the alliterative association of "worlde," "wanes," "wrechednes," and "wretchesse" building to the final link with "wele" which allows a rhyme with the culminating "falles into hell" which is the lowest level to which one can descend. Spatially, then, Rolle's song is associated with ascent in contrast to the "descent" of worldly concerns, but it also has a larger significance. Boenig comments that "[t]his emphasis on the sweetness of music brings us close to the very centre of Rolle's thought. In the Prologue to his English Psalter, he transforms Augustine's psaltery with his mathematical analogy between its ten strings and the Ten Commandments into something affective" (1995, 83). In his *canor,* we find the culmination of Rolle's mystical experience. While *calor* and *dulcor* are inner experiences that find their true place in God, *canor* not only allows Rolle an access to the heavenly realm but provides the basis for a way to share the fruit of his experience. Patrick Grant summarizes this idea when he observes that "[Rolle] dissociates 'song' from its outward expression as sound. . . . The poetic or literary effect of Rolle's prose comes, therefore, from interplay between a singular identity of experience and its manifold relevance for humanity at large" (1983, 12). Thus, Rolle translates the heavenly *canor* into earthly words and rhythms in his texts in order that others may also find their "settle" near God.

By exhibiting these cosmological, mathematical, and musical associations in the elaboration of his mystical experience, Rolle creates a mystical space that is revealed as being far more thoughtfully and carefully conceived than is generally acknowledged. The amenability of his mystical apprehensions to an examination of some modern theories of perception and space also point to a greater depth of mystical experience than that with which Rolle is credited. Equally, however,

---

draws them to death. / All the wickedness of this world are drawing toward a dale / Where they may see sorrowing, where woe is ever present. / But he may sing of solace who loves Jesus Christ, / When the wretched from their well-being fall into hell."

when considered in terms of the conceptual *mise en abîme,* Rolle's mystical space is seen to be one that is particularly representative of the dominant medieval worldview that conceived of an ineluctable mingling of material and spiritual aspects with Rolle's perceptual and sensible experiences of the former being capable of replication in the latter and vice versa. In his predominantly medieval worldview and his avowed love of words and images, Rolle creates a mystical space that stands in contrast to the mystical space that the *Cloud* author elaborates. It is to a consideration of that space that I turn in the following chapter.

Chapter Five

THE MYSTICAL SPACE OF THE *CLOUD* AUTHOR

Wisest is he who knows what he does not know.

(Socrates)

THE LITERARY *MISE EN ABYME*

The mystical space, that space of the intimate experience of God, is present in, and encompassed by, all the strata of the *mise en abîme* as God is the precipitator and the focus of the mystical experience. However, for the *Cloud* author, that space is elaborated not as one in which God is met and known but one where God is experienced by "unknowing." It is a space that is at once empty of all things, thoughts, and images and yet is full of God. Thus, though the *Cloud* author's mystical space is elusive, it is, in a way, a truly "mystical" space—in the original definition of the word—in that it is "hidden" and barely "spoken of" within the texts. It is, however, represented in ways that reflect the author's conviction that God "may wel be loued, bot not þou3t" (Cl. 6.26: 4).[1] By advocating the negation of thought, the *Cloud* author is offering a reflection of the mystical space itself that is posited as being situated between a cloud of forgetting and a cloud of unknowing. The reflection amply demonstrates Lucien Dällenbach's definition of the

---

1. God "may well be loved but not thought."

(literary) *mise en abyme*[2] as "any aspect enclosed within a work that shows a similarity with the work that contains it" (1989, 8). Pertinent here, too, is Dällenbach's further point that "[t]he practice of most critics shows that the *mise en abyme* and the mirror are sufficiently interchangeable for us to combine the two and refer to 'the mirror in the text'" (1989, 35). My interpolation of the literary *mise en abyme* into the overarching *mise en abîme* paradigm of mystical space yields a conception of the *Cloud* author's mystical space as one of countless mirror images of the central abyss in which God is encountered and loved. That is, the empty space in the center of contemplation, though full of God, is reflected in multiple ways in the particular practice of contemplation, as recommended by the *Cloud* author, in the physical and social space that the *Cloud* author recommends. In general, all the reflections are of an absence: absence of interest in worldly things, absence of thought, absence of knowing, absence of self, and, frequently, the apparent absence of God.

The postulation of the mirror in the mystical text leads me to focus my discussion on certain key features in relation to *The Cloud of Unknowing* and *The Book of Privy Counselling*. Primarily, the figure of the mirror and the multiple representations of reflection in the texts are considered from a spatial perspective. Both medieval and modern conceptions of the speculum are incorporated in the consideration. The image of the cloud itself is also explored, particularly in relation to its metaphorical spatiality.

Furthermore, as I have suggested, the space of contemplation is posited as an empty space, a space of absence that is "suspended" between two clouds: of forgetting and unknowing. Like the gap between presence and representation in language, which I explored in Chapter Three, the *Cloud* author's mystical place seems to be locat-

2. The differentiation in spelling here is due to the specific literary use of the term here, though my examination will expand to include the other (i) spelling and its definition as well.

ed in a gap between the material world and the eternal world of the spirit. It is this gap that the *Cloud* author's contemplative readers are asked to enter and in which they remain until God reaches out for them. Thus, the gap, though an empty space, holds the possibility of being full of God.

In a way, the *Cloud* author himself is an example of the literary *mise en abyme* at work. By that I mean that he is contained within his texts as an unknown author and his texts contain an endorsement of "unknowing." In line with Dällenbach's definition of the *mise en abyme,* then, the *Cloud* author is an "aspect enclosed within a work that shows a similarity with the work that contains it" (1989, 8). His personal absence from the texts, too, can be considered as a representation of his theological approach to mysticism which follows, for the most part, the *via negativa.* His corpus of vernacular works is generally considered to consist of *The Cloud of Unknowing* and *The Book of Privy Counselling,* which are the main interests of this chapter; *The Epistle of Prayer; The Epistle of Discretion of Stirrings; Hid Divinity;* a translation and partial adaptation (via intermediate Latin texts) of the work of Dionysius the Areopagate; *Benjamin Minor; The Study of Wisdom,* freely adapted from *The Twelve Patriarchs* of Richard of St. Victor; and *A Treatise of Discerning of Spirits* (Glasscoe 1993, 165).[3] While the *Cloud* author's anonymity continues to pique curiosity, only a few probabilities about the *Cloud* author can be adduced. The period of composition of his works can be placed approximately between c. 1345 and 1386, and linguistic evidence points to an East Midland origin for the texts (Knowles 1961). Marion Glasscoe notes that the *Cloud* author "has strong connections with the

3. Glasscoe notes, with reference to the probable order of composition of these works, that "[t]he major work, *The Cloud of Unknowing,* is explicitly elucidated by further thought in *The Book of Privy Counselling,* in which the author also refers to *The Epistle of Prayer* and *Hid Divinity* as his. This establishes the fact that these three texts preceded *The Book of Privy Counselling.* There is, however, no other certain knowledge about the other works or the order in which they were written" (1993, 166).

Carthusian order" (1993, 167), basing this conclusion on the author's mode of thought as exemplified in his works and on the order's role in the transmission of the texts.

In general, his writings on mysticism, resulting from, it is assumed, an exemplary mystical life, are accorded the highest praise. William Johnston, for example, considers him to be "at once a mystic, a theologian, and a director of souls" (1978/1967, 1). Eric Colledge compares him with Richard Rolle and finds the *Cloud* author superior in every way and declares him to be one of "the two greatest fourteenth century writers" (1961, 50). However, while Rolle has been variously criticized for injecting too much of his personality into his texts, the opposite criticism is leveled occasionally at the *Cloud* author, even to the extent of calling into question the actuality of his mystical experience. Kevin Hart, for example, commenting on Johnston's assertion that *The Cloud of Unknowing* "testifies to the author's personal mystical experience," remarks:

> [To] the argument . . . that personal experience is necessary for persuasive writing [m]any objections could be raised. One could point to a number of poems or novels which effectively describe events of which the author has had no direct experience. Conversely, rhetoric skill is requisite for persuasive writing, even if one is writing from direct experience. *The Cloud of Unknowing* may seem realistic but the very concision of the text suggests that material has been selected and framed, which implies that the text does not so much report raw experience as deploy a realist code. There may be traces of direct experience in the text but the argument from literary persuasiveness to personal experience will not help us isolate them. (1989, 182)

Similarly, while David Knowles considers the *Cloud* author as substantially more advanced in spiritual matters than Rolle, for example, he nonetheless points out that "for all the apparently esoteric quality of some of its instruction [*The Cloud of Unknowing*] is in fact a manual of traditional ascetic teaching, based on current orthodox theology and assuming the customary sacramental and devotional life of medieval England" (1961, 74). In effect, what Hart and Knowles are intimating is that the *Cloud* author's apparent lack of originality in the basic matter of his texts classes him more readily as a spiritual teacher than, necessarily, a spiritual "practitioner." Certainly it is true that evidence of the major influences on his thinking and approach are easily discernible, but it is also true, as Cheryl Taylor point outs, that his use of the vernacular "supports a colloquial spontaneity and fragmentary organization that suggest an origin in oral composition and dialogue" (2005, 34). However, despite the *Cloud* author's efforts "to pour cold water on the tendency of previous churchmen to produce taxonomies, segregating and grading the stages of growth of the soul towards God" (Whitehead 1998, 203), he cannot avoid at least chapter divisions and summaries of his work and the elaboration of the four states of Christian life, with the fourth "stretching" all the way to heaven: "& þe ferþe may bi grace be bigonnen here, bot it schal euer laste wiþ-outen eende in þe blis of heuen (Cl. 1.13: 11–13).[4] On balance, though, evidence of the author's own solitary life and dedication to the mystical ideals that he proclaims are there in his texts. It is, perhaps, a credit to his writing skill that these clues are often overlooked. It is an indication of a synchronicity between his purpose and his writing style that he manages to effect the almost complete effacement of himself from his own texts, just as he recommends an effacement of all earthly things when one enters the contemplative life. He purposely "forgets" his existence and advises his readers to follow this same practice of self-effacement: "& þerfore breek doun alle wetyng & felyng of alle maner of creatures; bot most besily of þi-self" (Cl. 43.82: 19–20).[5] Thus the author "forgets" his own name and his writings are delivered without the overlay or interference of a "real" person. In fact he places himself within the same space as he recommends for his readers—between a cloud of forgetting and a cloud of unknowing. That is, in his retreat into anonymity,

4. "and the fourth may by grace be begun here, but it shall be everlasting in the bliss of heaven."
5. "and therefore break down all knowledge and feeling of all forms of creatures; but most thoroughly of yourself."

the author himself comes to reflect the very void that he seeks to construct for his readers' encounter with God.

THE REFLECTIVE SPACE

The mystical space of the *Cloud* author seems to be a space that, conceptually, has attributes in common with the mirror. Lefebvre regards the mirror as "a surface at once pure and impure, almost material yet virtually unreal; it presents the Ego with its own material presence, calling up its counterpart, its absence from—and at the same time its inherence in—this 'other' space" (185). His definition is surprisingly resonant with the *Cloud* author's mystical space. By that I mean that the *Cloud* author, in recommending that his reader enter the metaphorical space between the cloud of forgetting and the cloud of unknowing, is suggesting, in effect, an abandonment of the ego and of the consciousness of the self to the extent that, within the mystical experience, the contemplative is the "counterpart" of the self in the material world, a negative image of his "own material presence" and an "absence" in an "'other' space."

Lefebvre goes further, stating that

[t]he mirror discloses the relationship between me and myself, my body and the consciousness of my body—not because the reflection constitutes my unity *qua* subject, but because it transforms what I am into the sign of what I am. This ice-smooth barrier, itself merely an inert sheen, reproduces and displays what I am—in a word, signifies what I am—within an imaginary sphere which is yet quite real. (Ibid.)

Similarly, for the *Cloud* author's contemplative reader, the disclosure of the relationship between the self in the material world and the self in the contemplative world reveals a deep sorrow which "clensiþ þe soule, not only of synne, bot also of peyne þat he haþ deseruid for synne" (Cl. 44.84: 3–4)[6] and institutes an accompanying desire

---

6. "cleanses the soul, not only of sin, but also of the pain it has deserved for sin"

which paradoxically produces an awareness of one's being and the "desire vnsesingly for to lakke þe wetyng & þe felyng of his beyng" (Cl. 44.85: 1–2).[7] That is, there is an awareness of self and, in the contemplative space, a desire for a liberation from the knowledge and feeling of that being—a simultaneous reinstatement of being and erasure of it and a need for presence in order to replace it with absence.

The absence that is substituted for the presence is, in fact, a bare acknowledgment of being that finds its reflection in God. Thus the *Cloud* author recommends that

Þat meek derknes be þi mirour & þi mynde hole. Þenk no ferþer of þi-self þan I bid þee do of þi God, so þat þou be on wiþ hym in spirit as þus, with-outyn departyng & scatering of mynde. For he is þi being, & in him þou arte þat at þou arte, not only bi cause & bi beyng, bot also he is in þee boþe þi cause & þi beyng. & þerfore þenk on God as in þis werk as þou dost on þi-self, & on þi-self as þou dost on God, þat he is as he is & þou arte as þou arte, so þat þi þou3t be not scaterid ne departid, bot onid in hym þat is al; euermore sauyng þis difference bitwix þee & him, þat he is þi being & þou not his. (P.C. 136: 7–16)[8]

The author's stressing of the difference between God and the reader, which is that "he is þi being & þou not his," is indicative of the way in which a mirror reflects. Thus, as Julia Kristeva has pointed out in terms of the physical sense of sight, the eye "sees only because it reflects the light of a single source" (1987, 120).[9] In the *Cloud* author's

7. "unceasing desire to be free of the knowledge and feeling of his being."

8. "[Make] humble darkness your mirror and your whole mind. Think no more of yourself than I bid you think of God, so that you are one with him in spirit, though without loss or disintegration of your mind. For he is your being, and in him you are what you are, not only by cause and by being, but also because he is in you as your cause and your being. And therefore think of God in this work as you do of yourself, that is, he is as he is and you are as you are, and in this way, your thoughts will not be distracted or lost, but united with him who is all; but remember the difference between you and him: he is your being but you are not his."

9. See Julia Kristeva, "Narcissus: The New Insanity," in *Tales of Love,* trans. Leon S. Roudiez (New York: Columbia University Press, 1987), 103–21. There, Kristeva discusses in detail the idea of God and reflection, in particular in regard to the Narcissus myth.

elaboration, the "source" is God and the apprentice reflects the source in the simple actuality of his being.[10] This "being," unencumbered and unembellished by knowledge, is offered back to God who IS. That is, the reader, as all humanity, has his being *in* God and offers his being *to* God. We are returned to Northrop Frye's postulation (which I presented in Chapter Three) of God as a verb, as a process rather than a noun, a thing. The *Cloud* author offers no qualification for God other than "he is" and likewise the reader is reminded only that "þou arte." In the *Cloud* author's mystical space, then, the dynamic effects of process rather than static materiality are foregrounded. In such a space, "no-thing" and "no-where" seem to be far more legitimate descriptors than nouns with connotations tied to earthly images. Thus, when the author advises his reader "Þat meek derknes be þi mirour & þi mynde hole," he is recommending that the contemplative's mind literally reflect nothing of the world or the self; instead "naked being" and "naked intent" represent the being and the will, stripped of the earthly props of imagination, knowledge, and even language.

The mirror's reflection of darkness is resonant, too, with Lefebvre's concept of an "anti-mirror effect" which he defines as "a lived experience of blank opacity" (184). That is, the central mirror of the mystical space reflects back only darkness to the viewing subject, the contemplative.

In regard to this "dark mirror" Johnston believes that

even though the metaphor of a cloud in the sky is central to the principal treatise, the main endeavor of the author is not so much to fix our eyes on an outer world charged with the presence of God in all things, but rather to direct our eyes into the depth of our own soul in the darkness of which "mirror" we will find God. This way of thinking occupies the opening pages of Privy Counsel where the author, instructing his disciple to empty his mind

10. Augustine had observed God as the source of all reflection and was insistent "that the soul can only be reformed in the image of God by God: "'the beginning of the image's reforming must come from him who first formed it' (xiv.xvi.22)" (Louth 1981, 157).

of all thoughts and images so that it may remain in supraconceptual darkness, says: "Let that darkness be thy mirror and thy mind wholly" [P.C. 136: 7]. The mind is a mirror; void of images and thoughts but filled with faith, it is in darkness; and in the darkness one sees God. (1978, 3)

The oxymoronic quality of a mirror reflecting only darkness is reflected in the notion of a mind devoid of thinking. The *Cloud* author elucidates this notion in two similar and juxtaposed warnings to his reader. First, he advises of the necessity to "beware in þis werk, & trauayle not in þi wittes ne in þin ymaginacion no wise" (Cl. 4.23: 9–11)[11] and, second, to understand that "when I sey derknes, I mene a lackyng of knowyng" (Cl. 4.23: 20).[12] Of course, the first warning contains both the designation of contemplation as "werk" and the direction to "trauayle not" in the work. The noun and verb represent simultaneously a similarity and an opposition. Likewise, to recognize a lack of knowing, one must "know" what "knowing" is. That is, "a lackyng of knowing" is both similar and opposite to "knowing." Both warnings can be understood, therefore, as presentations of mirror images. The difficulty is, of course, that in the material world a mirror cannot reflect without a light source, just as an individual would be hard-pressed to "unknown" that which he had not known previously. Similarly, just as a dark mirror provides no information, so the cloud of unknowing has no relationship to any of the reasoning or sensible faculties.

However, if the reflection received from the mirror is only darkness, then the contemplative is well placed to approach God with a type of blindness, exemplified in the author's recommendation of an approach enlivened by "a louyng steryng & a blinde beholdyng vnto þe nakid beyng of God him-self only" (Cl. 8.32: 7–8).[13] That blindness is itself paradoxical as the *Cloud* author exemplifies with

11. "beware in this work that you in no way employ your knowledge or your imagination"
12. "when I say darkness, I mean an absence of knowing."
13. "a loving outreaching and a blind beholding of only the naked being of God himself."

ȝif I schal soþlier sey, a soule is more bleendid in felyng of it for habundaunce of goostly liȝt, þen for any derknes or wantyng of bodely liȝtte. What is he þat clepiþ it nouȝt ? Sekirly it is oure vtter man, & not oure inner. Oure inner man clepiþ it Al. (Cl. 68.122: 11–15)[14]

The blindness, the absence of sight, then, is really an excess of the true light. By extrapolation, perhaps unknowing is an admittance to the true knowing that is in God. The concept of blindness collocates with the notion of the eye as a mirror and such a metaphor is taken from Augustine's theory of perception (Grabes 1982/1973). Conversely, though, Edward Nolan has noted in Augustine's *De Trinitate* 10 what he labels an "antisimilitude": "For eyes can never see themselves except in looking glasses; but it cannot be supposed in any way that anything of that kind can also be applied to the contemplation of incorporeal things, so that the mind should know itself, as it were, in a looking glass" (1990, 58).

The association between the mirror and spiritual matters has its scriptural origin in 1 Corinthians 13.12 in which Paul highlights the impossibility of truly "seeing" and "knowing" in this life.[15] St. Augustine, taking up the theme, elaborates that "we see in the mirror ... an image that is unlike as well as like the interior image of reality we have in our mind."[16] Nolan expands on this idea and explains that

[o]ne saw, in medieval mirrors, either an image that showed the world as it is or one that showed the world as it should be; mirrors reflected either reality or ideality. And one saw images of the Other (God or neighbor) or of the self. Thus one could extrapolate, by contemplating the discrepancy between what one saw and what one was, agendas for reform or despair. (116)[17]

14. "if I speak more truly, a soul is more blinded by the abundance of spiritual light, rather than any actual darkness or lack of physical light. Who is he that calls it nothing? Certainly, it is our outer self, and not our inner self. Our inner self calls it All."

15. "videmus nunc per speculum in aenigmate: tunc autem facie ad faciem. Nunc cognosco ex parte: tunc autem cognoscam sicut et cognitus sum" (Paul, 1 Cor 3.12).

16. Quoted in Nolan 1990, 278.

17. Grabes warns against taking an image as metaphor (in this case, the mirror) and believing it to have the same figurative meaning wherever it appears. He cautions

Thus, by the later Middle Ages, the mirror was both a literal and a metaphorical image that could represent the actual and the aspirational ideal. And the ideal image in the mirror was, first and foremost, God. As early as the third century Origen had spoken "of the soul being a mirror in which it can see the image of the Father . . . when the soul has put off every stain of sin" (Louth, 1981, 79). The *Cloud* author demonstrates a view of the mirror as both actual and ideal when he implies that the text, *The Cloud of Unknowing,* acts as a mirror:

Goddes worde, ouþer wretyn or spokyn, is licnid to a mirour. Goostly, þe iȝe of þi soule is þi reson; þi concience is þi visage goostly, & riȝt as þou seest þat ȝif a foule spot be in þi bodily visage, þe iȝe of þe same visage may not see þat spotte, ne wite wher it is, wiþ-outyn a myrour or a teching of anoþer þan it-self: riȝt so it is goostly. (Cl. 35.72: 4–9)[18]

Here, in relation to the idea of "reflective space," the *Cloud* author is paralleling the nature of reflection in the physical and spiritual worlds with "Goddes words." Those words are posited as being the initiator of a chain of action in which human reason and conscience are stirred by the "worde" to enact an inward examination and, presumably, rectification of spiritual faults and failings. In addition, in

---

that context and author's intention are paramount in matters of interpretation (39). With this in view, he elaborates four basic types of mirrors (in literature): 1. The mirror reflects things as they are . . . (informative); 2. It shows the way things should or should not be . . . (exemplary); 3. It shows the way things will be . . . (prognostic); 4. It shows what only exists in the mirror or in the writer's imagination . . . (fantastic) (1982/1973, 39).

18. "God's word, either written or spoken, is like a mirror. Spiritually, the eye of your soul is your reason; the conscience is the spiritual face, and just as if there is a dirty spot on the physical face, the eye of that same face cannot see that spot, nor know where it is, without a mirror or the information of someone else; and it is the same spiritually."

Note that Grabes (1982) stresses that "[t]he employment of the mirror in metaphorical contexts is so frequent and deliberate a strategy in the English literature of the thirteenth to seventeenth centuries that the mirror can be said to constitute the central image for a particular world-view" (4).

referring to "Goddes words," the *Cloud* author is including his own text in the appellation, inferring that the contemplative who reads his texts is receiving God's instruction to assist him in his chosen pursuit. Of course, the author goes on to advise that any sort of instruction is unnecessary for the contemplative truly called by God because "þees sodeyn conseytes & þees blynde felynges ben somner lernyd of God þen of man" (Cl. 36.73: 4–6).[19]

The paradoxical situation of the author's assertion of the necessity of God's written (or spoken) word and the simultaneous superfluity of it when God is the initiator of contemplation is partially resolved if the actuality of the book is considered as a mirror that, in its material presence, reflects an absence of materiality. Gellrich observes that "the metaphor of writing does not get in the way of the truth with its 'artificial inscription' and 'difference' but reveals divine wisdom like a brilliant mirror (speculum)" (1985, 39). It seems that this is the purpose which the *Cloud* author envisages for his own texts. That is, he offers his own writing as a mirror in which the contemplative can see himself and his faults and failings reflected, in the hope that he will reform himself in God's image.

The *Cloud* author's own texts are not the only "mirrors" that he offers his readers. Holy Church and its ministrations and sacraments are stressed so that the contemplative may obtain "amendement in contricion & in confession & in aseeþ makyng after þe statute & ordinaunce of alle Holy Chirche" (Cl. 15.43: 22–24).[20] In addition, "oure Lady Seinte Marye" (Cl. 15.44: 2)[21] and the angels (ibid., 5) are upheld as models of perfection. The primary model for the reader, however, is Mary Magdalene. She is shown to be a reflection "in persone of alle sinners þat ben clepid to contemplatiue liif" (Cl. 16.44:

19. "these sudden concepts and blind feelings are sooner learned from God than from man."
20. "amendment by contrition and by confession and by penance according to the statutes and ordinance of holy Church."
21. "our Lady, St. Mary"

22–45: 1)²² particularly because "sche loued mochel—lo! here mowe men see what a priue loue put may purchase of oure Lorde, before alle oþer werkes þat man may þink" (Cl. 16.45: 4–6).²³

In a way, the *Cloud* author, in his considerable discussion of the relative merits of "contemplatives" as compared to "actives," proffers Mary and Martha as reflective models. In general, the importance that the *Cloud* author places on Mary and Martha as models, respectively, for the contemplative and the active lives, cannot be disregarded.²⁴ Chapters 16 to 23 (inclusive) of *The Cloud of Unknowing* are devoted, almost exclusively, to discussion and elaboration of the various merits of the two types of life and of their respective representatives. Thus the reader is encouraged to see a reflection of himself and his own undertaking in the example of Mary.

Further signs of the mirror within the text are not always empty spaces that point to God. Sometimes the mirror reflects very negative aspects. By that I mean that the reflections presented in the text are not always positive models that point the way to God. On the contrary, other issues are brought into the space of the text by the author himself. The discussion of fiends and, tangentially, necromancy are cases in point.²⁵ So, too, is the discussion of false contemplatives. A clue to the reason for the author's apparent digressions seems to

22. "representing all sinners called to the contemplative life"

23. "she loved so much—Look! Here we may see what a secret love can purchase from our Lord, beyond all other works that we may think of."

24. Denise Baker identifies three main paradigms for the way in which active and contemplative life was conceived of, and presented, in religious texts: complementary, oppositional, and alternating (or mixed) models. Though Baker finds evidence of the *Cloud* author's endorsement of all three models, she finds that in Chapters 18 and 19 of *The Cloud of Unknowing* "he nonetheless emphasizes the oppositional paradigm by insisting that only those in the contemplative state, and especially solitaries, can achieve the third stage and enter the cloud of unknowing" (1999, 97).

25. Julian of Norwich includes references to the devil but makes no mention of angels, while Richard Rolle includes both notions but gives more attention to angels, particularly in his elaboration of the angelic hierarchies, following pseudo-Dionysius.

be given very early in the text when he cautions his reader to "kepe þou þe windowes & þe dore for flies & enemies assailyng" (Cl. 2.15: 19–20),[26] thereby pointing to the dangers of the work. At the most basic level, then, the seeming digressions are warnings about possible threats to contemplation. Additionally, such inclusions represent a material inversion of that which the contemplative is striving for spiritually. That is, the world of the false contemplatives with their overt signs of "sanctity," and of the fiends associated with physical temptation, are the manifestations of all that should be avoided. Their displays are empty signs that indicate spiritual emptiness while true contemplatives eschew all outward signs to enter the divine emptiness within. All that they exteriorly exhibit is the opposite to that which the true contemplative aims to experience interiorly. Thus the interior spiritual qualities of humility and love are reversed in the outward and physical manifestation of pride and self-aggrandizement.

René Tixier regards these presentations of seemingly tangential issues as necessary to the text as a whole, for while "some passages may seem to be digressions . . . on the contrary, by returning regularly to the central themes of the author's teaching, they maintain the reader's concentration on the main argument" (1997, 134).

That is, the *Cloud* author directs his readers to external models, the "ideal" mirror image, and toward an inwardly focused gaze that finds an absence. The mystical space of the *Cloud* author, therefore, encompasses a true representation of the literary *mise en abyme*—the mirror in the text—in that, when the reader looks into the text, he sees himself reflected with all his faults; he sees exemplary models presented for his consideration; and he encounters the darkness of unknowing that presages God. The first two reflections are positive in that they are discernible in the material world, while the third re-

---

26. "keep your windows and door closed against fleeing and assailing enemies." This advice is very similar to the advice given to three anchoresses to whom the *Ancrene Wisse* is addressed. The author advises: "lokið þe parlures beo on eauer euche half feste & wel itachet. & wited þer ower ehnen leaste þe heorte edfleo & wende ut" (f.13a.12–15).

flection is a negative reflection in that it is without light and its full implications will only become clear after life. Together, however, the positive and the negative reflections are the two parts of a whole and both are necessary components of the mystical life.

THE SPACE OF THE *CLOUD*

The *Cloud* author metaphorically locates the mystical space between two clouds, though the "cloud of unknowing" is described as the actual site of mystical experience. He establishes this in relation to the exemplary contemplative, Mary:

Þat þer was neuer ȝit pure creature in þis liif, ne neuer ȝit schal be, so hiȝe rauischid in contemplacion & loue of þe Godheed, þat þer ne is euermore a hiȝe & wonderful cloude of vnknowyng bitwix him & his God. In þis cloude it was þat Marye was ocupied wiþ many a preue loue put. & whi? For it was þe best & þe holiest party of contemplacion þat may be in þis liif. (Cl. 17.47: 17–48: 2)[27]

Christiana Whitehead points to "the nervous mistrust with which the *Cloud* author responds to the tradition of conveying spiritual concepts via the evocation of spatial and motor imagery" (1998, 201) and proceeds to suggest that "something like a third of *The Cloud of Unknowing* is given over to articulating the danger of misreading spatial expression" (ibid., 203). While this suggestion is an overstatement, it does highlight the pervasiveness in the text of the author's denouncement of literalism, particularly with regard to spatiality. (I considered aspects of this denouncement in Chapter Three.) Nevertheless, the *Cloud* author uses some images in his texts that incorporate spatial allusions; predominant among them is the image of the cloud.

27. "There never was, nor ever shall be in this life, so pure a creature who was so highly enraptured in contemplation and the love of God, that he did not have this high and wonderful cloud of unknowing between himself and God. It was in this cloud that Mary was occupied with many a secret love. And why? Because it was the best and the holiest part of contemplation that may be attained in this life."

In spatial terms, a cloud signifies something that, in the material world, is unfailingly found "above." However, though the *Cloud* author's use of the word seems to incorporate a notion of spiritual ascent, he consistently seeks to minimize the image's spatial connotation. Thus, though the author advises his reader that "þis cloude of vnknowyng is abouen þee, bitwix þee & þi God" (Cl. 5.24: 2–4),[28] and that "alle þing þat þou þinkest apon it is abouen þee for þe tyme, & bitwix þee & þi God" (Cl. 5.24: 21–25: 1),[29] he is adamant, as I have discussed already, that prepositions of place are, in his schema, metaphorical. In the above examples, the metaphorical interspersion of thoughts "above" the reader and, consequently, "bitwix þee & þi God," is posited as creating a barrier between the reader and his approach to God, and therefore "above" is inscribed with a negative connotation.

The central image of *The Cloud of Unknowing,* the cloud, is elusive in its signification. In Lefebvre's schema, the cloud could be considered as a *representational space* and, simultaneously, a *representation of space* in that it is both a symbol and a conceptual location for contemplation. In both its symbolism and situational conception, however, the cloud is exclusively metaphorical and therefore not truly absorbent of any of Lefebvre's categories.

Nike Pokorn explains that the association of a cloud with God has its scriptural origin in the "descript[ion] [of] Moses' ascent to Mount Sinai: 'But Moses went to the dark cloud wherein God was' (Exodus 20:21)" (1997, 410).[30] However, from the earliest time of biblical

28. "this cloud of unknowing is above you, between you and God."

29. "everything that you think about is above you for the time, and [therefore] between you and God."

30. Pokorn further explains that "[t]he allegorical interpretation of the cloud Moses entered was most probably first made by Philo in his *Life of Moses,* where entering into the cloud denoted the progressive stripping away of material elements which hamper human apprehension of the divine. St. Gregory of Nyssa further defined this biblical image. For him, the soul in its ascent to God progresses from light to deeper and deeper darkness, until it is eventually cut off from all that can be grasped by sense and reason" (1997, 410).

interpretation, a distinction was made between the notion of "darkness" *(skótos)* and "the dark cloud" *(gnóphos)* (ibid.). Later, Gregory of Nyssa clearly separates the two ideas and "speaks of the soul's successive entry into light, cloud and darkness" (Louth 1981, 83). The pseudo-Dionysius apparently used the two words synonymously in *De Mystica Theologia* and the *Cloud* author maintains the synonymity in his translation of the work, titled *Deonise Hid Diuinite*.[31] Interestingly, though, the *Cloud* author distinguishes the terms in *The Cloud of Unknowing*. Pokorn considers the distinction to be a result of the author's influence by Victorine precepts to the extent that

the Dionysian term *caliginem ignorantiae,* which can be found in Sarracenus' translation (completed c. 1167) of the Dionysian corpus and in Extractio of Dionysian treatises by Thomas Gallus (+1246), is changed into *nubes ignorantiae* in Richard [of St. Victor]'s version and reproduced in the clowde of vnknowing of the English text, and Richard's argument that the cloud operates differently in respect of earthly and divine realities is reflected in the Cloud author's additional clowde of forȝetyng. (1997, 411)[32]

It is possible that the *Cloud* author's image of a cloud in general is representative of both a "mistiness" and a "darkness." Conversely, though, the *Cloud* author declares that he is incorporating neither connotation in his mystical teaching as he clearly elaborates a literal-metaphorical distinction in his use of the term, stating that

31. Prior to the *Cloud* author's translation of *De Mystica Theologiae* many translators and commentators "insisted on distinguishing the two terms: *gnóphos* is consistently rendered by *caligo* and *skótos* by *tenebrae*" (Pokorn 1997, 411).

32. Glasscoe posits that as Dionysius's works were "particularly influential in the West from the twelfth century onwards in a tradition of negative theology and teaching on the contemplative life. . . . It is thus probable that [the *Cloud* author] did not derive the image which gives *The Cloud of Unknowing* its title directly from Dionysius at all. He talks of darkness rather than a cloud of unknowing, whereas Richard of St. Victor's treatise on mystical theology, *Benjamin Major,* uses the exact image of 'the cloud of unknowing' *(nubes ignorantiae)* and also describes the cloud of forgetting which, like that in the *Cloud*-author, wipes out memory of the knowledge of created things" (1993, 173).

& wene not, for I clepe it a derknes or a cloude, þat it be any cloude congelid of þe humours þat fleen in þe ayre, ne ȝit any derknes soche as is in þin house on niȝtes, when þi candel is oute. For soche a derknes & soche a cloude maist þou ymagin wiþ coriouste of witte, for to bere before þin iȝen in þe liȝtest day of somer; & also aȝensward in þe derkist niȝt of wynter þou mayst ymagin a clere schinyng liȝt. Lat be soche falsheed; I mene not þus. For when I sey derknes, I mene a lackyng of knowyng; as alle þat þing þat þou knowest not, or elles þat þou hast forȝetyn, it is derk to þee, for þou seest it not wiþ þi goostly iȝe. & for þis skile it is not clepid a cloude of þe eire, bot a cloude of vnknowyng, þat is bitwix þee & þi God. (CL. 4.23: 13–24)[33]

Here, the *Cloud* author gives an explanation of his "cloud of unknowing" which fails to clarify the idea. Initially he suggests, in line with pseudo-Dionysius, that "darkness" and "cloud" are virtually interchangeable terms. In addition, however, he aligns "darkness" and "a lackyng of knowing," effecting a further synonymy between "cloud" and "unknowing." That is, the two nouns of the phrase "cloude of vnknowyng" exist in a syntagmatic chain of referents that point to a field of signification that is beyond earthly connotative parameters. John Stephens and Ruth Waterhouse have described, in reference to figurative language in general, that "what characteristically initiates figurative movement along such a chain of signifieds can be described as a dislocation of surface meaning, of the obvious relationships between signifiers" (1990, 214–15). In the above example, the *Cloud* author effects not only a dislocation of relationships between signifiers but a dislocation along the paradigmatic axis as well, by using the ap-

---

33. "And do not think, because I call it a darkness or a cloud, that it is any cloud made up of the constituents of the air, nor is it a darkness such as you have in your house at night, when your candle is out. For such darkness and such a cloud may be imagined by your mind to be such as being before your eyes on the brightest summer day, as, again, in the darkest night of winter may imagine a clear and shining light. Leave aside such falsehood. I do not mean that. For when I say darkness, I mean an absence of knowing; just as everything that you do not know, or that you have forgotten, is said to be dark to you, because you are not seeing it with your spiritual eye. And for this reason, it is not called a cloud of the sky, but a cloud of unknowing, that is between you and God."

parently concrete descriptors "cloude" and "derk" to point not only to abstract signifieds but negative abstract signifieds. That is, the author describes, literally and metaphorically, what is *not*. His meaning, then, is shown to be elusive of "worldly" signification and, equally, unable to be envisaged in the imagination. In fact, the "cloud of unknowing" is constructed as a notion that is itself unknowable, suggestive of solid connotation yet beyond definition. The epithet thus hints at meaning and simultaneously evades it.

Whatever the composition of the cloud, physical or spiritual, a connotation of enclosure emerges. That is, in between the cloud of forgetting and the cloud of unknowing, the contemplative waits in the faith, hope, and love of God. This spiritually enclosed space is thus the reflection of the contemplative's physical enclosure as a solitary. The *Cloud* author's use of the figure of a house is similarly evocative of enclosure. Referring to the "werk" of contemplation, he advises that "be þou bot þe hous, & lat it be þe hosbonde wonyng þer-in" (Cl. 34.70: 16–17).[34] The "werk" of contemplation is here presented as being safely "housed" within the contemplative and yet, like a medieval "hosbonde," the "werk" controls the house. Thus, contemplation both encloses and is enclosed within the contemplative.

When the *Cloud* author poses the rhetorical question, from the point of view of his reader, "How schal I þink on him-self & what is hee?" (Cl. 6.25: 13–14),[35] he admits that the question is unanswerable and that it brings him to that same place of unknowing in which he seeks to locate his reader. He explains that with this question "þou hast brouзt me wiþ þi question into þat same derknes, & into þat same cloude of unknowyng þat I wolde þou were in þi-self" (Cl. 6.25: 16–18).[36] His explanation here is both a textual and spatial locating of the central premise of *The Cloud of Unknowing*. That is, as I have

34. "you be but the house, and let it be the husband living therein."
35. "How shall I think of [God] and what is he?"
36. "you have brought me with this question into that same darkness, and into that same cloud of unknowing that I want you to be in yourself."

already proposed, for the *Cloud* author, the mystical space *is* contemplation. And while the text can show a way into the space of contemplation, with its site between earthly forgetting and mystical unknowing, it can go no further than forgetting and unknowing allow.

THE EMPTY SPACE: THE SPACE OF ABSENCE

The theoretical application of the literary *mise en abyme* allowed me, earlier in this chapter, to consider the reflective nature of the *Cloud* author's mystical space. The notion of the *abîme* as abyss is also illuminating when applied to the *Cloud* author's texts as it admits of the great gap that seems to separate God and humanity in life and is reflected in the *Cloud* author's locating of the contemplative in the space between the cloud of forgetting and the cloud of unknowing. Such a metaphorical space represents the epitome of a space of absence: a space in which material things, thoughts, and actions are forgotten and God, the object of contemplation, is unknown; the space in which nothing is remembered and nothing is known. Notionally, beneath the cloud of forgetting exists the physical world and above the cloud of unknowing exists God. The space of contemplation, therefore, is an empty space and represents a negative reflection of the earthly space full of things and the heavenly space full of God. Thus, the mystical space contains both an absence (with the hope of a presence in life) and the promise of an eternal presence after life. In relation to this notion of alternating emptiness and fullness Gillespie and Ross believe that

[t]he play of absence and presence characterizes the human experience of engagement with the ineffable. The search for the Transcendental Signified which is God requires not only a struggle with the fallen will but also the necessity of wrestling with the fallen language which resolutely anchors itself in the world of signifiers. As Rowan Williams has written, "any speech is a speech about an absence." This absence, as Derrida has noted, "extends the domain and play of signification infinitely." The game of mystical hide and seek acted out over the centuries generates a longing for release from the play of language. (1992, 53)

The association between negative theology and Derridean deconstruction has been noted frequently. I do not intend to engage with the idea here beyond admitting that such an association is certainly demonstrable and to note one essential difference that seems relevant and which is summarized by Pokorn:

> Although it is true that both [deconstruction and negative theology] discuss the subject which is ineffable, escaping the possibility of determination and total description, only mystical language and mystical imagery seek to form liminal signifiers "which gesture beyond themselves into the realm of unmediated wisdom and the practice of the Transcendental signified from which we have been excluded by the fall" [Gillespie 1992, 140]. . . . [T]he ineffability that concerns and amazes the theologian thus profoundly differs from the ineffability that perplexes and haunts the deconstructionist. (1997, 414)[37]

The *Cloud* author's words, which are often negative signifiers, certainly can be understood to be "gesturing beyond themselves" into an empty mystical space. Conversely, though, in using so many words with seemingly negative connotations, the author endeavors to direct the reader's attention wholly toward God who contains all within Him and is contained within negation. That is, if the very center of the *Cloud* author's space were a true void within the language within the text, then we would have no knowledge of it. It is because the *Cloud* author also allows the empty space to be full of, reflective of, God that the author reflects the presence in his writings for the edification of others.

The positioning of the contemplative in the empty space is analogous to locating him "nowhere," which is the author's intention. The aim is to attain the cloud but, before that is possible, the contemplative must enter an in-between space that is devoid of all earthly attachments and, for much of the time, also devoid of God: "& ȝif euer þou schalt come to þis cloude & wone & worche þer-in as I bid þee,

---

37. For a thorough discussion of negative mystical theology and Derridean deconstruction, see Kevin Hart, *The Trespass of the Sign: Deconstruction, Theology and Philosophy* (Cambridge: Cambridge University Press, 1989).

þee byhoueþ, as þis cloude of vnknowyng is abouen þee, bitwix þee &
þi God, riȝt so put a cloude of forȝetyng bineþ þee, bitwix þee & alle
þe cretures þat euer ben maad. (Cl. 5.24: 1–4)[38]

Such metaphorical locating of the contemplative follows the author's positioning of the reader in humility: "Look up now, weike
wreche, & see what þou arte. What arte þou, & what hast þou dese-
rued, þus to be clepid of oure Lorde?" (Cl. 2.14: 16–17)[39]

Despite the author's wariness about the positioning of spiritual
things in terms of literal locations, he nevertheless makes frequent
use of spatial metaphors to "locate" the contemplative within the
mystical realm. Thus, for example, in elaborating some of the differences between the active and the contemplative life, he explains that

In þe lower partye of actiue liif a man is wiþ-outen him-self & bineeþ himself. In þe hiȝer party of actyue liif & þe lower party of contemplatiue liif, a
man is wiþ-inne him-self & euen wiþ him-self, Bot in þe hiȝer partie of contemplatiue liif, a man is abouen him-self & vnder his God. Abouen him-self
he is, for whi he purposeþ him to wynne þeder bi grace, wheþer he may not
come bi kynde; þat is to sey, to be knit to God in spirite, & in oneheed of
loue & acordaunce of wile. (Cl. 8.32: 9–16)[40]

The prepositions literally indicate a rise from "bineeþ" to "euen" to
"abouen" and are aligned with the notion of a parallel spiritual ascent
that finds its final destination in the highest spiritual attainment of
a "knit[ting] to God in spirite." These prepositions are intertwined

38. "And if you are to come to this cloud and live and work in it as I bid you to do,
you will find, just as this cloud of unknowing is above you, between you and God, so
you must put a cloud of forgetting beneath you, between you and all creation."

39. "Look up now, weak wretch, and see what you are. What are you, and why
have you deserved to be called by our Lord."

40. "In the lower part of active life a man [acts] outside himself and thus is beneath himself. In the higher part of active life and the lower part of contemplative
life, a man is inward looking/acting and on an even level with himself. But in the
higher part of contemplative life, a man is above himself and under God. He is above
himself because he directs his intention to winning by grace that which he cannot
win by nature; that is, to be united to God in spirit, in oneness with him in love and
will."

with the prepositions "wiþ-outen" and "wiþinne" that indicate a change of focus and intention from outward to inward. Thus, this ascent to transcendence is enabled "bi grace" (which finds its opposite reflection in the term "bi kynde") and is concurrently accomplished by the suppression of the rational mind. If the suppression of the understanding is not achieved then, the author explains, no ascent can be expected. This failure to rise is expressed in terms of the preposition "doun": "And þerfore þe scharp steryng of þin vnderstondyng, þat wile alweis press apon þee when þou settest þee to þis blynd werk, behoueþ always be born doun; and bot þou bere him doun, he wile bere þee doun" (Cl. 9.33: 17–20).[41] Metaphorically, then, the author suggests that the distance created between "up" and "doun" is synonymous with the distance between spiritual and material, between soul-space and body-space, between the need to aspire to God and the need to suppress the workings of the material mind.

The *Cloud* author seems to envision this gap as residing in the breach between God and mankind in his fallen nature. The two borders of the gap are summed up by the author in the two words "God" and "sin." He explains that

þerfore schalt þou chaungeably mene þees two wordes—Synne & God; wiþ þis general knowyng: þat & þou haddest God, þen schuldest þou lacke synn, & miȝtest þou lacke synne, þen schuldest þou haue God. (Cl. 40.79: 16–19)[42]

Sin, as part of the human condition, is what keeps humanity from God. The only way to "distroie[ ] . . . þe grounde & rote of sinne" (Cl. 12.39: 11)[43] is to reach for God with love. Within the mystical

41. "And therefore the sharp stirring of your understanding, which will always be pressing when you set out on this blind work [of contemplation], must always be pushed down; and if you do not push it down, it will push you down."

42. "Therefore you should constantly concentrate on these two words—'sin' and 'God'; with the knowledge that if you had God, you would not have sin, and if you did not have sin, you would have God."

43. "destroy . . . the ground and root of sin"

space, then, the contemplative's work is to attempt to bridge the gap by overcoming sin by love. The author states that

& þerfore, ʒif þou wilt stonde & not falle, seese neuer in þin entent, bot bete euermore on þis cloude of vnknowyng þat is bitwix þee & þi God wiþ a sharpe darte of longing loue. (Cl. 12.38: 11–13)[44]

Part of the process of embracing this gap is tied to the experience of sorrow. The sorrow is born out of the realization of this distance between God and humanity as a result of the human condition. Thus, the *Cloud* author points out that

Alle men han mater of sorow, bot most specyaly he feliþ mater of sorow þat wote & feliþ þat he is. Alle oþer sorowes ben vnto þis in comparison bot as it were gamen to ernest. For he may make sorow ernestly þat wote & feliþ not onli what he is, bot þat he is. & who-so felid neuer þis sorow, he may make sorow, for whi he felid ʒit neuer parfite sorow. (Cl. 44.83: 20–84: 2)[45]

That is, true sorrow is the result of the awareness of one's own existence as separate from God, and it is only after the "nakid weting & a felyng of þin owne beyng" (Cl. 43.83: 3–4)[46] is destroyed that the epitome of contemplation, the "onyng" with God, can be attained.[47]

In making the approach to the bridging of this gap via contemplation, the *Cloud* author recommends several ploys to his reader. In addition to the covering "any newe þouʒt or steryng of any synne" with "a þicke cloude of forʒetyng" (Cl. 31.66: 3 & 6),[48] it is suggested that

44. "and therefore, if you want to stand and not fall, do not cease in your intention, but beat even more on this cloud of unknowing that is between you and God with a sharp dart of longing love."

45. "All men have reasons for sorrow, but most especially he has reason to sorrow who knows and feels that he is. All other sorrows by comparison are as games to reality. For he really sorrows who knows and feels not only what he is, but that he is. And he who has never felt this sorrow, let him be really sorry, for he has never felt perfect sorrow."

46. "a naked knowing and feeling of your own being"

47. St. Augustine similarly aligns seeking and sorrow. See, in particular, O'Connell (1989/1969, 56), who gives a clear summary of Augustine's approach to sadness.

48. "any new thought or stirring of any sin" with "a thick cloud of forgetting"

the contemplative either look beyond the intrusive thoughts to God or surrender to them. Both ploys, in fact, involve the adoption of absolute humility in the recognition of "þi-self as þou arte, a wrecche & a filþe, fer wers þen nouȝt" (Cl. 32.67: 8–9).[49] In recognizing the self as less than nothing, the self is totally emptied and becomes an absence seeking the "absent" God across the empty space.

The suggestion of the use of spiritual ploys finds its full expression in the author's recommendation that the reader "schuld fele good gamesumli pley wiþ [God], as þe fadir doþ wiþ þe childe" (Cl. 46.88: 2–3).[50] René Tixier identifies three "games of love" (1990, 235) in the *Cloud* author's elucidation of this recommendation, the first of which is particularly relevant here. Tixier designates it "Hide-and-Seek" (236) in response to the *Cloud* author's advice to

bewar wiþ þis beestly ruedness, & leerne þee to loue listely wiþ a softe & a demure contenaunce, as wel in body as in soule. & abide curtesly & meekly þe wil of oure Lorde, & lache not ouer hastely, as it were a gredy grehounde, hungre þee neuer so sore, & gamenly be it seyde, I rede þat þu do þat in þee is, refreynyng þe rude & þe grete steryng of þi spirite; ryȝt as þou on no wyse woldest lat hym wite hou fayne þou woldest see hym & haue hym or fele hym. (Cl. 46.87: 15–23)[51]

In attempting to hide his true desire from himself, the contemplative is, in effect, emptying himself of that desire so that the emotion and the imagination that frequently overlay material desire do not impinge on the naked spiritual desire.

Thus, inherent in the game, is an inversion of perspective: the cast-

49. "yourself as you are, a filthy wretch, far worse than nothing"
50. "should feel free to lovingly game-play with [God], as the father does with the child."
51. "Beware of acting like a rude beast and learn to love quietly with a soft and demure approach, in soul as well as in body. And wait courteously and humbly on the will of our Lord, and do not snatch too hastily, as if you were a greedy hound (hungry as you are). And, somewhat playfully, I suggest that what you should do is refrain from rude and exaggerated stirring of the spirit; as though in no way would you let him know how glad you would be to see him and to have him or to feel him."

ing of desire for God "into depnes of spirite, fer fro any rude mede-
lyng of any bodeliness, þe whiche wolde make it lesse goostly, & ferþer fro God in as moche" (Cl. 47.89: 16–18)[52] because "on o maner
schal a þing be schewid to man, & on an-oþer maner vnto God" (Cl.
47.90: 9–10).[53] The *Cloud* author offers a more detailed reason for
recommending this approach to God when he readdresses the same
reader in *The Book of Privy Counselling:*

For þof al I bid þee in þe biginnyng, bicause of þi boistouste & þi goostly
rudenes, lappe & cloþe þe felyng of þi god in þe felyng of þi-self, ʒit schalt
þou after whan þou arte maad by contynowaunce more sleiʒ in clennes of
spirit, nakyn, spoyle & vtterly vncloþe þi-self of al maner of felyng of þi-self,
þat þou be able to be cloþid wiþ þe gracyous felyng of God self. (P.C. 156:
9–15)[54]

In terms of metaphorical spatiality, therefore, in the ploys, the author
advises the effecting of an absence within the mystical space (of absence) that is representative of the literary *mise en abyme* as well as
the mystical casting into the abyss. That is, in terms of the *mise en
abyme,* the contemplative's absence of desire is a reflection of the absence of God in the mystical space and, in terms of the *abîme* of mysticism, it is a casting of desire into the deepest part of the spirit.

Part of the usefulness of these games and ploys reside in their un-
usualness, and thus their capability of putting the contemplative off-
guard and into a new position that privileges spiritual over physical
and mental perception. The *Cloud* author elucidates this idea with
an example:

52. "into the depth of your spirit, far from the rude interference of any physicality,
which would make it less spiritual, and much further from God."
53. "For in one manner is something shown to man, and in another manner to
God."
54. "Although I told you in the beginning, because of your exuberance and spiritual inexperience, to wrap and clothe the feeling of God in the feeling of yourself, yet
afterward, when you are made wiser through continuing in purity of spirit, you will
go naked, spoilt and utterly unclothed in regard to all manner of feeling of yourself,
to be clothed with the gracious feeling of God himself."

Ensaumple of þis maist þou see by þat þat I bid þee hele þi desire fro God in þat þat in þee is. For, parauenture, & I had boden þee schewe þi desire vnto God, þou schuldest haue conceyuid it more bodily þen þou dost now, when I bid þee hele it. For þou wost wel þat alle þat þing þat is wilful helid, it is casten into þe depnes of spiryt. (Cl. 51.94: 25–95: 5)[55]

The somewhat complicated reversal of focus is reflective of what the author seeks to do with language throughout the text, and, equally, to the positioning of the contemplative. That is, the reversal institutes new perspectives that destabilize and facilitate the forgetting of the familiar worldly attachments to concepts and ways of thinking as well as to words and actions. The *Cloud* author's emphasis on the idea that "Alle þe reuelacions þat euer sawe any man here in bodely licnes in þis liif, þei haue goostly bemenynges" (Cl. 58.107: 11–12)[56] is developed to include the notion of certain words having a "bodily" and a metaphorical significance that point beyond themselves to an anagogical level, thereby encapsulating an almost exegetical completeness in one word. For example, he explains that

By stondyng is vnderstonden a redynes of helping, & herfore it is seide comounly of oo frende to anoþer, whan he is in bodely batayle: "Bere þee wel, felaw & fi3t fast, & 3iue not up þe bataile over li3tly; for I schal stonde by þee." He meneþ not only bodely stondyng, for parauenture þis batayle is on hors & not on fote, & parauenture it is going & not stondyng. Bot he meneþ, whan he seiþ þat he schal stonde bi hym, þat he schal be redy to helpe him. (Cl. 58.109: 6–13)[57]

55. "An example of this can be seen in the way that I advised you to hide your desire from God. For, perhaps, if I had advised you to show your desire to God, you would have conceived of it more physically than you now do, since I advised you to hide it. For you know well that the thing that is deliberately hidden is cast into the depths of the spirit."

56. "All the revelations that anyone ever saw in physical form here in this life, have spiritual meanings."

57. "By standing is understood a readiness to help, and in this way it is commonly said by one friend to another, when he is in physical battle: 'Bear up well, friend and fight strongly, and do not give up the battle easily; for I will stand by you.' He does not only mean physical/literal standing, for perhaps the battle is on horseback and

The elaborate development of the meaning of the "stondyng" metaphor is intended, more probably, not to explain something that the reader would already know (that is, that "stondyng" in this context means a readiness to help and support another), but to draw the reader's attention to the way in which one word can have a different meaning in a different context. Similarly, then, the (worldly) literal meaning of words is presented, by the author, as functioning differently in the spiritual realm. Ellen Caldwell comments that

> ironically, the mind is still left with the images of language which the author of *The Cloud* cannot avoid, though he may distrust them. Beverly Brian describes these as "sunken images" which are visual, yet not pictorial. These metaphors, she comments, often refer to qualities (light, brightness, bloom) rather than to the objects they qualify. Moreover, she finds instances of one image imposed upon another incompatible with it so that neither image comes into focus. A good example occurs in the title of the treatise, *The Cloud of Unknowing.* By linking the simple image—a cloud—with a term of epistemological negation—unknowing—the author defies the imagination's power to apprehend the divine. (1984, 13)

Caldwell here overlooks the fact that "the cloud of unknowing" is not the *Cloud* author's original idea, but her point is pertinent. That is, the *Cloud* author's particular elucidation of a mystical space in the term "the cloud of unknowing" couples the ideas of the opacity of a physical cloud with the insubstantiality of "unknowing" to convey the impression of "something" that is beyond the scope of ordinary signification.[58]

Though straightforward literal signification is not a feature of the *Cloud* author's writing, Tixier detects a particular shape to *The Cloud of Unknowing* that points to spatial implications. Tixier notes that

---

not on foot, and perhaps it is moving and not standing still. But he means, when he says that he will stand by him, that he will be ready to help him."

58. Interestingly, Julian of Norwich also uses the word "unknowing," but with the more direct connotation of ignorance, when she says that "and in that same tyme the custome of our praier was brought to my mind, how that we vse for vnknowing of loue to make menie meanes" (LT. 6.304: 2–5).

"[t]he main arguments thus run through both the chapters and the argumentative units, while circling around the central teaching, in a progression which is both linear and circular, and by so doing they maintain unity while exploring related aspects of the work of contemplation" (1997, 135). If Tixier's suggested shape and arrangement of the text of *The Cloud of Unknowing* is accepted, an interesting parallel can be elicited in the particular practice of contemplation that the *Cloud* author is advocating, most especially in the approach to the understanding of spatiality. That is, in order to progress toward God, in which a metaphorical ascent is intimated, the contemplative must also be willing to be contained within a space of uncertainty, a space between forgetting and unknowing, within the life of contemplation with its attendant repetition of desire, brief attainment of that desire, and failure of attainment of that desire. The *Cloud* author summarizes this ebb and flow of God's presence thus:

For þof al it be hard & streyte in þe byginnyng, when þou hast no deuocion, neuerþeles ȝit after when þou haste deuocion, it schal be maad ful restful & ful liȝt vnto þee, þat bifore was ful harde; & þou schalt haue ouþer litil trauaile or none. For þan wil God worche som-tyme al by him-self; bot not euer, ne ȝit no longe tyme to-geders, bot when him lyst, & as hym list. & þan wil þee þink it mery to late hym alone.

þan wil he sumtyme parauenture seend oute a beme of goostly liȝt, peersyng þis cloude of vnknowing þat is bitwix þee & hym, & schewe þee sum of his priuete, þe whiche man may not, ne kan not, speke. Þan schalt þou fele þine affeccion enflaumid wiþ þe fiire of his loue. (Cl. 26.62: 7–18)[59]

59. "Although it is difficult and limited in the beginning when you have no devotion, nevertheless later when you have acquired devotion, it will be made very easy and very restful for you, that which before was very difficult; and you will either have little or no work to do. Because then God will sometimes work all by himself; not always and not for any length of time, but when it pleases him and as it pleases him. And then you will be happy to leave him alone [to work].

Then sometimes, perhaps, he will send out a beam of spiritual light, piercing the cloud of unknowing between you and him, and showing you some of his secrets, of which man may not and cannot speak. Then you will feel your affection inflamed with the fire of his love."

Here the author expresses the nature of the circularity, the necessary cycle that the contemplative accepts in life in order to follow
the direction of the dart of love to its source and final destination
after death. Inevitably, of course, with God as source and culmination, there is a circularity implied even in the linearity of desire. The
Cloud author emphasizes God's instigation of contemplation when
he states that

neuerþeles ȝit I fele verely, wiþ-outen errour or doubte, þat Almiȝty God
wiþ his grace behoueþ algates be þe cheef sterer & worcher, ouþer wiþ mene
or wiþ-outyn: & þou only, or eny oþer liche vnto þee, bot þe consenter &
suffrer. (P.C. 155: 7–11)[60]

In this way, the center of the circle and the end point of the line of
contemplation both contain and lead to God. And the center of
the circle is the empty space that contains God. This empty center
is reflected in the center of each reader's being, which variously feels
God's presence and the lack of God in the presence of sin.

This experience of absence in the mystical "hide and seek" is mir-
rored in the text. As I suggested in Chapter Three, in the *Cloud* author's schema the frequent detachment of signified and signifier in
some way reflects the detachment of the contemplative from the material world. In addition, however, the linguistic apophasis points to
the emptying of the self that the contemplative hopes to achieve in
contemplation. The text, then, is truly an example of a *mise en abîme*
presenting within itself words that point to empty significations in
a reflection of the state of its reader who also hopes for an apohatic
center to his being. Thus, the absence within the absence, the empty
space within the empty space, equates to the contemplative who, in
hiding his desires, also empties himself and finds his emptiness mir-
rored in the absence of God and the apophatic method of mysticism

60. "Nevertheless, I truly feel, without error or doubt, that Almighty God, with
his grace must always be the main initiator and worker [of contemplation], either
within or outside a method [of contemplation]: and you, and others like you, are but
to consent and suffer."

that he is attempting to pursue. Similarly, the author's words, which do not always fix on literal signification, and the author's absence from the text, each represent mirror-image emptiness of the contemplative's own situation.

Though the space is not described as such, the *Cloud* author indicates that he regards the contemplative life as a foretaste of heaven, albeit with the underpinning in life of an acute sense of humility. The author explains the nature and rewards of the undertaking to his reader in these words:

> & holde þee neuer þe holier ne þe beter for þe worþines of þis cleping & for þe singuler fourme of leuyng þat þou arte in; bot þe more wrechid & [werid], bot ȝif þou do þat in þee is goodly, bi grace & bi counsel, to lyue after þi cleping, & in-so-mochel þou schuldest be more meek & louyng to þi goostly spouse, þat he, þat is þe Almiȝty God, Kyng of kynges & Lorde of lordes, wolde meek hym so lowe vnto þee, &, amonges alle þe flok of his scheep, so graciously wolde chese þee to be one of his speciales, & siþen set þee in þe stede of pasture, where þou maist be fed wiþ þe swetnes of his loue, in erles of þin heritage, þe kingdom of heuen. (Cl. 2.14: 20–15: 9)[61]

As the author has stressed elsewhere and intimates here, the complete union with God is not attainable in life. Here, however, he uses spatial images to effect a paralleling of body-space and soul-space in the experience of contemplation. That is, by being chosen to be set "in þe stede of pasture" in life, the contemplative is being "fed" in preparation for entry into "þe kingdom of heuen" after life. Having been specially chosen of God, the contemplative is urged, in further spatial terms, to "Look now forwardes, & lat be bacwardes" (Cl. 2.15: 10–

---

61. "And never hold yourself to be holier or better because of the honor of being called to the singular form of living that you are in; rather be more wretched and worried if you are not doing all you can that is good, by grace and by counsel, to live up to your calling, and you should be so much more humble and loving to your spiritual spouse because he, who is Almighty God, King of kings and Lord of lords, humbled himself unto you, and all the sheep of his flock. So graciously did he choose you to be one of his specials, and then set you in place of his pasture, where you could be fed with the sweetness of his love, in anticipation of your heritage, the kingdom of heaven."

11).[62] The means of looking forward, however, is not with the eyes, but with unimpeded desire for God, as the author advises:

Alle þi liif now behoueþ algates to stonde in desire, ȝif þou schalt profite in degre of perfeccion. þis desire behoueþ algates wrouȝt in þi wille, bi þe honde of Almiȝti God & þi consent. (Cl. 2.15: 12–15)[63]

The particular nature of this reflection is well represented in the way in which the contemplative, on entering the new space, is both called there by God and directs the will and the intent only toward God in order to remain there. Thus, the role of the application of the will is also of interest in this chapter, especially as the desire for contemplation and the work of contemplation are presented by the author as being one and the same:

Þe condicion of þis werk is soche, þat þe presence þerof abliþ a soule for to haue it & for to fele it. & þat abilnes may no soule haue wiþ-outyn it. Þe abilnes to þis werk is onyd to þe selue werk, wiþ-outyn departyng; so þat who-so feliþ þis werk is abil þerto, & elles none; in so mochel, þat wiþ-outyn þis werk a soule is as it were deed, and can not coueite it ne desire it. (Cl. 34.69: 23–70: 6)[64]

THE SPACE OF THE WILL

According to the *Cloud* author, the perfect state of Christian life "may bi grace bigonnen here, bot it schal euer laste wiþ-outen eende in þe blis of heuen" (Cl. 1.13: 12–13).[65] And though the author indi-

62. "Look forward, and not backward."
63. "All your life now requires that you persist in desire, if you are to reach the degree of perfection. This desire must be effected in your will, by the hand of Almighty God and your consent."
64. "The condition of this work is such that the very presence of it enables a soul to have it and to feel it. And no soul may have that ability without it. The ability to do this work is united to self-work, without diversion; so that whoever feels this work is able to do it, but no-one else; so much so that without this work a soul is as if it were dead, and can neither conceive of or desire it."
65. "may by grace be begun here, but it shall be everlasting in the bliss of heaven."

cates that momentary union with God is attainable in life, particularly in the contemplative life, he emphasizes, of course, that "Bot now
þou mayst not come to heuen not bodely, bot goostly" (Cl. 59.110:
9–10).[66] The situation is to be somewhat different after the Judgment
Day, the *Cloud* author stating that

at þe Day of Dome . . . we schul be maad so sotyl in body & in soule to-
geders, þat we schul be þan swiftely where us liste bodely, as we ben now in
oure þou3t goostely; wheþer it be up or doune, on o syde or on oþer, bihinde
or before. (Cl. 59.110: 5–8)[67]

This change in the potentiality of movement after life finds a parallel
in the author's elaboration of the effectiveness of the application of
the will during the contemplative's life. The key to the negotiation of
the gap between the earthly and the mystical realms is tied, it seems,
to the application of the will. Thus, the *Cloud* author explains that
though heaven is not in a physical location, it is an actual space that it
is possible to access, however briefly, spiritually in life:

For heuen goostly is as nei3 doun as up, & up as down, bihinde as before,
before as behynde, on o syde as oþer, in so moche þat who-so had a trewe
desire for to be at heuyn, þen þat same tyme he were in heuen goostly. For
þe hi3e & þe next wey þeder is ronne by desires, & not by pases of feet. &
herfore seiþ Seinte Poule of him-self & many oþer þus: "þof al oure bodies
ben presently here in erþe, neuerþeles 3it oure leuyng is in heuen." He ment
þeire loue & þeire desire, þe whiche is goostly þeire liif. & sekirly as verrely
is a soule þere where it louiþ, as in þe body þat leueþ bi it, & to þe whiche it
3eueþ liif. & þerfore 3if we wil go to heuen goostly, it nediþ not to streyne
oure spirit neiþer up ne doune, ne on o syde ne on oþer. (C. 60.112: 10–21)[68]

66. "you cannot come to heaven bodily, but spiritually."
67. "on Judgment Day . . . we shall be fused so subtly in body and soul, that we will
be able to go where we want physically as swiftly as we can now go in our thoughts;
whether it be up or down, to one side or the other, behind or in front."
68. "For, spiritually, heaven is as near down as up, and up as down, behind as in
front of, in front of as behind, on one side as the other, insofar as whoever has had a
true desire to be in heaven, at that same time he was there spiritually. For the highway
to heaven is reached by desire, and not by steps of the feet. And here St. Paul speaks

Metaphorically, then, a change of place is effected by an application of the will to the extent that wherever the desire is, there also is the soul. The direction of the desire to God thus enables the penetration of the cloud of unknowing, albeit briefly, and the author advises his reader without hesitation to "smyte apon þat þicke cloude of vnknowyng wiþ a scharp darte of longing loue" (Cl. 6.26: 11)[69] for God "may wel be loued, bot not þouȝt" (Cl. 6.26: 4).[70]

In assuming the contemplative life, an individual has already followed this desire to be dedicated to God and so the "werk" of contemplation "is not elles bot a nakid entente directe vnto God for him-self" (Cl. 24.58: 15–16).[71] This "nakid entente" on the contemplative's part, however, is merely a reflection of God's will, so that in directing the will toward God the contemplative is fulfilling the will of God and in the process, paradoxically, his own will is both "onyd" to God and subsumed in Him, to the extent that personal will is obliterated and the will of God *is* the will of the contemplative and vice versa. The *Cloud* author intimates this simultaneous union and virtual erasure of self-will when he explicates the meaning of "nakid entente":

A nakid entente I clepe it, for whi in þis werke a parfite prentis askiþ neiþer relesing of peyne, ne encresing of mede, ne ... nouȝt bot him-self; in-so-moche þat nouþer he rechiþ ne lokiþ after wheþer þat he be in peyne or in blisse, elles þat his wille be fulfyllyd þat he loueþ. (Cl. 24.58: 16–20)[72]

---

for himself and many others: 'Although our bodies are presently here on earth, nevertheless, we are living in heaven.' He meant their love and their desire which, spiritually, is their life. And surely, a soul is truly where it loves as a body is where it lives, and to which it gives life. And therefore if we want to go to heaven spiritually, we need not strain our spirit either upward or downward or sideways."

69. "strike upon that thick cloud of unknowing with a sharp dart of longing love."

70. "may well be loved, but not thought."

71. "is nothing else but a bare intention directed toward God for himself."

72. "I call it a bare intention, for in this work a perfect apprentice asks neither for release from pain nor increase in reward, nor ... for nothing but [God] himself; to the extent that he does not care or look for whether he is in pain or bliss, only that the will of him whom he loves is fulfilled."

This translocation of the will into God is registered by the *Cloud* author in an inversion of image and signification. Or, more precisely, the author uses words of negative signification to allude to the erasure of personal will. Thus, when the contemplative is "nowhere" doing "nothing," he is accomplishing the true "werk" of contemplation. "Everywhere" is exchanged for "nowhere," but his absence of place is really an absence of mental and emotional "presence" in the material world so that his "true" presence is in the spiritual realm within God. Thus it is an exchange of spaces, a negative for a positive, for "noȝwhere bodely is euerywhere goostly" (Cl. 68.121: 15).[73]

The space of the will, then, is the space of infinite possibility in *God* and the mystical space of contemplation seems to be where the will is exercised in the hope of God. The final chapter of *The Cloud of Unknowing* reemphasizes this conflation of will and possibility when the author stresses: "For not what þou arte, ne what þou hast ben, beholdeþ God wiþ his mercyful iȝe; bot þat þou woldest be" (Cl. 75.132: 19–20).[74] This final pronouncement is a very clear statement, emphasizing the effectiveness of the will in attaining God. In this sentence, the past tense is negated as is the present. Grammatically, the word "woldest" does not indicate futurity but absolute desire and direction of volition. Spatially "woldest" encompasses multiple possibilities of action that condense to the one simple action of wanting God with the whole will. The "will" is the inseparable partner of the "naked intent" unencumbered by reason, knowledge, or imagination. The *Cloud* author sums up the preeminence of this unfettered desire by quoting St. Augustine:

Al þe liif of a good Cristen man is not elles bot holy desire. (Cl. 73.133: 2–3)[75]

---

73. "nowhere physically is everywhere spiritually"

74. "For not what you are, nor what you have been, does God see with his merciful eyes, but what you will [to] be."

75. "All the life of a good Christian is nothing else but holy desire."

In fact, the will in God is all that remains of the self in the mystical space of the *Cloud* author. But in the absence of the self, the presence of God is reflected and the cloud of unknowing has the potential to evaporate in the blinding light of that presence.

In all levels of the *mise en abîme,* therefore, the *Cloud* author's mystical space is the space of contemplation existing in the will of God. As such it is indescribable beyond an allusion to an all-encompassing nothingness. In the metaphor of spatiality, God is the apophatic center around which all other levels of space revolve. Thus, the mystical space of the *Cloud* author may seem fundamentally different from the sensually envisaged space of Richard Rolle, which was considered in the previous chapter, and the rich visionary space of Julian of Norwich, to be considered in the next chapter, but, in fact, the *Cloud* author's space offers the negative reflection of their positive depictions and, together, both views encompass the possibilities of mystical space.

Chapter Six

THE MYSTICAL SPACE OF
JULIAN OF NORWICH

*One word frees us from the weight and pain of
life; that word is love.*

(*Sophocles*)

DEFINING JULIAN'S MYSTICAL SPACE

In terms of Henri Lefebvre's formulation of space, the mystical
space of Julian of Norwich would be best placed, though not exclusively, in the category designated *representational space*. That space, as
explained in the Introduction, encompasses nonverbal signs and images. Lefebvre further defines it as

space directly lived through its associated images and symbols . . . [which] is
the dominated—and hence passively experienced—space which the imagination seeks to change and appropriate. It overlays physical space, making
symbolic use of its objects. Thus representational physical space may be said
. . . with certain exceptions, to tend towards more or less coherent systems of
non-verbal symbols and signs. (1991/1974, 39)

Julian, in her vivid descriptions of the "showings" that she received
on May 8th, 1373, certainly reports an experience that both "overlays"
and "appropriates" physical space and material objects. The difficulty in wholly designating Julian's experience as *representational space*,
however, lies particularly in the appending of the concept of "imagi-

nation" to the experience. That is, to Julian, and other mystics, there was nothing imaginary about the experience, despite its amenability to expression in images.

Roland Maisonneuve refers to Julian's space of mystical encounter as a

very rich visionary universe, a *mundus imaginalis,* which is neither the physical world nor the intelligible world, but an intermediate world where the spiritual takes shape, and where the terrestrial, the physical, the visible are spiritual flashes. This is a median and mediating world, theomorphic, that of the divine intelligence which becomes apprehensible by the senses. (1980, 93)

Maisonneuve's summary is germane here because it both encompasses notions of the liminality of mystical space, which was elaborated in Chapter Two, and points to the role of the material sphere in the apprehension and interpretation of Julian's mystical experience. In addition, such a representation is compatible with the suggested overarching paradigm of the *mise en abîme* as Julian's texts disclose layers of experience that are representative of the physical and social world of the time and yet also indicate a new conception of space that is experienced deep within the soul and is conveyed back to the physical and social world via texts and language.

In observing Julian through the filter of her text, we see that she, in turn, is observing herself within her own physical and social world and within a textual consciousness that facilitates the relating of her visionary experiences. Despite Julian's "big picture" approach, however, she shows herself capable of distinguishing the multiple layers of her mystical space. The distinctions are both part of her own experience of the revelations in which she seems to have had access to multiple perspectives, and her stated desire to share her experience with all "evyn cristens."[1] The differentiation is established almost from the outset and is maintained throughout Julian's text. Most obviously,

1. "fellow Christians"

Julian is spatially fixed and physically immobilized in the everyday material space, confined to bed because of her illness. Here she remains, immobile, for the entire duration of the revelations. In terms of the Foucauldian formulation of space, which I presented in Chapter Two, Julian's bed (or pallet) can be considered to be a heterotopic site, the site of illness which no one else can enter but in which Julian can be easily observed by others. Her bed exemplifies Foucault's "contested space" as in it life and death, health and sickness, spiritual and material, are juxtaposed and coexistent. It is here that Julian is liminally poised as she receives her last rites and her revelations.[2] Her illness rapidly progresses to the point where she is virtually paralyzed, as she explains: "Thus I indured till day, and by then was my bodie dead from the miedes downward, as to my feeling" (LT. 3.290: 17–18).[3] However, though Julian cannot move in the physical world, within her mystical space she is able to shift perspective frequently, moving about with great facility. In the beginning, though, an equally immobile object mirrors Julian's situation across a small intimate space. That object is the crucifix. While Lefebvre might view this crucifix as an object put to symbolic use in *representational space,* for Julian it is far more than an object that is part of a "coherent system of non-verbal symbols and signs" (39). Certainly the crucifix represents Christ's Crucifixion and acts as the primary symbol of Christianity. For Julian, however, the crucifix set before her face gestures beyond

2. Pierre Bourdieu has also observed the importance of the sickbed as a place of "gathering" for the friends and relatives of the sick person and of the social function of sickness in preindustrial societies. He quotes the comments of a Kabyle woman, from his extensive study of that society, on the role of sickness and dying in the society: "When someone was ill, the news soon spread everywhere, not just in the village but all over the *arch.* Besides, a sick man's house is never empty; in the daytime all his relatives, men and women, come for news. . . . At nightfall, all the women relatives, even the youngest, would be taken to his bedside" (1994, 161). This description seems to have some similarities to the situation that Julian briefly describes in regard to the visitors to her bedside.

3. "I endured in this way until day, and by then my body felt as if it were dead from the middle downward."

its usual field of signification to become the precipitating symbol for the revelations. It becomes a symbol of translocation to the mystical space. In Margaret Wertheim's schema of medieval space, the crucifix might be understood as a bridge between body-space and soul-space but, contrary to Wertheim's view, Julian does not cross the bridge after death but in life and she remains in her body's space even as she experiences the incorporation of that body into mystical space. Julian is able to fix her vision on Christ on the cross to the exclusion of all else. However, as she continues to concentrate on the cross her illness progresses and she notes that

After this my sight began to feyle. It waxid as darke aboute me in the chamber as if it had ben nyght, saue in the image of the crosse, wher in held a common light; and I wiste not / how. All that was beseid the crosse was oglye and ferfull to me as it had ben much occupied with fiends. (LT. 3.291: 28–32)[4]

It is in this moment of intense visual concentration, as Julian's physical sight fails, that she sees the light of Christ on the cross, to the exclusion of all else. In this moment, Julian begins to die in true fulfillment of her desire to suffer as Christ did. She explains that "After this the over part of my bodie began to die so farforth that vnneth I had anie feeling. My most payne was shortnes of breth and faielyng of life" (LT. 3.291: 33–292:35).[5] The opening phrase—"after this"—of each description of bodily decline, contrasts with the use of the adverb "sodenly" which, it seems, Julian frequently uses when describing occurrences that are not only unexpected but almost miraculous in quality. In addition, the adverb sometimes seems to signal the approach of her entry into the mystical space. For example, she states

4. "After this my sight began to fail. It became as dark all around me in my chamber as if it had been night, except for the image of the cross which maintained a natural light, I did not know how. All that was around the cross was ugly and frightening to me as if it were occupied by many fiends."

5. "After this the upper part of my body began to die insofar as I had hardly any feeling there. My greatest pain was shortness of breath and the ebbing of life."

that "Then went I verily to haue passed. And in this sodenly all my paine was taken from me, and I was as hole, and namely in þe parte of my bodie, as ever I was befor" (LT. 3.292: 35–37).[6] The unexpected alleviation of pain leads Julian to "sodenly" think that she "should desyer the second wound of oure lordes gifte and of his grace" (LT. 3.292: 43–44) and the sudden thought leads to the actualization of the desire as Julian explains that "sodenly I saw the reed bloud rynnyng downe from vnder the garlande" (LT. 4.294: 3–4)[7] and the revelations begin and Julian experiences "in the same shewing sodeinly the trinitie fulfilled my hart most of ioy" (9–10).[8] Thus, Julian seems here to differentiate semantically—between the (ordinary) physical space in which sickness is part of the human experience and the mystical space in which sickness can be part of the embodiment of the mystical experience—by using "after this" with its connotation of temporally successive occurrences in the physical space and "sodenly" to imply the instantaneousness of events in the mystical space. That is, though Julian details the passing of time in the physical world during her revelations, *within* the revelations time seems to be suspended, with many things happening "sodenly." The repetition of this word, particularly in the opening chapters when the revelations are beginning, suggests that all things are happening in the moment, out of time, as much as they suggest the surprising nature of those things. Gillespie and Ross note that as Julian "[f]eel[s] herself to be on the point of death, [she] is *sodenly* relieved of her pain (the adverb is repeated three times in seven lines and is one of her most common descriptors, signalling the suspension of "ordinary" time)" (1992, 60). Glasscoe agrees that Julian maintains the integrity of the two sorts of time, earthly and spiritual, when she comments that "[t]here is a clear

6. "Then I was truly near death. And at that moment suddenly all my pain was taken from me, and I was as well, especially in the upper part of my body, as I was ever before."

7. "suddenly I saw the red blood running down from under the crown [of thorns]"

8. "in the same revelation suddenly the Trinity filled my heart with the greatest joy."

shape to the basic sequence of visions common to both texts which as it unfolds, communicates a vivid simultaneous awareness of time and eternity" (1993, 220). In a way, "after this" can be considered to represent an impression of the horizontal movement in time whereas "sodenly" implies nonmovement, a suspension of time in which experience might be visualized as accumulating in the vertical direction.[9]

The suggested paralleling of the horizontal and vertical directions with concepts of temporality and eternity, respectively, particularly in regard to Julian's fixating of her gaze on the crucifix, finds some resonance with the ideas of Thomas Torrrance that were discussed in Chapter Three. That is, Torrance considers the cross to be a representation of the intersection of the horizontal axis of earthly time and the vertical axis of eternity. Similarly, Julian's concentration on the crucifix seems to enable her simultaneous experience of temporality and eternity. That is, as has already been suggested, the crucifix functions as an image and a product of *representational space,* but also signifies Julian's translocation to a mystical space that is not contained in Lefebvre's formulation.

Furthermore, the fixing of her gaze on the fixed point of intersection of the cross's vertical and horizontal axes and the fixed position of her body in the sick bed finds a textual reflection in the first revelation that Julian describes as containing all subsequent revelations:

This is a reuelacion of loue that Jhesu Crist our endles blisse made in xvi shewynges, of which the first is of his precious crownyng of thornes; and ther in was conteined and specified the blessed trinitie with the incarnacion and the vnithing betweene god and mans sowle. (LT. 1.281: 2–5)[10]

9. St. Thomas Aquinas explains that "[t]ime differs from eternity not primarily because it begins and ends . . . but because it measures changes whereas eternity is an instantaneous whole measuring abiding existence" (*Summa* 24, 4).

10. "This is a revelation of love that Jesus Christ our endless bliss made in sixteen showings, of which the first is of his precious crowning of thorns; and therein was contained and specified the blessed Trinity with the Incarnation and the union between God and man's soul."

Here Julian presents both a textual containment and summary and a metaphorical, notionally spatial, containment of all possibilities within the circle of the crown of thorns. The written account of the revelation in the text acts as an example of *spatial practice* in the way it negotiates between body-space and soul-space while the crown of thorns simultaneously represents Christ's kingship and Christ's humanity. Spatially, the crown of thorns is, in Lefebvre's formulation, a *representational space*, a symbol of Christianity, of Christ's suffering in the beginning of the Passion which resulted in human liberation from eternal death. Likewise, Julian's own situation is analogized: the crown of thorns, a circle of pain, encloses a sacred space, the sacred head of God-made-man, just as Julian is enclosed, encircled in her own physical pain, and is brought to contemplate that which is sacred and God-like within her own enclosed space of "lived" experience.

The first revelation is also described as the "ground" of all the revelations, the showing in which "all the shewynges that foloweth be grovndide and ioyned" (LT. 1.281: 7).[11] From the initial intense focus on Christ's crown of thorns, the first revelation progresses to a subtle transfer of Julian's attention from the circle of thorns to the effect of those thorns: a flowing of Christ's blood. The living dynamism inherent in the blood flow prompts Julian to consider the Trinity of God and she emphasizes that

The trinitie is god, god is the trinitie. The trinitie is our maker, the trinitie is our keper, the trinitie is our everlasting louer, the trinitie is our endlese ioy and our bleisse, by our lord Jesu Christ, and in our lord Jesu Christ. And this was shewed in the first syght and in all, for wher Jhesu appireth the blessed trinitie is vnderstand, as to my sight. (LT. 4.295: 11–296: 16)[12]

---

11. "all the showings that follow are grounded and joined."

12. "The Trinity is God, God is the Trinity. The Trinity is our creator, the Trinity is our keeper, the Trinity is our everlasting lover, the Trinity is our endless joy and our bliss, by our Lord Jesus Christ, and in our lord Jesus Christ. And this was shown to me in the first vision and in all [of them], for where Jesus appears, the blessed Trinity is understood, as I see it." ·

This is an important point as, although Julian cites Jesus' humanity as pivotal in her experience, she expounds all her showings with attention to orthodoxy, in this case with regard to the particular teaching on the Trinity.[13] An emphasis on Christ's suffering humanity leads to a spiritual vision of "our ladie sainct Mari" (LT. 4.297:28) and of her place as the highest created being after Jesus. Julian then understands Christ as "oure clothing, that for loue wrappeth vs and wyndeth vs, halseth vs and all becloseth vs, hangeth about vs for tender loue" (LT. 5.299: 4–6).[14] The metaphor is evocative of God's spaciousness which was elaborated in Chapter Four and, equally, of the idea of God as the container for creation. The whole of creation, however, is shown to be as nothing in comparison to uncreated God and the soul finds its desired rest only when it realizes the relative nothingness of all created things. Despite the insignificance of creation—its smallness comparable in size to a hazelnut—God shows Julian that He loves and cares for it. Love is shown to be the impetus and reason for creation and God is revealed to be all that is good.

All these aspects, presented in the first revelation, are revisited and expanded (or inverted) in subsequent revelations. Andrew Sprung proposes that "[t]he sixteen [revelations] are made one, first of all by the structure of the whole: the first and last are mirror images of each other, revealing respectively that we are in Christ and Christ is in us" (1993, 53). Here, Sprung is intimating the importance of the concepts of enclosure and reflection both in Julian's revelations and in her textual representation of them. While these concepts will be elaborated in a later section of this chapter, the point to be made here is that Julian's mystical space is revealed, from the first detailing of it

---

For pertinent discussion on the theological connection between the Trinity and Christ's Passion in Julian's showings, see Pelphrey (1998, 292).

13. See, specifically, Thomas Aquinas's doctrinal explication of the medieval Church's teaching on the Trinity (pp. 65–81 in Timothy McDermott's translation and edition of the *Summa Theologiae*).

14. Christ is "our clothing, who for love wraps and enfolds us, holds and encloses us, covers us with tender love."

in the opening showing, as a malleable, reflective world in which inversions of perspective assist the communication of the revelations and in which parts can represent the whole and vice versa.[15] Furthermore, the proposition that the first revelation is a "grounde" for all that follows intimates that certain aspects of earthly logic and order operate within the mystical space despite the apparent suspension of ordinary time. In many ways, the first revelation reinforces the advice Julian received to take things generally, not specifically. This is not unfailingly the case, though, for there are many times throughout the showings when Julian's attention is specifically focused. For example, Julian vividly describes the copious bleeding from Christ's head:

The grett droppes of blode felle downe fro vnder the garlonde lyke pelottes, semyng as it had comynn ouȝte of the veynes. And in the comyng ouȝte they were bro(wn)e rede, for the blode was full thycke; and in the spredyng abrode they were bryght rede. And whan it camme at the browes, ther they vanysschyd; and not wythstonding the bledyng contynued tylle many thynges were sene and vnderstondyd. Nevertheles the feyerhede and the lyuelyhede continued in the same bewty and lyuelynes.

The plentuoushede is lyke to the droppes of water that falle of the evesyng of an howse after a grete shower of reyne, that falle so thycke that no man may nomber them with no bodely wyt. And for the roundnesse they were lyke to the scale of heryng in the spredyng of the forhede. (LT. 7.311: 14–312: 26)[16]

15. Spatially, this is akin to recent theories on the universe as a hologram. The defining property of a hologram is that the whole can be seen in the part. See, e.g., Michael Talbot, *The Holographic Universe* (New York: HarperCollins, 1991).

16. "The great drops of blood fell from under the crown like pellets, looking as if they had come from the veins. And in the flowing they were brownish red, for the blood was very thick; and as it spread out it was bright red. And when it reached the brows, [the drops] vanished; but despite this, the bleeding continued until I had seen and understood many things. Nevertheless, the fairness and the liveliness continued with the same beauty and vividness.

The plenitude is like the drops of water that fall from the eaves of a house after a great shower of rain, falling so thickly that no one can humanly count them. And in their roundness they were like the scales of a herring as they spread over the forehead."

The attention to the detail in this description affirms that Julian was looking at the scene with intense concentration. The similes—"pelottes," "droppes of water" on house eaves, and the "scale of heryng"—are ordinary features of everyday life, suggesting that, though she was intent on the showing, Julian simultaneously was translating the extraordinary and mesmerizing effect of the revelation into everyday tangible terms.[17] That is, the vision and the similes occurred to Julian together, the spiritual and the material coexisting so that Julian simultaneously received the revelations and the means to interpret them. She acknowledges this simultaneity of perception when she says that

Thes thre thynges cam to my mynde in the tyme: pelettes for the roundhede in the comyng ou3te of the blode, the scale of the herying for the roundhede in the spredyng, the droppes of the evesyng of a howse for the plentuoushede vnnumerable. Thys shewyng was quyck and lyuely and hidows and dredfule and swete and louely. (LT. 7.312: 27–31)[18]

Further, Julian recognizes, within this showing, that "oure good lorde, that is so reverent and dredfulle, is so homely and so curteyse" (LT. 7.313: 32–33).[19] That is, God is both extraordinary in His Godhead and ordinary in His humanity. His bleeding is the token of His true humanity while, paradoxically, the showing of the humanity to Julian is indicative of his transcendence. Julian effects the representation of the two facets by using the everyday similes to elucidate the

17. Carroll Hilles takes the opposite view, positing that "[t]hese metaphors do not much help the reader envision the sight Julian is describing. . . . [She] seems to be less concerned with making the sacred familiar than with making the familiar sacred" (1998, 561). This, though, is the view of a late twentieth-century reader; to an inhabitant of fourteenth-century Norwich, the scales of a herring would have been a very familiar sight. As Pelphrey (1982) points out, Norwich was a center of trade whose huge open-air markets drew traders from all parts of England and the Continent.

18. "These three things came to mind at the time: [the drops were] as round as pellets as the blood was flowing, as round as the scale of a herring as they were spreading, and as plentifully uncountable as raindrops from a house's eaves."

19. "our good lord who is so revered and feared, is so familiar and so courteous."

extraordinary, neatly reflecting the figure of the *mise en abîme*. She further emphasizes the simultaneous merging and separating of the spatial layers, particularly those that might be broadly described as indicative of body-space and soul-space, by the frequent juxtaposing of the images of blood and water. For example, as shown above, Julian compares Christ's flowing blood with rainwater. In the second revelation she describes seeing the blood dried and caked and then subtly introduces another "water" image of the sea ground. In the fourth revelation, Julian sees Christ's blood flowing again, this time as a result of the scourging. This "blood" image is juxtaposed with the thought that "god hath made waters plentuous in erth to our servys, and to our bodely eese" (LT. 12: 13–14).[20] These three juxtapositions, viewed as a whole, present an impression of the ebb and flow of both blood and water. That is, blood and water are both necessary fluids of life but Julian seems to experience the blood (of Christ) as life-giving within the space of the revelations and then the water in the space of earthly experience. It is the reflection of the eucharistic consecration in which water and wine become Christ's blood. Thus, water is posited as mundane, blood as sacred, the one operating on the material level, the other on the spiritual level. In addition, water is cleansing for earthly stains while the spiritual stain of sin is removed by Christ's suffering as Julian highlights when she says that

lykyth hym better that we take full holsomly hys blessyd blode to wassch vs of synne; for ther is no lycour that is made that lykyth hym so wele to yeue vs. For it is most plentuous, as it is most precious and that by the vertu of the blessyd godhead. (LT. 12.343: 15–18)[21]

20. "God has made water plentiful on earth for our use and for our bodily comfort."

21. "nothing pleases him more than our total acceptance of his precious blood to cleanse us of sin; for there is no drink that is made which he is so well pleased to give us. For it is most plentiful, as it is most precious, and by virtue of the blessed Godhead."

Julian, too, is careful to distinguish between the power of Christ's blood in the mystical space in which she is experiencing the revelations and in the physical space of everyday experience. Thus, for example, in the showing of the scourging, Julian views it bodily and yet simultaneously registers in her consciousness that it is happening in another space—the mystical space—as she exemplifies when she says that

And after this I saw beholdyng the body plentuous bledyng in semyng of the scoregyng, as thus. The feyer skynne was broken full depe in to the tendyr flessch, with sharpe smytynges all a bout the sweete body. The hote blode ranne out so plentuously that ther was neyther seen skynne ne wounde, but as it were all blode. And when it cam wher it shuld haue falle downe, ther it vanysschyd. Not with standing the bledyng continued a whyle, tyll it might be seen with avysement. And this was so plentuous to my syght that me thought if it had ben so in kynde and in substance, for that tyme it shulde haue made the bedde all on bloude, and haue passyde over all about. (LT. 12.342: 3–343: 12)[22]

That is, Julian remains aware of herself as observer, being able to think about her own reactions to the showings even as she is in the midst of them. She describes the blood as living and flowing and yet demonstrates that she is aware that its living qualities are not directly transferable to the material world. Julian's showings and material reality are rendered mutually exclusive. In the general terms of Lefebvre's theory, the blood and water are both images and objects of *representational space*. However, though they are symbols of Christ's Passion

---

22. "And after that I saw as I beheld the body, plentiful bleeding as a result of the scourging. The fair skin was broken deeply into the tender flesh because of the sharp blows all over the sweet body. The hot blood ran out so plentifully that there was neither skin nor wound [to be seen], but all blood, as it were. And when it reached where it should have flowed down [off the body], there it vanished. Notwithstanding, the bleeding continued for a while, till it could be clearly seen. And this was so plentiful to my sight that I thought that if it had been happening in life and in substance, in that time it would have soaked the bed in blood, and covered everything nearby."

and salvation of humanity, and of transubstantiation in the Eucharist, they also represent the mundane in the physical space and the sacred in the mystical space. Like the crucifix, in its multiplicity of significations, the symbols of the blood and the water therefore require Julian's particular interpretation and translation into word before any theoretical spatial category can be superimposed upon them. Because of this, the blood and water might fulfil Lefebvre's criterion of being objects that are "passively experienced" as symbols in the physical world but, in Julian's experience, they also facilitate and define the distinction between ordinary material space and the mystical space. Such a distinction is not part of the usual field of symbolic signification for blood and water.

INSIDE THE MYSTICAL SPACE: TRANSLOCATION

Within the mystical space, the field of symbolic signification is extended even further. Christ's blood is posited as being able to transcend metaphorical spatial boundaries and, in doing so, to effect a translocation of all those whom it touches:

The dere worthy blode . . . descendyd downe in to helle and brak her bondes and delyuerd them all that were there which belongh to the courte of hevyn. The precious plenty of his dere worthy blode ovyrflowyth all erth, and is redy to wash all creatures of synne which be of good wyll, haue ben and shall be. The precious plenty of his dereworthy blode ascendyth vp into hevyn in the blessed body of our lorde Jesu Crist, and ther is in hym, bledyng, preyeng for vs to the father, and is and shal be as long as vs nedyth. And ovyr more it flowyth in all heauen, enjoying the saluacion of all mankynd that be ther and shall be, fulfylling the number that faylyth. (LT. 12.344: 22–345: 31)[23]

23. "The precious blood . . . descended into hell and broke its bonds and delivered all who were there who belonged in the court of heaven. The precious plenty of his precious blood overflows all the earth and is ready to wash all creatures of sin who are, have been, and shall be of good will. The precious plenty of his precious blood ascended into heaven in the body of our Lord Jesus Christ and is there in him, bleeding, praying for us to the Father now and for as long as we need. And moreover, it

Such a description of the motility and power of Christ's blood approaches Lefebvre's notion of the decrypting of space that I considered in Chapter One. That is, here Christ's blood effects a decrypting
by descending "in to helle" in order to raise from the depths all those
who rightfully "belongh" to another spiritual space, that is, "the
courte of hevyn." In addition, Julian seems to suggest that the blood
contained "in the blessed body of our lorde Jesu Crist" is working to
effect a further spiritual decryption in the form of enabling an ascent
to heaven for "all mankynd."

Julian herself experiences multiple translocations, particularly of
perspective. In a way, the blood of Christ can be regarded as precipitating these metaphorical translocations. That is, as I said earlier in
this chapter, before her revelations actually begin, Julian describes a
disappearance of her pain as she concentrates on the image of Christ
on the crucifix. Not believing, however, that the remission of pain signals a return to health, but rather her imminent death, Julian decides
that she "should desyer . . . that [her] bodie might be fulfilled with
mynd and feeling of his blessed passion" (LT. 3.292: 43–45).[24] Her
desire is granted instantly as she sees "the reed bloud rynnyng downe
from vnder the garland" (LT. 4.292: 3)[25] and, thus, her revelations begin with the blood of Christ. Its flowing vividness and copiousness
attract and fix Julian's attention and subsume her previous fixation
on the static crucifix. Julian's earlier positing of blood as sacred here
assumes greater meaning as it signals Julian's own translocation into
the mystical space of her revelations. There she experiences altered
and multiple perspectives.[26] Initially, within the mystical space, Julian

flows in all heaven, rejoicing in the salvation of all mankind that is and shall be, making up for the number that fails."

24. "should desire . . . that [her] body be filled with thoughts and feelings of his
blessed Passion."

25. "the red blood running down from under the crown [of thorns]."

26. Roland Maisonneuve considers in regard to Julian's emphasis on color in the
description of her showings that ". . . le symbolisme sacré des couleurs chez . . . Julienne de Norwich nous introduit, lié à d'autres symboles, dans un monde imaginal,

is privileged not only with heightened metaphorical understanding but also with a more literally heightened viewpoint. As I suggested in Chapter One, when she is shown "a little thing, the quantitie of an haselnotte" (LT. 5.299: 9)[27] she is, in effect, experiencing "all that is created" from a much higher vantage point, possibly as high as the *primum mobile* in the medieval cosmological context, perhaps even sharing God's view of creation for a moment.

Then, as briefly mentioned above, after she witnesses the drying and caking of Christ's blood, Julian elaborates an experience in stark literal contrast to the dryness when she proceeds to state that "One tyme my vnderstandyng was lett down in to the sea grounde, and ther saw I hilles and dales grene, semyng as it were mosse begrowyng with wrake and gravell" (LT. 10: 21–23).[28] That is, from the highest vantage point Julian descends to the lowest imaginable point. This is a most remarkable metaphorical change of place and perspective for a fourteenth-century woman.[29] On the one hand, it is a very foreign concept that Julian is representing as she follows her description with the consideration that "If a man or a woman wer there vnther the brode water, and he might haue syght of god, so as god is with a man continually, he shoulde be safe in sowle and body, and take no harme" (LT. 10.326: 23–26).[30]

On the other hand, while Julian expresses the point in the third person, she implicates herself most directly within the qualification

---

où la couleur est palpitation vivante du divin et non simple traduction d'un concept, même théologique. Il fait expérimenter simultanément l'unité et la polyvalence des contraires" (1988, 267).

27. "a little thing, the size of a hazelnut."

28. "Once my understanding was taken down to the bottom of the sea and there I saw green hills and dales which seemed like moss growing among seaweed and gravel."

29. Colledge and Walsh cite two scriptural precedents for this image: Ecclesiasticus 24.7–8 and Psalm 138.9–10. However, while both examples refer to the "bottom of the sea," neither gives any description of it, as Julian does.

30. "If a man or a woman were there under the wide sea, and he could have sight of God, as God is continually with man, he would be safe in soul and body and come to no harm."

because she *is* a "woman … vnther the brode water" who, simultaneously, has "syght of god." Her translation from the highest to the
lowest location, therefore, is expressed both experientially and didac-
tically, in an instance of teaching by example. That is, Julian seems to
suggest that she has gone above the *primum mobile* and below the
sea, at God's behest, and she has remained "safe [enough] in sowle
and body" to be able to report the experience to her readers for their
own edification.

The spatial implications of Julian's descriptions of the translocations are perhaps best understood in terms of a medieval, rather than
modern, conception of space. Wertheim points out that, for medieval (Christian) humanity, "the physical world was always and ever
a reflection of the 'true' underlying realm of the soul" (55). In those
terms, Julian's apparent vast translocations can be considered as being perceived, and understood, by medieval readers as occurring dually in body-space and soul-space, on literal and metaphorical levels,
and can be seen to be suggestive of the appropriateness of trusting in
God for physical as well as spiritual well-being. A link between spiritual and physical acquiescence to God's will is also suggested. Thus,
on the occasions when Julian states that her "vnderstondyng was lyftyd vppe in to hevyn" (LT. 14.351: 4–5: 22.382: 7),[31] she first sees "our
lorde god as a lorde in his owne howse" (LT. 14.351: 5),[32] and later she
also experiences God as dwelling within her soul in "his restyng place
and his wurschypfulle cytte" (LT. 81: 10–11).[33] Julian marvels at the
paradox of this, declaring that though

owre good lorde shewde hym to his creature in dyverse manner both
in hevyn and in erth; but I saw hym take no place but in mannes soule.
(LT. 81.713: 2–3)[34]

31. "understanding was lifted up to heaven"
32. "our lord God as a lord in his own house"
33. "his resting place and honorable city"
34. "Our good Lord showed himself to his creature in various ways both in heav-
en and on earth; but I saw him take no place but in man's soul."

Julian's declaration is in line with the Christian belief that God is everywhere and most particularly within the human soul, and is spatially indicative of the notion of God as both container and that which
is contained. Julian's revelations and remarkable changes of perspective, then, can be understood to have occurred in both physical and
spiritual modalities. Despite the general medieval conception of an
ineluctably intertwined body-space and soul-space, it seems that she
distinguishes between the two for the sake of clarity for her readers.
That is, her careful reporting is not only of what she saw and experienced but of the mode of the experience's apprehension. Julian's detailing of three categories of mystical perception also seems to suggest
an inseparable interconnectedness. Glasscoe's interpretation of the
categories is pertinent here as she proposes that" 'gostly sight'refers to
the spiritual understanding which coincides with, and develops from,
insights received both in visual and linguistic terms, what she calls
'bodily sight' and 'word formyd in my understonding'" (1993, 223).

The medieval understanding of a link between body-space and
soul-space finds further reflection in Julian's elaboration of the "lord
and servant" allegory in two particular points of coincidence in relation to spatial notions. First, the allegory reveals a servant who is
journeying at the lord's behest. That is, the servant undertakes a metaphorical traversing of space, representing microcosmically Julian's
own spiritual journey and her metaphorical traversing of mystical
space which, in turn, represents humanity's traversing of life in the
journey toward God. Second, these "journeys within a journey" are
also structurally analogous to the proposed *mise en abîme* of mystical space in that the allegory lies deeply embedded within one of the
revelations of Julian's mystical experience and yet this deep layer can
also be considered to invert its position to impact on the physical,
social, and textual layers that constitute all of Julian's mystical space.
For example, socially, the allegory incorporates all "evyn christens"
in its meaning and, textually, it turns back on itself to shed light on
all the revelations that precede and follow the revelation in which

the allegorical vision occurs. The situating of such an allegory with-in Lefebvre's schema is problematical. On the one hand, while the "journey within the journey" notion of the allegory is generally anal-ogous to Lefebvre's postulating of the negotiation of space that he designates *spatial practice,* he limits such spatial negotiation to the physical realm. On the other hand, the rich symbolism of the alle-gory places it within Lefebvre's definition of *representational space* in that it "tend[s] towards more or less coherent systems of non-verbal symbols and signs" (39). Nevertheless, the allegory overflows its genre boundaries to inform other aspects of Julian's showings and subse-quently to enter the social sphere in textual form. Clearly, however, the translation of the symbols of the allegory into written explana-tion partially reinstates it into the sphere of *spatial practice* which, as I have said, does not accommodate metaphorical journeys.

After the "lord and servant" allegory, Julian expands the idea of the physical and spiritual traversing of space, applying it directly to Christ. She states, in reference to Christ's Resurrection:

And at this poynt he beganne furst to show his myght, for then he went in to helle; and whan he was ther, than he reysed vppe the grett root oute of the depe depnesse, whych ryghtfully was knyt to hym in hey hevyn. The body ley in the grave tyll E(as)ter morow; and fro that tyme he ley nevyr more. (LT. 51: 302–3)[35]

The positioning of this statement, immediately following the elabo-ration of the allegory, points to the suggestion that the servant's fall is reversed in Christ's Resurrection just as Christ's Descent into Hell prior to the Resurrection not only fulfils the scriptural precedents but reinstates his "myght" from the lowest to the highest point in, and beyond, creation. Here, too, the metaphorical vastness of the

35. "And at this point he first began to show his might, for then he went into hell; and when he was there, he raised up the great root out of the deep depth, which rightly was joined to him in heaven. The body lay in the grave until Easter morning; and from that time he lay no more." For scriptural allusions related to this passage, see Colledge and Walsh (1978, 542 nn. 301 and 302).

salvation that Christ effected, from "the depe depnesse" to the "hey hevyn," reiterates the extensive reach of Christ's sacred blood. Concurrently, Julian's own understanding is raised at this point. Just prior to the mention of the Resurrection, referring to the allegory in general, Julian declares that

Also in thys merveylous example I haue techyng with in me, as it were the begynnyng of an A B C, wher by I may haue some vnderstondyng of oure lordys menyng, for the pryvytes of the reuelacion be hyd ther in, not withstondyng that alle þe shewyng be full of prevytes. (LT. 51.539: 268–72)[36]

This "begynnyng of an A B C" finds its completion in the sixteenth revelation when Julian understands that

By thre thynges man stondyth in this lyfe, by whych iij god is wurschyppyd and we be sped, kepte and savyd. The furst is vse of mannes kyndly reson. The seconde is the comyn techyng of holy chyrch. The iij is the inwarde gracious werkyng of the holy gost; and theyse thre be alle of one god. (LT. 80.707: 2–6)[37]

Julian goes on to describe the way in which reason, the Church, and the Holy Spirit "wurke in vs contynually, alle to geder and thoo be gret thinges; of whych gretnesse he wylle we haue knowyng here, as it were in an A B C" (LT. 80.708: 9–11).[38] Paradoxically, these three things can also be understood to be the "A B C" by which Julian came to have insight into the "lord and servant" allegory and, concomitantly, into all the preceding and subsequent revelations. Having received her earthly ABC in the form of reason, holy Church,

36. "also in this marvelous example I was taught inwardly as if it were the beginning of an ABC, whereby I may have some understanding of our Lord's meaning, for the secrets of the revelation are hidden therein, even though all the showings are full of secrets."

37. "Man stands by three things in this life, by which three God is honored and we are advanced, kept and saved. The first is the use of man's natural reason. The second is the common teaching of holy Church. The third is the inward working of the grace of the Holy Spirit; and these three are all from one God."

38. "work in us continually, altogether and those are great things; of this greatness he wants us to have knowledge here, as it were in an ABC."

and Holy Spirit and her spiritual ABC by way of the "lord and servant" allegory, Julian proceeds more boldly, interspersing didactic
elaborations into her text in addition to her own continuing experience of revelation. In effect, Julian becomes a teacher of both earthly
and spiritual ABCs. That is, though she describes being within the
revelatory space, her vision and understanding is heightened and
enlarged theologically. Thus, Chapters 52 to 63 offer further interpretations and elucidations of the allegory and the general matter
of the fourteenth revelation. Julian moves into an area of extended
and more complex metaphor than in her earlier revelations. As she
acknowledges a "risen" Christ, her experience is also poised between
an understanding of the rise and fall of humanity and she becomes
particularly concerned with the inward and "upward" aspects—soul,
heaven, and an alignment of humanity with God in his glory—just
as the earlier revelations focused on the alignment of humanity with
the suffering Christ. For example, Julian explains that

thus was my vnderstandyng led of god to se in hym and to wytt, to vnderstonde and to know that oure soule is made trynyte lyk to the vnmade
blessyd trynyte, knowyn and lovyd fro with out begynnyng and in þe makyng onyd to the maker. (LT. 55.568: 39–42)[39]

Similarly, the insights that Julian has received regarding sin coalesce
with her received ideas of the rise and fall of humanity to the extent
that, toward the end of her text, Julian is able to offer a description of
sin and its place in the world as being somewhat circular in its effect,
with sin leading to sorrow which, in turn, leads to the seeking for,
and obtaining of, mercy and love:

in fallyng and in rysyng we are evyr preciously kepte in o[ne] loue. For in the
beholdyng of god we falle nott, and in þe beholdyng of oure selfe we stonde

39. "Thus was my understanding led by God to see in him and to know, understand and acknowledge that our soul is a created trinity like the uncreated blessed
Trinity, known and loved without beginning and in the creation united to the creator."

nott; and boyth theyse be soth, as to my syght, but the beholdyng of oure
lorde god is the hygher sothnes. Than are we moch bounde to hym, that he
wylle in this lyvyng shew vs this hygh sothnes; and I vnderstode whyle we be
in this lyfe, it is full spedfull to vs that we se theyse boyth at onys. For the hygher beholdyng kepyth vs in gostly joy and trew enjoyeng in god, that other,
þat is the lower beholdyng, kepyth vs in drede, and makyth vs a shamyd of
oure selfe.

But oure good lorde wylle evyr that we holde vs moch more in þe beholdyng of the hygher, and nought leue the knowyng of the lower in to the
tyme that we be broughte vppe aboue, where we shalle haue oure lorde Jhesu
to oure mede, and be fulfyllyd of joy and blysse with oute ende. (LT. 82.720:
28–37)[40]

That is, Julian sees two perspectives here (or sees one and intuits the
other)—God's and humanity's—as she depicted in the "lord and servant" allegory. Here she sees the truth of both perspectives, coexisting in an inseparable sympathy, with one being the consequence of
the human condition and the other the reverse that leads us to God.

CHANGING PLACES

At its deepest level, Julian's mystical space is the meeting place
of God and Julian, who represents all humanity. In Julian's mystical
space, however, this meeting is not an ecstatic union beyond description but a true "onyng"[41] of perspectives and possibilities in which Ju-

40. "in falling and in rising we are forever preciously kept in one love. For in the
sight of God we do not fall and in our own sight we do not stand; and both these are
true, as I see it, but the sight of our Lord God is the higher truth. Thus we are greatly
bound to him, that he will in this life show us this high truth; and I understood that
while we are in this life, it is expedient for us that we see both these at once. For the
higher sight keeps us in spiritual joy and true rejoicing in God; the other, which is
the lower sight, keeps us in fear and makes us ashamed of ourselves.

But our good Lord wants always that we cling much more to the higher sight and
not leave the knowledge of the lower until the time that we are brought up above,
where we shall have our Lord Jesus for our reward, and be filled with joy and bliss
without end."

41. Though in many parts of Julian's elaboration "onyng" can be readily translated

lian receives an insight into God's view of humanity. Particularly, it is a place of "onyng" of the apparent opposites, suffering and love, and a place where Julian and Jesus can be understood to metaphorically change places in their respective pain and love for each other. Julian explains that, in His Passion, "thus was oure lord Jhesu payned for vs; and we stonde alle in this maner of payne with hym" (LT. 18.369: 36–37).[42]

Cynthea Masson's summation of Julian's theology here is pertinent. She regards it as a "theology of necessity of opposites existing together . . . [and] she admits that love in God could never be known without woe preceding it" (1998, 157). This coexistence of opposites is particularly obvious in the eighth and ninth showings. Here, in the numerical center of the revelations, Julian and Jesus seem to change places in their suffering and their love, in an intimate empathy.[43] That is, in these central showings, Julian relates an inverted description of her own illness and the sufferings of Christ such that the text functions as a meeting point, a mirror, and a true mirror, in which the reverse image of suffering is present and represented. Lefebvre's definition of the mirror, which I applied in the previous chapter to the mystical space of the *Cloud* author, is also relevant to Julian's situation. Thus I reiterate that

---

as "union," there are other times when, I contend, she uses the word with a slightly different and stronger connotation. Here, in particular, "onyng" is not simply a "union"; it is a melding, an obliteration of difference, a true "becoming as one."

42. "thus our Lord Jesus suffered for us; and we all suffer with him in this way."

43. Roland Maisonneuve considers the "lord and servant" allegory as pivotal in the revelations. He states that "the most complete insight received by Julian about the revelations is not a conceptual explanation but a new vision given to her: the parable of the lord and the servant, which is at the centre of the work, and which is the centre of the work. Anguishing over the problem of the real meaning of her visions, Julian does not receive an answer through argumentation, but rather through a kind of symbolic vision, that of the fall and final transfiguration of a servant sent by his lord into a desert in search of treasure. In short, it is a new and very enigmatic vision which sheds the ultimate light on the revelations. We are at the heart of a visionary universe, the real meaning of which is difficult to perceive" (1980, 87).

[t]he mirror discloses the relationship between me and myself, my body and the consciousness of my body—not because the reflection constitutes my unity *qua* subject, as many psychoanalysts and psychologists apparently believe, but because it transforms what I am into the sign of what I am . . . within an imaginary space which is yet quite real. (185)

Lefebvre's consideration is relevant to Julian's eighth and ninth showings because here she sees Christ suffering as He "dries" and dies on the cross in an exact reflection of her own bodily illness and spiritual thirst, and the intimate, physical space across which this revelation is reflected becomes subsumed in the metaphorical space of understanding and enlightenment. That is, Julian sees Jesus' sufferings as He sees hers. In a moment, she understands that Jesus' greatest suffering is to see her, as representative of all humanity, suffer, just as Julian's greatest pain is to see Jesus, the one whom she most loves, suffering so greatly. In this way, Julian's bodily suffering is elevated to a higher spiritual plane in which bodily illness and spiritual insight become paired in the same way that Christ's dying represents both bodily death and spiritual life for humanity. Julian's greatest suffering, which is Christ's greatest suffering, becomes the pivotal point of her understanding. Julian says that, in the showing,

Here saw I a grett onyng betwene Crist and vs, to my vnderstondyng; for when he was in payne we ware in payne, and alle creatures that myght suffer payne sufferyd with hym. (LT. 18.367: 14–16)[44]

Physically, there is some correspondence between Julian's illness and the pains of Christ's Crucifixion. For example, Julian's description, first, of her "bodie [being] dead from the miedes downward, as to my feeling" (LT. 3.290: 17–18),[45] then the "over part of my bodie beg[inning] to die so farforth tha vnneth I had anie feeling" (LT.

44. "Here I saw a great 'oneing' between Christ and us, as I understood it; for when he was in pain we were in pain, and all creatures that could suffer pain suffered with him."

45. "body [being] dead from the middle downward, as it felt to me"

3.291: 33–34),[46] and finally the declaration that "My most payne was shortnes of breth and faielyng of life" (LT. 3.291: 34–292:35)[47] could allude to suffocation, which some scholars have considered to be the final pain of Christ and of crucifixion in general.[48]

In fact, Julian considers Christ's "drying" to be His last pain, stating that "me thought the dryeng of Cristes flessch was the most peyne and the last of his passion" (LT. 16.359: 29–30).[49] This does not necessarily efface the reflection of Christ's and Julian's sufferings, however, as Julian elaborates a multiplicity of meanings for "drying" on both physical and spiritual levels. Thus when Christ uttered "I thurst" (LT. 17.360: 3), Julian understands "a dowbylle thurst, oon bodely and a nother gostly" (ibid., 3–4),[50] and while she does not propose that she was physically thirsting at the time of this revelation, a spiritual thirst is implied from the outset, most particularly in the expression of her desire for "thre gyftes by the grace of god. The first was mynd of the passion. The secund was bodilie sicknes. The thurde was to haue of godes gyfte thre woundys" (LT. 2.285: 4–6)[51]

46. "upper part of my body beg[inning] to die to the extent that I had hardly any feeling"

47. "My greatest pain was shortness of breath and the ebbing of life"

48. I would like to thank Fr. Vincent Hurley, S.J., for bringing this point to my attention and sharing his considerable knowledge of the practice of crucifixion in Roman times. He explains that when the crucified body begins to sag from pain and exhaustion, breathing is interrupted and the person must place all his weight on his feet in order to push himself upward so as to be able to breathe again. When the pain in the feet becomes too intense to bear, the person will again allow his body to sag, thus starting the process again. This seems to resemble the pains that Julian describes though I am aware that Colledge and Walsh, in their Introduction to *A Book of Showings to the Anchoress Julian of Norwich*, cite Julian's symptoms as indicative of heart disease (see p. 69 of that edition). In addition, a very convincing case for botulism as the cause of Julian's symptoms is presented by James T. McIlwain (1984). Equally convincing is the argument presented by Richard Lawes (2000) for a diagnosis of a febrile illness such as pneumonia.

49. "I thought that the drying of Christ's flesh was his greatest and final pain of his Passion."

50. "a double thirst, on physical and the other spiritual"

51. "three gifts by the grace of God. The first was thoughts of the Passion. The second was bodily sickness. The third was to have, of God's gift, three wounds."

That is, in her early desires for God, Julian expressed a willingness to suffer in her own body and in spiritual sympathy with Christ in His Passion. In the fulfilment of the desires, therefore, Julian experiences doubly her physical illness and Christ's final sufferings, in both body-space and soul-space.[52]

In addition to wishing that Christ's pains were her pains, Julian also hoped that the resulting compassion would lead to a longing for God. This wish has also been fulfilled before Julian has realized that she is asking for it. That is, there is what might be termed a reciprocal reflection in the manner in which Julian's illness increases her longing for God and yet equally her longing for God has subtly prompted her request for an illness.

The empathic exchange between Christ and Julian is not limited to illness and dying but is reflected in Julian's return to health as well. Thus, when Jesus' appearance changes to one of joy, Julian reports that "the channgyng of hys blessyd chere channgyd myne" (LT. 21.379: 7–8).[53] Glasscoe considers this change of "chere" to be

one of the most moving epiphanies in medieval writing. After it, Julian's remaining revelations unpack what is concentrated in this change of *chere:* the glory of a life-giving energy that brought it about, and the capacity of this energy to process all the works of darkness to feed its own light. In the final vision of the kingdom the outward shows of time have dissolved into a solution on joy. Changing of *chere* is the quick of the whole revelation and at the heart of the eighth showing. (1997, 117)[54]

The epitome of the reciprocal "change of *chere*" between Julian and Christ is displayed here when Julian is "restored to health at the point of her own death" (ibid.). It is a reflection not only of Christ's change of *chere* but of His ultimate triumph over death in His Resurrection and the reversal of the Fall in that same rising. Julian ex-

---

52. Barratt (1998, 244) notes that there is even a temporal correspondence implied between the sufferings of Julian and of Christ.

53. "the changing of his blessed appearance changed mine"

54. Glasscoe disagrees with Colledge and Walsh's editorial positioning of this "change of '*chere*'" in the ninth showing.

pounds the essential interconnectedness between the Fall and the Resurrection:

For þe tyme of this lyfe we haue in vs a mervelous medelur both of wele and of woo. We haue in vs oure lorde Jhesu Cryst vp resyn, and we haue in vs the wrechydnesse and the myschef of Adams fallyng. Dyeng by Cryst we be lastynly kept, and by hys gracyous touchyng we be reysed in to very trust of saluacyon. And by Adams fallyng we be so broken in oure felyng on dyverse manner by synne and by sondry paynes, in whych we be made derke and so blynde that vnnethyes we can take any comforte. But in oure menyng we abyde god, and feythfully trust to haue mercy and grace; and this is his owne werkyng in vs, and of his goodnesse openyth the ey of oure vnderstanding, by which we haue syght, some tyme more and somtyme lesse, after þat god gevyth abylte to take. And now we be reysyde in to that one, and now we are sufferyd to fall in to that other. And thus is that medle so mervelous in vs þat vnnethis we knowe of oure selfe or of oure evyn crysten in what wey we stonde, for the mervelousnes of this sondrye felyng, but þat ech holy assent þat we assent to god when we fele hym, truly wyllyng to be with hym with all oure herte, with all oure soule and with all oure myghte. (LT. 59.546: 9–548: 26)[55]

Thus Julian melds Christ's rising and Adam's (and humanity's) falling into the two aspects of salvation, and the metaphorical spatial directions that are implicit in the notions of rising and falling are obliter-

55. "During the time of this life we have in us a marvelous mixture both of well-being and woe. We have in us our risen Lord Jesus Christ, and we have in us the wretchedness and the mischief of Adam's fall. Dying, we are lastingly protected by Christ, and by the touch of his grace we are raised to an absolute trust in salvation. And because of Adam's fall we are so broken in our feelings in various ways by sin and by sundry pains that we become so dark and blind that we can hardly receive any comfort. But in our intention we remain with God, and faithfully trust to have mercy and grace; and this is his own working in us, and in his goodness he opens the eye of our understanding, by which we have sight, sometimes more and sometimes less, depending on God's giving of the ability to receive. And now we are raised to this one, and now we are allowed to fall into the other. And thus there is that mix so marvelous in us that we barely notice that we and our fellow Christians are in that condition, so marvelous are these various feelings, except for each holy move toward God which we make when we feel him, truly willing to be with him with all our heart, with all our soul and with all our might."

ated in the melding. That is, in Julian's mystical schema, the literal directional signification of "rising" and "falling," "up" and "down," are no longer representative of binary opposition but of completeness. Similarly, Christ's and Julian's "change of place" points to a "onyng" of opposites and an obliteration of the metaphorical space between Christ and humanity.

WHOLENESS: ASPECTS OF GENDER AND ENCLOSURE

The melding of opposites finds particular expression within Julian's texts in the way that conventionally gendered notions such as "fatherhood" and "motherhood" are frequently posited as aspects of one whole.[56] In Lefebvre's theory of space, the concept of motherhood fits dually into the categories of *representations of space* and of *representational spaces*. Its location in the first category is related to the notion of motherhood as a socially and sexually constructed role in relation to the "production" of children. Its concurrent location in the other category is related to the term's symbolic association with ideas of love and nurture. Julian's use of the notion of the "motherhood of God" is frequently admired but, of course, the image did not originate with her. As Bynum, for example, explains,

56. A link is discernible between Julian's elaboration of God in his completeness and the dynamism of the Trinity. The expression of such dynamism in spatial terms is perhaps approached, in contemporary terms, by modern particle theory. Pelphrey sees a parallel between Julian's Trinitarian theology and modern atomic physics, postulating that "[i]f contemporary physicists were theologians, they might say with Julian that the Trinity is an absolute interpenetration or reciprocity of Persons. Scientists speak of matter as composed of interacting sub-particles which swarm like bees, more like concentrations of energy than substantial objects. These sub-particles are so dynamic that in a sense they cannot be said to 'be' anywhere, unless they are viewed as everywhere-at-once in their spheres of possibility. Similarly, Julian sees the Persons of the Trinity as continually in and with one another, not identical but never separate" (1998, 296).

It was Clement of Alexandria who in the 2nd century elaborated the explicitly eucharistic image of Christ as mother feeding the soul from his breasts and the direct source in the later Middle Ages for such imagery was the writings of Anselm (d. 1109) and of several 12th century Cistercian monks, among them Bernard, Guerric of Igny and William of Thierry. (1987, 94)

In Julian's use of the term, the symbolic level generally displaces the culturally determined parameters of motherhood though she does not completely disregard them. For example, in expounding her view of God's motherhood Julian explains that she

Vnderstode thre manner of beholdynges of motherhed in god. The furst is grounde of oure makyng, the seconde is takyng of oure kynde, and ther begynnyth the moderhed of grace, the thurde is moderhed in werkyng. And therin is a forth sp[r]edyng by the same grace of lengt and brede, of hygh and of depnesse without ende, and alle is one loue. (LT. 59.593: 43–48)[57]

In the first point, Julian acknowledges the biological aspect of motherhood in the "makyng." In the third point she speaks of the "werkyng" of motherhood, which seems to refer to the caring and nurturing attributes of a mother. The second point in Julian's summation is that God is our mother because He assumed our humanity. This point combines the notions of physical and spiritual "motherhood" and knits the first and third points, the "making" and the "werkyng," as God is responsible for our creation and "werk[s]" within us by grace. In the medieval schema, such an elaboration represents motherhood in terms of both body-space and soul-space. Additionally, this middle point reflects the manner in which Christ in His humanity effects a reconciliation between material and spiritual reality.

In speaking of God's motherhood, Julian places notions of motherhood (and fatherhood) beyond the simple gender binary and fo-

---

57. "understood three ways of considering motherhood in God. The first is [as] the ground of our making/creation, the second is the taking/assuming of our [human] kind, and there begins the motherhood of grace, the third is motherhood in working/practice. And therein is a spreading forth by the same grace in length and breadth, in height and depth without end, and all is one love."

cuses attention on the completeness of God and the way in which humanity finds its completeness in God.[58] She emphasizes God's multifaceted relationship to humanity when she states that

And thus I saw that god enjoyeth that he is our fader, and god enjoyeth that he is our moder, and god enjoyeth that he is our very spouse and our soule his lovyd wyfe. And Crist enjoyeth þat he is our broder, and Jhesu enioyeth that he is our savyour. (LT. 52.546: 2–5)[59]

That is, in Julian's mystical space, the association of "male" and "female" to the notions of father and mother, brother and wife, is no longer especially relevant, though the socially and biologically bestowed attributes of each familial position remain apposite. Furthermore, God's completeness is related to the image of His containment of all of humanity within Him as, logically, all of creation is a necessary part of God's wholeness. Julian combines the concepts of God's enclosure of humanity and familial relationships in a series of metaphors that simultaneously equate and elevate the earthly intimacy of human relationships to the highest level of intimacy with God when she says that

I sawe no dyfference between god and oure substance, but as it were all god; and yett my vnderstandyng toke that oure substance is in god, that is to sey that god is god and oure substance is a creature in god. For the almyghty truth of the trynyte is oure fader, for he made vs and kepyth vs in hym. And the depe wysdome of þe trynyte is oure moder, in whom we be closyd. And the hye goodnesse of the trynyte is our lord, and in hym we be closyd and he is vs. We be closyd in the fader, and we be closyd in the son, and we are closyd in the holy gost. And the fader is beclosyd in vs, the son is beclosyd in vs, and the holy gost is beclosyd in vs, all myght, alle wysdom and alle goodnesse, one god, one lorde. (LT. 54.562: 17–563: 22)[60]

58. For elaboration of the opposite argument which regards Julian's use of imagery, especially that which deals with "motherhood," as being strongly associated with the feminine, see in particular Liz Herbert McAvoy (1998, 2004).

59. "And thus I saw that God rejoices that he is our father, and God rejoices that he is our mother, and God rejoices that he is our true spouse and our soul his loved wife. And Christ rejoices that he is our brother, and Jesus rejoices that he is our savior."

60. "I saw no difference between God and our substance, but as it were all God;

In this explication, the words "closyd" and "beclosyd" carry connotations of spatiality that are suggestive of God's all-embracing containment of humanity and of God's willingness to be enclosed by humanity. In addition, the words gesture toward the multiplicity of aspects
that coalesce in God and that metaphorically are enclosed in God.

Julian's representation of enclosure in the texts works in a similar
way, centering on the notion of the reciprocal indwelling of God in
humanity and of humanity in God and highlights the inextricable
link between God and humanity. Thus, in the above example, God
contains truth, wisdom, and goodness; God is the Trinity; each Person of the Trinity, Father, Son, and Holy Ghost is an expression of
the truth, wisdom, and love of God; and God encloses the substance
of humanity. Contingent on the consideration of God as all-encompassing, Julian advises that "if we wylle haue knowyng of oure soule
and comenyng and dalyance ther with, it behovyth to seke in to oure
lord god in whom it is enclosyd" (LT. 56.571: 16–18).[61] The concept of
reciprocal indwelling, inherent in much of Julian's elaboration, is op-
erative here, too, however, when she adds "And not withstandyng all
this, we may nevyr come to the full knowyng of god tylle we knowe
furst clerely oure owne soule" (LT. 56.573: 32–33).[62] Here Julian can
be understood to be reiterating her earlier statement that "oure substance is in god." Equally, she alludes to the idea of God as mother in
that God is the ground of our "makyng" and, thus, we find our spiritual familiarity in Him because our soul's substance is in God.

---

and yet my understanding accepted that our substance is in God, that is to say that
God is God and our substance is a creature in God. For the almighty truth of the
Trinity is our Father, for he made us and keeps us in him. And the deep wisdom of
the Trinity is our mother, in whom we are enclosed. And the high goodness of the
Trinity is our Lord, and in him we are enclosed and he is in us. We are enclosed in the
Father, and we are enclosed in the Son, and we are enclosed in the Holy Spirit. And
the Father is enclosed in us, the Son is enclosed in us, the Holy Spirit is enclosed in
us, all might, all wisdom and all goodness, one God, one Lord."

61. "if we want to have knowledge of our soul and communion and contemplation therein, it is necessary to seek in our Lord God in whom it is enclosed."

62. "And not withstanding all this, we may never come to a full knowing of God
until we first clearly know our own soul."

The alignment of enclosure and God's motherhood is established in the ideas of "making" that refers dually to material and spiritual generation. In soul-space, God is the progenitor in which humanity is enclosed; in body-space the mother's womb is the space of primary physical enclosure. This collocates with other enclosure images throughout the text. Julian's recommendation, for example, that we ". . . be fastenyd and onyd to oure moder holy Church, that is Crist" (LT. 61607: 63)[63] effects a link between spiritual nurture and earthly authority. Most importantly, though, the motherhood allusion admits of the enclosure of humanity in God, of God in our souls, and of Christ in our humanity.

In admitting of Christ's Incarnation which, in common with the rest of humanity, began with enclosure in the womb, Christ's own mother Mary is thus specifically incorporated into the larger connotation of motherhood and she is vicariously inferred as humanity's spiritual mother.[64] Likewise, Mary's presentation in other parts of Julian's revelations is reinscribed with greater meaning. Mary is particularly shown in three ways: "The furst was as she conceyved, the secunde as she was in her sorowes vnder the crosse, and the thurde was as she is now in lykynge, worschyppe and joy" (LT. 25.401: 38–41).[65] Earlier Julian had been shown Mary "as she beheld her god, that is her maker, marvayling with great reuerence that he would be borne of her that was a symple creature of his makyng" (LT. 4.297: 32–34).[66] Glasscoe, in considering that these two showings of Mary present her as a representative for all, suggests that

63. "be fastened and 'oned' to our mother, Holy Church, which is Christ."

64. "The doctrine of Mary's spiritual motherhood is explicit in the West from the time of Augustine; and his treatise *De sancta virginitate* remained a classic in the contemplative tradition" (Colledge and Walsh 1978, 580 n. 47).

65. "The first was as she conceived, the second as she was in her sorrow under the cross, and the third was as she is now in delight, worship and joy."

66. "as she beheld her God, who is her creator, marveling with great reverence that he would be borne of her who was a simple creature of his creation."

[h]ere Julian understands that her vision of the Virgin at the Annunciation enabling Christ to be born and thus participating in his *kenosis,* and at the Crucifixion sharing his suffering, is completed by her knowledge of Mary exalted in glory; and all these perceptions are a means to her spiritual understanding that Mary projects the pattern of transfiguration possible for all men to "worshippe and ioye" in Christ whose glory is ineffably the completion of all partiality. (1993, 221)

The presentation of Mary as a creature of God's making who would be instrumental in the making of God restates the concept of humanity's enclosure in God and God's enclosure in humanity. Julian restates the Church's authority, too, when she posits the earthly dwelling places for God as the Church and the human soul:

Here may we see that we be all bounde to god for kynd, and we be bounde to god for grace. Her may we see that vs nedyth nott gretly to seke ferre out to know sondry kyndys, but to holy church into oure moders brest, that is to sey in to oure owne soule, wher oure lord dwellyth. And ther shulde we fynde alle, now in feyth and in vnderstandyng, and after verely in hym selfe clerely in blysse. (LT. 62.612: 22–613: 27)[67]

The aligning of the Church and the soul as God's earthly enclosures transposes the symbolic *representational space* of God's heavenly realm into a physically accessible space for the medieval faithful. Furthermore, the Church and the soul are representative of a coexistent body-space and soul-space.

The linking of the physical and the spiritual seems to be part of Julian's didactic intent which, she indicates, was facilitated by God in the revelations. Julian's efforts to convey a quality of wholeness in her texts, therefore, seem to reflect the completeness that she saw in God. That is, the spiritual wholeness finds a physical reflection in the tex-

---

67. "Here we may see that we are all bound to God by [our human] nature, and we are bound to God by grace. Here we may see that we need not seek very far to know various natures, but to holy Church, into our mother's breast, that is to say our own soul, where our Lord dwells. And there we will find everything, now in faith and understanding, and afterwards truly in himself, clearly in bliss."

tual drawing together and enclosing of the showings. The following statement is a particular example as Julian stresses that

And ryght as in the furst worde that oure good lorde shewde, menyng his blessyd passyon: Here with is the fende ovyr come, ryght so he seyde in the last worde with ful tru feytfulnes, menyng vs alle: Thou shalt not be ovyr come. (LT. 68.646: 59–63)[68]

Here the words have multiple possibilities of meaning: they imply the possibility for all Christians of overcoming sinfulness and physical death; for Julian personally, they imply the overcoming of her illness and her spiritual doubts, her mastering of the understanding of the revelations, and her overcoming of the difficulty of writing the text for others' benefit. It is an enclosure of all the implications of the revelations in a capsule of hope.

Shortly after this insight, Julian returns her sight to the cross, the point of her departure into mystical space. She explains that

Mi bodely eye I sett in the same crosse there I had seen in comforte afore þat tyme, my tong with spech of Cristes passion and rehersyng the feyth of holy church, and my harte to fasten on god with alle the truste and þe myghte, that I thought to my selfe, menyng: thou hast now great besenes to kepe the in þe feyth, for þat thou shuldest nott be taken of thyne enemys. (LT. 70.650: 2–7)[69]

Here Julian encloses the revelations in faith, as she reviews the cross as a symbol of *representational space*. As a consequence of the revelations, however, the cross's symbolism has been multiplied to incorporate not only the previous symbolism inscribed by medieval Chris-

68. "And just as in the first word that our good Lord showed, regarding his blessed Passion: Herewith is the fiend overcome, just as he said in his last words with full, true faithfulness, regarding us all: You shall not be overcome."

69. "My physical eye I set on the same cross where I had seen comfort before, my tongue on words of Christ's Passion and repeating the faith of holy Church, and my heart fastened on God with all my trust and might, so that I thought to myself: you have now great business to keep you in the faith, so that you may not be taken by your enemies."

tian *habitus,* but additionally the revealed insights attained by Julian in mystical space.

The ultimate, and most important enclosure, however, is the final enclosure in love. Thus, Julian summarizes the preceding layers of enclosure when she declares that "charite kepyth vs in feyth and in hope. And feyth and hope ledyth vs in charite and at þe ende alle shalle be charite" (LT. 84.727: 8–9).[70] In doing so, she fulfils, literally and textually, the metaphorical mystical message, which surrounds and enlivens, as well as ends, the revelations:

Thus was I lernyd, þat loue is oure lordes menyng. And I sawe fulle surely in this and in alle that or god made vs he lovyd vs, whych loue was nevyr slekyd ne nevyr shalle. And in this loue he hath done alle his werkes, and in this loue he hath made alle thynges profytable to vs, and in this loue oure lyfe is evyr lastyng. In oure makyng we had begynnyng, but the loue wher in he made vs was in hym fro with out begynnyng. In whych loue we haue oure begynnyng, and alle this shalle we see in god with outyn ende. (LT. 86.733: 20–734: 27)[71]

God is shown to be the initiator of Julian's desire for God, the preciptator of the revelations, the content and focus of her revelations, and her guide within the mystical space. Ultimately He is shown to be analogous to "Love" that has instigated, informed, and enclosed Julian's mystical experience, as she explains:

And fro the tyme þat it was shewde, I desyerde oftyn tymes to wytt in what was oure lords menyng. And xv yere after and mor, I was answeryd in gostly vnderstondyng, seyeng thus: What, woldest thou wytt thy lordes menyng in this thyng? Wytt it wele, loue was his menyng. Who shewyth it the? Loue.

70. "charity keeps us in faith and hope. And faith and hope lead us in charity and in the end all shall be charity."

71. "Thus I learnt that love is our Lord's meaning. And I saw full surely in this and in all that before God made us he loved us, and that love has never lessened nor ever shall. And in this love he has done all his works, and in this love he has made all things profitable to us, and in this love our life is everlasting. In our creation we had beginning, but the love in which he made us was in him from without beginning. In this love we have our beginning and all this we shall see in God without end."

(What shewid he the? Love.) Wherfore shewyth he it the? For loue. Holde the therin, thou shalt wytt more in the same. But thou schalt nevyr witt
therin other withoutyn ende. (LT. 86.732: 13–733: 19)[72]

The answer gives assurance to Julian that Love is all-encompassing
and eternal. Love in not confined to body-space but extends infinitely
into soul-space. Thus, Love is simultaneously immanent and transcendent. Likewise, Julian's mystical space is an all-encompassing space in
which time offers no resistance to the seamless blending of physical
and spiritual experience. In her mystical space, Love encloses Julian just
as Julian encloses Love and the two medieval postulations of space as a
receptacle and that which is contained are reconciled.

72. "And from that time that it was revealed, I desired many times to know what
our Lord's meaning was. And after fifteen years and more, I was answered in my
spiritual understanding, thus: What, you want to know your Lord's meaning in this
thing? Know it well, love was his meaning. Who revealed it to you? Love. (What
did he reveal to you? Love.) Why does he reveal it to you? For love. Stay firm in this,
you shall know more of the same. And you shall never know anything other without
end."

EPILOGUE

Space in all its conceptual and perceptual possibilities is an essential aspect of our human experience. However, unlike time, which absorbs our attention to the extent that we mark off our lives in constructed increments of it, space is generally taken for granted.

To date, the importance of space in the examination of all kinds of medieval and modern texts has been largely overlooked. In the case of medieval mystics in particular this is a surprising omission because mystics like Richard Rolle, *The Cloud of Unknowing* author, and Julian of Norwich demonstrate in their texts a clear awareness of the pervasiveness of the physical, social, and spiritual dimensions of their lives. For them, these spatial dimensions assumed a far greater importance than did chronology as they lived their lives with their intentions fixed firmly on eternity. At the same time, too, God's immanence was tangible to them and informed their everyday undertakings. This simultaneous recognition of God's transcendence and immanence is possibly what the definition of mysticism as an unmediated apprehension of the Divine is really encapsulating. That is, mystical experience is unmediated by time and is therefore a transcendent experience even though the expression of that experience is immanent and reflective of contemporary social mores. Mystical space, then, is also transcendent and immanent, absorbing and reflecting physical, social, textual, and spiritual dimensions simultaneously.

Just as Julian, the *Cloud* author, and Rolle were called to contemplate in the fourteenth century, so we in the twentieth-first century also contemplate the Divine through the texts and the lives of the mystics themselves. The mystics survive, contained in the space of the text, but in addition the texts point backward to the authors as actual people. Simultaneously, the texts point beyond time and history to an experience that is beyond material containment. Thus, in committing their experiences to writing, the mystics fulfilled the requirements of their privileged experience, that they disseminate their "fruit" for all Christians. Notably, this dissemination did not only take effect within their own lifetimes but has continued to the present day. Their texts have provided a three-dimensional container for their mystical space, and as such have assured their transcendence.

The reflective quality of the *mise en abîme* of mystical space transcends time, too, to remain active as a mirror, even today. That is, in reading the texts, modern readers encounter a space full of traces of lives lived in the pursuit of a spiritual ideal. Their texts thus reveal the mystics and their methods and, just as exemplars were important in the medieval society for the purposes of imitation and edification, so these same mystics become present day exemplars. Thus we add another layer to the *mise en abîme* by enclosing the mystical space within the framework of contemporary spiritual and theoretical inquiry. Within this space of theoretical inquiry, within the vast space of the cosmos, within the society of the Middle Ages, within an enclosed solitary space, within the physical body, within the soul, there exists a space of mystical experience that resonates with all the surrounding spaces and yet is located in none of them exclusively. The *mise en abîme* of mystical space is rendered infinite.

WORKS CITED

PRIMARY TEXTS

Anonymous. 1944. *The Cloud of Unknowing* and *The Book of Privy Counselling.* Ed. Phyllis Hodgson. EETS o.s. 218. London: Oxford University Press.

Anonymous. 1962. *Ancrene Wisse.* Ed. J. R. R. Tolkien. EETS o.s. 249. Oxford: Oxford University Press.

Aquinas, St. Thomas. 1989. *Summa Theologiae.* Ed. Timothy McDermott. London: Methuen.

Athanasius, St. 1950. *The Life of St. Antony.* Trans. Robert T. Meyer. New York: Newman Press.

Augustine, St. 1991. *Confessions.* Trans. Henry Chadwick. Oxford: Oxford University Press.

Bernard of Clairvaux. 1976. *Five Books on Consideration: Advice to a Pope.* Trans. John D. Anderson and Elizabeth T. Kennan. Kalamazoo: Cistercian Publications.

Boethius. 1969. *The Consolation of Philosophy.* Trans. V. E. Watts. Ed. Betty Radice. London: Penguin Books.

Chaucer, Geoffrey. 1987. *The Riverside Chaucer.* Ed. Larry Benson. Oxford: Oxford University Press.

Gregory of Tours. 1985. *Life of the Fathers.* Trans. Edward James. Liverpool: Liverpool University Press.

Hilton, Walter. 1923. *The Scale of Perfection.* Ed. Evelyn Underhill. London: John M. Watkins.

———. 1988. *The Ladder of Perfection.* Trans. Leo Sherley-Price. Ed. Clifton Wolters. London: Penguin Books.

Julian of Norwich. 1978. *A Book of Showings: Part One and Part Two.* Eds. Edmund Colledge and James Walsh. Toronto: Pontifical Institute of Medieval Studies.

Kempe, Margery. 1997. *The Book of Margery Kempe.* Ed. Sanford Brown Meech. EETS o.s. 293. London: Oxford University Press.

Rolle, Richard. 1896. *The Fire of Love.* Trans. Richard Misyn. EETS o.s. 106. London: Kegan, Paul, Trench, Trübner & Co.

———. 1915. *Incendium Amoris of Richard Rolle of Hampole.* Ed. Margaret Deansely. Manchester: Manchester University Press.

———. 1963. *English Writings of Richard Rolle.* Ed. Hope Emily Allen. Oxford: Clarendon Press. (Orig. pub. 1931.)

———. 1972. *The Fire of Love.* Trans. Clifton Wolters. London: Penguin Books.

———. 1988. *Prose and Verse.* Ed. S. J. Ogilvie-Thomson. EETS o.s. 293. London: Oxford University Press.

SECONDARY TEXTS

Abert, John. 1996. "Pseudo-Dionysius as Liberator: The Influence of the Negative Tradition on Late Medieval Female Mystics." *Downside Review* 114, no. 395: 96–115.

Aers, David. 1975. *Community, Gender and Individual Identity.* London: Routledge.

Allen, Hope Emily, ed. 1963. *English Writings of Richard Rolle.* Oxford: Clarendon Press. (Orig. pub. 1931.)

Allen, Rosamund. 1984. "'Singuler Lufe': Richard Rolle and the Grammar of Spiritual Ascent." In *The Medieval Mystical Tradition in England: Papers Read at Dartington Hall, July, 1984.* Ed. Marion Glasscoe. Cambridge: D. S. Brewer.

Almond, Philip. 1982. *Mystical Experience and Religious Doctrine: An Investigation of the Study of Mysticism in World Religions.* Berlin: Mouton.

Armstrong, Elizabeth Psakis. 1995. "Womanly Men and Manly Women in Thomas a Kempis and St. Teresa." In *Vox Mystica: Essays on Medieval Mysticism.* Eds. Anne Clark Bartlett et al. Cambridge: D. S. Brewer.

Astell, Ann. 1989. "Feminine Figurae in the Writings of Richard Rolle: A Register of Growth." *Mystics Quarterly* 15, no. 3: 117–24.

Atkinson, Clarissa W. 1983. *Mystic and Pilgrim: The Book and the World of Margery Kempe.* Ithaca: Cornell University Press.

Bachelard, Gaston. 1969. *The Poetics of Space.* Trans. Maria Jolas. Boston: Beacon Press.

Baker, Denise N. 1993. "Julian of Norwich and Anchoritic Literature." *Mystics Quarterly* 19, no. 4: 148–60.

———. 1994. *Julian of Norwich's Showings: From Vision to Book.* Princeton: Princeton University Press.

———. 1998. "The Image of God: Contrasting Configurations in Julian of Norwich's 'Showings' and Walter Hilton's 'Scale of Perfection.'" In *Julian of Norwich: A Book of Essays.* Ed. Sandra McEntire. New York: Garland.

———. 1999. "The Active and Contemplative Lives in Rolle, the *Cloud*-author and Hilton." In *The Medieval Mystical Tradition: Exeter Symposium VI.* Ed. Marion Glasscoe. Cambridge: D. S. Brewer.

Bakhtin, Mikhail. 1984. *Rabelais and His World.* Trans. Helen Iswolsky. Bloomington: Indiana University Press. (Orig. pub. 1968.)

———. 1990. *The Dialogic Imagination: Four Essays by M. M. Bakhtin.* Ed. Michael Holquist. Austin: University of Texas Press.

Barratt, Alexandra. 1995. "How Many Children Had Julian of Norwich? Editions, Translations and Versions of Her Revelations." In *Vox Mystica: Essays on Medieval Mysticism.* Eds. Anne Clark Bartlett et al. Cambridge: D. S. Brewer, 1995.

———. 1998. "'In the Lowest Part of Our Need': Julian and Medieval Gynecological Writing." In *Julian of Norwich: A Book of Essays.* Ed. Sandra McEntire. New York: Garland.

Bartlett, Anne Clark. 1992. "Miraculous Literacy and Textual Communities in Hildegard of Bingen's 'Scivias.'" *Mystics Quarterly* 18 (2): 43–55.

———. 1994. "Foucault's 'Medievalism.'" *Mystics Quarterly* 20 (1): 10–15.

Bartlett, Anne Clark, et al., eds. 1995. *Vox Mystica: Essays on Medieval Mysticism.* Cambridge: D. S. Brewer.

Bauerschmidt, Frederick Christian. 1997. "Seeing Jesus: Julian of Norwich and the Text of Christ's Body." *Journal of Medieval and Early Modern Studies* 27, no. 2: 189–214.

Beckwith, Sarah. 1993. *Christ's Body: Identity, Culture and Society in Late Medieval Writings.* London: Routledge.

Beer, Frances. 1992. *Women and Mystical Experience in the Middle Ages.* Woodbridge: Boydell Press.

Beggiani, Seely J. 1996. "Theology at the Service of Mysticism: Method in Pseudo-Dionysius." *Theological Studies* 57, no. 2: 201–223.

Biddick, Kathleen. 1993. "Genders, Bodies, Borders: Technologies of the Visible." *Speculum* 68: 389–419.

Boenig, Robert. 1984. "The God-as-Mother Theme in Richard Rolle's Biblical Commentaries." *Fourteenth Century English Mystics Newsletter* 10, no. 4: 171–74.

———. 1995. "St. Augustine's Jubilus and Richard Rolle's Canor." In *Vox Mystica: Essays on Medieval Mysticism.* Eds. Anne Clark Bartlett et al. Cambridge: D. S. Brewer.

Bothe, Catherine M. 1994. "Writing as Mirror in the Work of Marguerite Porete." *Mystics Quarterly* 20, no. 3: 105–111.

Bourdieu, Pierre. 1977. *Outline of a Theory of Practice.* Cambridge: Cambridge University Press.

———. 1990. *The Logic of Practice.* Trans. Richard Nice. Cambridge: Polity Press.

———. 1991. *Language and Symbolic Power.* Trans. Gino Raymond and Matthew Adamson. Ed. John B. Thomson. Cambridge: Polity Press.

———. 1994. "Structures, Habitus, Power: Basis for a Theory of Symbolic Power." In *Culture/Power/History: A Reader in Contemporary Social Theory.* Eds. Nicholas B. Dirks et al. Princeton: Princeton University Press.

Bowman, Mary Ann. 1978. *Western Mysticism: A Guide to the Basic Works.* Chicago: American Library Association.

Boyd, Beverly. 1995. "Chaucer's Moments in the Kneeling World." In *Vox Mystica: Essays on Medieval Mysticism.* Eds. Anne Clark Bartlett et al. Cambridge: D. S. Brewer.

Boyne, Roy. 1990. *Foucault and Derrida: The Other Side of Reason*. London: Unwin Hyman.

Bradley, Ritamary. 1984. "The Speculum Image in Medieval English Mystical Writers." In *The Medieval Mystical Tradition in England: Papers Read at Dartington Hall, July, 1984*. Ed. Marion Glasscoe. Cambridge: D. S. Brewer.

———. 1995. "Beatrice of Nazareth (c. 1200–1268). A Search for Her True Spirituality." In *Vox Mystica: Essays on Medieval Mysticism*. Eds. Anne Clark Bartlett et al. Cambridge: D. S. Brewer, 1995.

———. 1997. "Julian of Norwich: Everyone's Mystic." In *Mysticism and Spirituality in Medieval England*. Eds. William F. Pollard and Robert Boenig. Woodbridge: D. S. Brewer.

Brown, Peter. 1981. *The Cult of the Saints*. Chicago: University of Chicago Press.

———, ed. 1999. *Reading Dreams: The Interpretation of Dreams from Chaucer to Shakespeare*. Oxford: Oxford University Press.

Burke, Sean. 1992. *The Death and Return of the Author*. Edinburgh: Edinburgh University Press.

Bynum, Caroline Walker. 1982. *Jesus as Mother: Studies in the Spirituality of the High Middle Ages*. Berkeley and Los Angeles: University of California Press.

———. 1987. *Holy Feast and Holy Fast: The Religious Significance of Food to Medieval Women*. Berkeley and Los Angeles: University of California Press.

———. 1992. *Fragmentation and Redemption: Essays on Gender and the Human Body in Medieval Religion*. New York: Zone Books.

———. 1995. *The Resurrection of the Body in Western Christianity*. New York: Columbia University Press.

Caldwell, Ellen. 1984. "The Rhetorics of Enthusiasm and Restraint in 'The Form of Living' and 'The Cloud of Unknowing.'" *Fourteenth Century Mystics Newsletter* 10, no. 1: 9–16.

Casey, Edward. 1997. *The Fate of Place: A Philosophical History*. Berkeley and Los Angeles: University of California Press.

Cassidy-Welch, Megan. 2001. *Monastic Spaces and Their Meanings: Thirteenth Century Cistercian Monasteries*. Turnhout: Brepols.

Chewning, Susannah Mary. 2005. "Gladly Alone, Gladly Silent: Isolation and Exile in the Anchoritic Mystical Experience." In *Anchorites, Wombs and Tombs: Intersections of Gender and Enclosure in the Middle Ages*. Ed. Liz Herbert McAvoy. Cardiff: University of Wales Press.

Clark, John. 1992. "Late Fourteenth-Century Cambridge Theology and the English Contemplative Tradition." In *The Medieval Mystical Tradition in England: Exeter Symposium V. Papers Read at the Devon Centre, Dartington Hall, July, 1992*. Ed. Marion Glasscoe. Cambridge: D. S. Brewer.

Clay, Rotha Mary. 1914. *The Hermits and Anchorites of England*. London.

Colledge, Edmund, and James Walsh. 1978. Introduction to *A Book of Showings: Part One and Part Two,* by Julian of Norwich. Toronto: Pontifical Institute of Medieval Studies.

Colledge, Eric. 1956. "Recent Work on Walter Hilton." *Blackfriars* 37, no. 435: 265–70.

———, ed. 1961. *The Medieval Mystics of England.* New York: Charles Scribner & Sons.

Comper, Frances M. M. 1969. *The Life and Lyrics of Richard Rolle.* New York: Barnes & Noble. (Orig. pub. 1928.)

Conner, Edwin L. 1995. "'Goostly Freend in God': Aelred of Rievaulx's 'De Spirituali Amicitia' as a Source of 'The Cloud of Unknowing.'" In *Vox Mystica: Essays on Medieval Mysticism.* Eds. Anne Clark Bartlett et al. Cambridge: D. S. Brewer.

Copeland, Rita. 1984. "Richard Rolle and the Rhetorical Theory of the Levels of Style." In *The Medieval Mystical Tradition in England: Papers Read at Dartington Hall, July, 1984.* Ed. Marion Glasscoe. Cambridge: D. S. Brewer.

Copleston, Frederick C. 1961. *Medieval Philosophy.* New York: Harper Torchbooks.

Cousins, Ewert H. 1992. "Bonaventure's Mysticism of Language." In *Mysticism and Language.* Ed. Steven T. Katz. New York: Oxford University Press.

Curtius, Ernst Robert. 1963. *European Literature and the Later Middle Ages.* Trans. William R. Trask. New York: Harper & Row.

Dällenbach, Lucien. 1989. *The Mirror in the Text.* Cambridge: Polity Press, 1989.

Darnton, Robert. 1984. *The Great Cat Massacre.* Hammondsworth: Penguin Books.

Davies, Paul. 1982. *Other Worlds.* London: Sphere Books.

———. 1984. *God and the New Physics.* London: Penguin Books.

———. 1992. *The Mind of God.* London: Penguin Books.

———. 1992. *How to Build a Time Machine.* New York: Penguin Putnam.

Davies, Paul, John D. Barrow, and Charles Harper. 2004. *Science and Ultimate Reality.* Cambridge: Cambridge University Press.

De Ford, Sara. 1980. "Mystical Union in the Melos Amoris of Richard Rolle." In *The Medieval Mystical Tradition in England: Papers Read at the Exeter Symposium, July, 1984.* Ed. Marion Glasscoe. Exeter: University of Exeter.

Deshman, Robert. 1997. "Another Look at the Disappearing Christ: Corporeal and Spiritual Vision in Early Medieval Images." *Art Bulletin* 79, no. 3: 518–46.

Despres, Denise, L. 1996. "Ecstatic Reading and Missionary Mysticism: Orcherd of Syon." In *Prophets Abroad: The Reception of Continental Holy Women in Late Medieval England.* Cambridge: D. S. Brewer.

Dickman, Susan. 1980. "Margery Kempe and the English Devotional Tradition." In *The Medieval Mystical Tradition in England: Papers Read at the Exeter Symposium, July, 1980.* Ed. Marion Glasscoe. Exeter: University of Exeter.

Dillon, Janette. 1996. "Holy Women and Their Confessors or Confessors and Their Holy Women? Margery Kempe and Continental Tradition." In *Prophets Abroad: The Reception of Continental Holy Women in Late Medieval England.* Cambridge: D. S. Brewer.

Dinzelbacher, Peter. 1987. "The Beginnings of Mysticism Experienced in Twelfth Century England." In *The Medieval Mystical Tradition in England: Exeter Symposium IV. Papers Read at Dartington Hall, July, 1987.* Ed. Marion Glasscoe. Cambridge: D. S. Brewer.

Dronke, Peter. 1984. *Women Writers of the Middle Ages: A Critical Study of Texts from Perpetua to Marguerite Porete.* Cambridge: Cambridge University Press.

Duhem, Pierre. 1985. *Medieval Cosmology: Theories of Infinity, Place, Time, Void and the Plurality of Worlds.* Trans. and ed. Roger Ariew. Chicago: University of Chicago Press.

Eco, Umberto. 1986. *Art and Beauty in the Middle Ages.* Trans. Hugh Bredin. New Haven: Yale University Press.

———. 1997. *Kant and the Platypus: Essays on Language and Cognition.* London: Secker & Warburg.

———.1998. *Serendipities.* Trans. William Weaver. London: Weidenfeld & Nicholson.

Elkins, Sharon K. 1988. *Holy Women of Twelfth Century England.* Chapel Hill: University of North Carolina Press.

Ellis, Roger. 1980. "A Literary Approach to the Middle English Mystics." In *The Medieval Mystical Tradition in England: Papers Read at the Exeter Symposium, July, 1980.* Ed. Marion Glasscoe. Exeter: University of Exeter.

Evans, Ruth. 1994. "Translating Past Cultures?" In *Medieval Translator 4.* Eds. Roger Ellis and Ruth Evans. New York: Medieval and Renaissance Texts and Studies.

Evans, Ruth, and Lesley Johnson, eds. 1994. *Feminist Readings in Middle English Literature.* London: Routledge.

Finke, Laurie A. 1992. *Feminist Theory, Women's Writing.* New York: Cornell University Press.

———. 1993. "Mystical Bodies and the Dialogics of Vision." In *Maps of Flesh and Light: The Religious Experience of Medieval Women Mystics.* Ed. Ulrike Wiethaus. New York: Syracuse University Press.

Forman, Robert K. 1987. "Mystical Experiences in *The Cloud* Literature." In *The Medieval Mystical Tradition in England: Exeter Symposium IV. Papers Read at Dartington Hall, July, 1987.* Ed. Marion Glasscoe. Cambridge: D. S. Brewer.

Foucault, Michel. 1979. "What Is an Author?" In *Textual Strategies: Perspectives in Post-Structuralist Criticism.* New York: Cornell University Press.

———. 1986. "Of Other Spaces." *Diacritics* 16: 22–27.

Frayling, Christopher. 1995. *Strange Landscapes: A Journey through the Middle Ages.* London: BCA.

Freeman, Elizabeth. 2005. "Male and Female Cistercians' Gendered Experiences." In *Anchorites, Wombs and Tombs: Intersections of Gender and Enclosure in the Middle Ages.* Ed. Liz Herbert McAvoy. Cardiff: University of Wales Press.

Frye, Northrop. 1982. *The Great Code: The Bible and Literature.* London: Routledge & Kegan Paul.

Gardiner, Eileen, ed. 1989. *Visions of Heaven and Hell before Dante.* New York: Italica Press.

Geldof, Koenraad. 1997. "Authority, Reading, Reflexivity: Pierre Boudieu and the Aesthetic Judgment of Kant." *Diacritics* 27: 20–43.

Gellrich, Jesse. 1985. *The Idea of the Book in the Middle Ages: Language, Theory, Mythology and Fiction.* Ithaca: Cornell University Press.

Gilchrist, Roberta. 1997. *Gender and Material Culture.* London: Routledge.

Gillespie, Vincent. 1992. "Postcards from the Edge: Interpreting the Ineffable in the Middle English Mystics." In *Interpretation: Medieval and Modern.* Cambridge: D. S. Brewer.

Gillespie, Vincent, and Maggie Ross. 1992. "The Apophatic Image: The Poetics of Effacement in Julian of Norwich. In *The Medieval Mystical Tradition in England: Exeter Symposium V. Papers Read at the Devon Centre, Dartington Hall, July, 1992.* Ed. Marion Glasscoe. Cambridge: D. S. Brewer.

Gilson, Etienne. 1961. *The Christian Philosophy of Saint Augustine.* Trans. L. E. M. Lynch. London: Victor Gollancz.

Glasscoe, Marion. 1989. "Visions and Revisions: A Further Look at the Manuscripts of Julian of Norwich." *Studies in Bibliography* 42: 103–20.

———. 1993. *English Medieval Mystics: Games of Faith.* London: Longman.

———. 1997. "Changing *Chere* and Changing Text in the Eighth Revelation of Julian of Norwich." *Medium Aevum* 66, no. 1: 115–121.

Grabes, Herbert. 1982. *The Mutable Glass.* Trans. Gordon Collier. Cambridge: Cambridge University Press. (Orig. pub. 1973.)

Grant, Patrick. 1983. *Literature of Mysticism in Western Tradition.* London: Macmillan.

Gregg, William O. 1992. "Presence of the Church in 'The Cloud of Unknowing.'" *American Benedictine Review* 43, no. 2: 184–206.

Grosz, Elizabeth. 1994. *Volatile Bodies: Towards a Corporeal Feminism.* Sydney: Allen & Unwin.

Gueron, Rene. 1953. *The Reign of Quantity and the Signs of the Times.* London: Luzac.

———. 1975. *The Crisis of the Modern World.* Trans. Marco Pallis and Richard Nicholson. London: Luzac. (Orig. pub. 1942.)

Hahn, Cynthia. 1997. "Seeing and Believing: The Construction of Sanctity in Early-Medieval Saints' Shrines." *Speculum* 72, no. 4: 1079–106.

Hale, Rosemary Drage. 1995. "'Taste and See, for God is Sweet': Sensory Perception and Memory in Medieval Christian Mystical Experience." In *Vox Mystica: Essays on Medieval Mysticism.* Eds. Anne Clark Bartlett et al. Cambridge: D. S. Brewer.

Hart, Kevin. 1989. *The Trepass of the Sign: Deconstruction, Theology and Philosophy.* Cambridge: Cambridge University Press.

Hawking, Stephen W. 1988. *A Brief History of Time from the Big Bang to Black Holes.* London: Bantam Press.

Hayes, Stephen E. 1995. "Of Three Workings in Man's Soul: A Middle English Prose Meditation on the Annunciation." In *Vox Mystica: Essays on Medieval Mysticism*. Eds. Anne Clark Bartlett et al. Cambridge: D. S. Brewer.

Heer, Friedrich. 1962. *The Medieval World: Europe 1100–1350*. Trans. Janet Sondheim. New York: World.

Herrin, Judith. 1987. *The Formation of Christendom*. London: Fontana.

Hertz, Neil. 1979. "Freud and the Sandman." In *Textual Strategies: Perspectives in Post-Structuralist Criticism*. Ithaca: Cornell University Press.

Hilles, Carroll. 1998. "The Sacred Image and the Healing Touch: The Veronica in Julian of Norwich's 'Revelations of Love.'" *Journal of Medieval and Early Modern Studies* 28, no. 3: 553–73.

Hirsh, John C. 1995. "Religious Attitudes and Mystical Language in Medieval Literary Texts: An Essay in Methodology." In *Vox Mystica: Essays on Medieval Mysticism*. Eds. Anne Clark Bartlett et al. Cambridge: D. S. Brewer.

Holbrook, Sue Ellen. 1987. "Margery Kempe and Wynkyn de Worde." In *The Medieval Mystical Tradition in England: Exeter Symposium IV. Papers Read at Dartington Hall, July, 1987*. Ed. Marion Glasscoe. Cambridge: D. S. Brewer.

Hollander, Robert. 1969. *Allegory in Dante's Comedy*. Princeton: Princeton University Press.

Holloway, Julia Bolton. 1990. "Crosses and Boxes: Latin and Vernacular." In *Equally in God's Image*. Eds. Julia Bolton Holloway et al. New York: Peter Lang.

Horstmann, C., ed. 1895. *Richard Rolle of Hampole, an English Father of the Church and His Followers*. London: S. Sonnenschein.

Huppe, Bernard, and D. W. Robertson. 1963. *Fruyt and Chaf*. Princeton: Princeton University Press.

Hussey, S. S. 1964. "The Text of *The Scale of Perfection*, Book II." *Neuphilologische Mitteilungen* 65: 75–92.

———. 1980. "Walter Hilton: Traditionalist?" In *The Medieval Mystical Tradition in England: Papers Read at the Exeter Symposium, July, 1980*. Ed. Marion Glasscoe. Exeter: University of Exeter.

Idel, Moshe. 1992. "Reification of Language in Jewish Mysticism." In *Mysticism and Language*. Ed. Steven T. Katz. New York: Oxford University Press.

Innes-Parker, Catherine. 2005. "The Anchoritic Elements of Holkham Misc. 41." In *Anchorites, Wombs and Tombs: Intersections of Gender and Enclosure in the Middle Ages*. Ed. Liz Herbert McAvoy. Cardiff: University of Wales Press.

Irvine, Martin. 1994. *The Making of Textual Culture: "Grammatica" and Literary Theory 350–1100*. Cambridge: Cambridge University Press.

Jantzen, Grace. 1995. *Power, Gender and Christian Mysticism*. Cambridge: Cambridge University Press.

Jenkins, Richard. 1992. *Pierre Bourdieu*. London: Routledge.

Johnson, Ian. 1996. "*Auctricitas?* Holy Women and Their Middle English Texts." In *Prophets Abroad: The Reception of Continental Holy Women in Late Medieval England*. Cambridge: D. S. Brewer.

Johnson, Lynn Staley. 1992. "Margery Kempe: Social Critic." *Journal of Medieval and Renaissance Studies* 22, no. 2: 159–84.

Johnston, William. 1978. *The Mysticism of "The Cloud of Unknowing."* Wheathampstead: Anthony Clarke Books. (Orig. pub. 1967.)

Katz, Steven T. 1992. "Mystical Speech and Mystical Meaning." In *Mysticism and Language*. Ed. Steven T. Katz. New York: Oxford University Press.

Kazarow, Patricia A. 1993. "Text and Context in Hildegard of Bingen's 'Ordo Virtutum.'" In *Maps of Flesh and Light: The Religious Experience of Medieval Women Mystics*. Ed. Ulrike Wiethaus. New York: Syracuse University Press.

Kerby-Fulton, Kathryn. 1996. "Hildegard and the Male Reader: A Study in Insular Reception." In *Prophets Abroad: The Reception of Continental Holy Women in Late Medieval England*. Ed. Rosalynn Voaden. Cambridge: D. S. Brewer.

Klocker, Harry R. 1980. "Ockhamism in Jean Gerson." *Michigan-Academician* 2, no. 3: 365–74.

Knowles, David. 1961. *The English Mystical Tradition*. London: Burns & Oates.

Knowlton, Mary Arthur. 1973. *The Influence of Richard Rolle and of Julian of Norwich on the Middle English Lyrics*. The Hague: Mouton.

Kristeva, Julie. 1987. *Tales of Love*. Trans. Leon S. Roudiez. New York: Columbia University Press.

Labarge, Margaret Wade. 1986. *Women in Medieval Life*. London: Hamish Hamilton.

Lacey, Robert, and Danny Danziger. 1999. *The Year 1000*. London: Little, Brown & Co.

Lagorio, Valerie. 1984. "The Medieval Continental Women Mystics." In *An Introduction to the Medieval Mystics of Europe*. Ed. Paul E. Szarmach. Albany: State University of New York Press.

Lawes, Richard. 2000. "Psychological Disorder and Autobiography." In *Writing Religious Women: Female Spiritual and Textual Practices in Late Medieval England*. Eds. Denis Renevey and Christiana Whitehead. Toronto: University of Toronto Press.

Lawrence, C. H. 1989. *Medieval Monasticism*. New York: Longman.

Leclercq, Jean. 1984. "Does St. Bernard Have a Specific Message for Nuns?" In *Distant Echoes: Medieval Religious Women*, Vol. 1. Eds. John A. Nicholls and Lillian Thomas Shank. Kalamazoo: Cistercian Publications.

Lefebvre, Henri. 1991. *The Production of Space*. Trans. Donald Nicholson-Smith. Oxford: Blackwell. (Orig. pub. 1974.)

Leroux-Dhuys, Jean-Francois. 1998. *Cistercian Abbey: History and Architecture*. Paris: Editions Menges.

Leuchak, Rebecca. 1997. "Imagining and Imaging the Medieval: The Cloisters, Virtual Reality and Paradigm Shifts." *Historical Reflections/Réflexions Historiques* 23, no. 3: 349–69.

Lewis, C. S. 1936. *The Allegory of Love*. London: Oxford University Press.

———. 1964. *The Discarded Image*. Cambridge: Cambridge University Press.

Lewis, Gertrud Jaron. 1995. "Music and Dancing in the 14th cent. Sister Books." In *Vox Mystica: Essays on Medieval Mysticism*. Eds. Anne Clark Bartlett et al. Cambridge: D. S. Brewer.

Llewelyn, Robert. 1981. "The Treatment of Distractions in Zen and 'The Cloud of Unknowing.'" *14th Century English Mystics Newsletter* 7, no. 2: 61–76.

Long, Julia. 1994. "Mysticism and Hysteria." In *Feminist Readings in Middle English Literature*. Eds. Ruth Evans and Lesley Johnson. London: Routledge.

Louth, Andrew. 1981. *The Origins of the Christian Mystical Tradition, from Plato to Denys*. Oxford: Clarendon Press.

Macris, Antony. 2003. "Claude Simon and the Emergence of the Generative Mise en Abyme." *AUMLA* 99: 50–66.

Maisonneuve, Roland. 1980. "Julian of Norwich and the Prison of Existence." *Studia Mystica* 3, no. 4: 26–32.

———. 1988. "Le symbolisme sacré des couleurs chez deux mystiques mediev-ales: Hildegarde de Bingen; Julienne de Norwich." In *Les Couleurs au Moyen Age*. Aix-en-Provence: Université de Provence.

Mann, Jill. 1994. "Allegorical Buildings in Medieval Literature." *Medium Ævum* 62, no. 2: 191–210.

Manter, Lisa. 2002. "Rolle Playing: 'And the Word Became Flesh.'" In *The Vernacular Spirit: Essays on Medieval Religious Literature*. Eds. Renate Blumenfeld-Kosinski, Duncan Robertson, and Nancy Bradley Warren. New York: Palgrave.

Markus, R. A., ed. 1972. *Augustine: A Collection of Critical Essays*. New York: Anchor Books.

Masson, Cynthea. 1998. "The Point of Coincidence: Rhetoric and the Apophatic in Julian of Norwich's 'Showings.'" In *Julian of Norwich: A Book of Essays*. Ed. Sandra McEntire. New York: Garland.

Matter, E. Ann. 1993. "Interior Maps of an Eternal External: The Spiritual Rhetoric of Maria Domitilla Galluzzi d'Acqui." In *Maps of Flesh and Light: The Religious Experience of Medieval Women Mystics*. Ed. Ulrike Wiethaus. New York: Syracuse University Press.

McAvoy, Liz Herbert. 1998. "'The Modyr's Service': Motherhood as Matrix in Julian of Norwich." *Mystics Quarterly* 24, no. 4: 181–97.

———. 2002. "'. . . a purse fulle fayer': Feminising the Body in Julian of Norwich's 'Revelations of Divine Love.'" *Leeds Studies in English* 34: 99–113.

———. 2004. *Authority and the Female Body in the Writings of Julian of Norwich and Margery Kempe*. London: D. S. Brewer.

McAvoy, Liz Herbert, and Mari Hughes-Edwards, eds. 2005. *Anchorites, Wombs and Tombs: Intersections of Gender and Enclosure in the Middle Ages*. Cardiff: University of Wales.

McEntire, Sandra. 1987. "The Doctrine of Compunction from Bede to Margery Kempe." In *The Medieval Mystical Tradition in England: Exeter Symposium IV*.

Papers Read at Dartington Hall, July, 1987. Ed. Marion Glasscoe. Cambridge: D. S. Brewer.

McGinn, Bernard. 1991. *The Presence of God: A History of Western Christian Mysticism.* New York: Crossroad.

————. 1992. "The Language of Love in Christian and Jewish Mysticism." In *Mysticism and Language.* Ed. Steven T. Katz. New York: Oxford University Press.

McIlwaine, James T. 1984. "The 'Bodelye Syeknes' of Julain of Norwich." *Journal of Medieval History* 10, no. 3: 167–80.

McNamara, Jo Ann. 1984. "Muffled Voices: The Lives of Consecrated Women in the Fourth Century." In *Distant Echoes. Medieval Religious Women,* Vol. 1. Eds. John A. Nicholls and Lillian Thomas Shank. Kalamazoo: Cistercian Publications.

————. 1993. "The Rhetoric of Orthodoxy: Clerical Authority and Female Innovation in the Struggle with Heresy." In *Maps of Flesh and Light: The Religious Experience of Medieval Women Mystics.* Ed. Ulrike Wiethaus. New York: Syracuse University Press.

Medcalf, Stephen. 1980. "Medieval Psychology and Medieval Mystics." In *The Medieval Mystical Tradition in England: Papers Read at the Exeter Symposium, July, 1980.* Ed. Marion Glasscoe. Exeter: University of Exeter.

Medcalf, Stephen, and Marjorie Reeves. 1981. "The Ideal, the Real and the Quest for Perfection." In *The Later Middle Ages.* Ed. Stephen Medcalf. London: Methuen & Co.

Mitchell, Marea. 2005. *The Book of Margery Kempe: Scholarship, Community and Criticism.* New York: Peter Lang.

Molinari, Paul. 1958. *Julian of Norwich: The Teaching of a 14th Century Mystic.* London: Longmans, Green & Co.

Moore, Peter. 1987. "Christian Mysticism and Interpretation: Some Philosophical Issues Illustrated in the Study of the Medieval English Mystics." In *The Medieval Mystical Tradition in England: Exeter Symposium IV. Papers Read at Dartington Hall, July, 1987.* Ed. Marion Glasscoe. Cambridge: D. S. Brewer.

Morris, T. J. 1989. "Rhetorical Stance: An Approach to 'The Cloud of Unknowing.'" *Mystics Quarterly* 15, no. 1: 13–20.

Morrison, Tessa. 2006. "The Symbol of the City: Utopian Symmetry." *International Journal of Humanities* 3, no. 5: 92–103.

Mulder-Bakker, Anneke. 2005. *Lives of the Anchoresses: The Rise of the Urban Recluse in Medieval Europe.* Trans. Myra Heerspink Scholz. Philadelphia: University of Pennsylvania Press.

Nash, Roy. 1999. "Bourdieu, 'Habitus' and Educational Research: Is It All Worth the Candle?" *British Journal of Sociology of Education* 20, no. 2: 175–87.

Needleman, Jacob, ed. 1974. *The Sword of Gnosis.* Baltimore: Penguin Books.

Nolan, Edward Peter. 1990. *Now Through a Glass Darkly: Specular Images of Be-*

ing and Knowing from Virgil to Chaucer. Ann Arbor: University of Michigan Press.

O'Connell, Robert J. 1989. *St. Augustine's Confessions: Odyssey of the Soul.* New York: Fordham University Press. (Orig. pub. 1969.)

O'Loughlin, Thomas. 1999. "Distant Islands: The Topography of Holiness in the 'Nauigatio Sancti Brendani.'" In *The Medieval Mystical Tradition: Exeter Symposium VI.* Ed. Marion Glasscoe. Cambridge: D. S. Brewer.

Ong, Walter J. 1988. "Before Textuality: Orality and Interpretation." *Oral Tradition* 3, no. 3: 259–69.

Panofsky, Erwin. 1967. *Gothic Architecture and Scholasticism.* Cleveland: Meridian Books. (Orig. pub. 1951.)

Pantin, W. A. 1963. *The English Church in the Fourteenth Century: Part III.* South Bend, Ind.: University of Notre Dame Press.

Partner, Nancy F. 1993. "No Sex, No Gender." *Speculum* 68: 419–43.

Patterson, Lee. 1987. *Negotiating the Past: The Historical Understanding of Medieval Literature.* Madison: University of Wisconsin Press.

Pelphrey, Brant. 1982. *Love Was His Meaning: The Theology and Mysticism of Julian of Norwich.* Salzburg: Institut für Anglistik und Amerikanistik.

————. 1998. "Leaving the Womb of Christ: Love, Doomsday and Space/Time in Julian of Norwich and Eastern Orthodox Mysticism." In *Julian of Norwich. A Book of Essays.* Ed. Sandra McEntire. New York: Garland.

Petersen, Zina. 1996. "'Every Manner of Thing Shall Be Well': Mirroring Serenity in the Shewings of Julian of Norwich." *Mystics Quarterly* 22, no. 3: 91–101.

Petroff, Elizabeth. 1994. *Body and Soul: Essays on Medieval Women and Mysticism.* New York: Oxford University Press.

Pokorn, Nike Kocijaneie. 1997. "The Language and Discourse of *The Cloud of Unknowing.*" *Literature and Theology* 11, no. 4: 408–21.

Pollard, William F., and Robert Boenig. 1997. "Richard Rolle and the 'Eye of the Heart.'" In *Mysticism and Spirituality in Medieval England.* Eds. William Pollard and Robert Boenig. Woodbridge: D. S. Brewer, 1997.

Power, Eileen. 1922. *Medieval English Nunneries.* Cambridge: Cambridge University Press.

Renevey, Denis. 1994. "Encoding and Decoding: Metaphorical Discourse of Love in Richard Rolle's Commentary on the First Verses of 'The Song of Songs.'" In *The Medieval Translator 4.* New York: Medieval and Renaissance Texts and Studies.

————. 1997. "Enclosed Desires: A Study of the Wooing Group." In *Mysticism and Spirituality in Medieval England.* Eds. William Pollard and Robert Boenig. Woodbridge: D. S. Brewer.

————. 1999. "Name above Names: The Devotion to the Name of Jesus from Richard Rolle to Walter Hilton's 'Scale of Perfection I.'" In *The Medieval Mystical Tradition: Exeter Symposium VI.* Ed. Marion Glasscoe. Cambridge: D. S, Brewer.

Riddy, Felicity. 1998. "Julian of Norwich and Self-Textualisation." In *Editing Women: Papers Given at the 31st Annual Conference.* Toronto: University of Toronto Press.

Riehle, Wolfgang. 1980. "English Mysticism and the Morality Play: Wisdom Who Is Christ." In *The Medieval Mystical Tradition in England: Papers Read at the Exeter Symposium, July, 1980.* Ed. Marion Glasscoe. Exeter: University of Exeter.

———. 1981. *The Middle English Mystics.* London: Routledge & Kegan Paul.

Ross, Eileen. 1988. "Submission or Infidelity? The Unity of Church and Mysticism in Walter Hilton's 'Scale of Perfection.'" *Downside Review* 106, no. 363: 134–44.

Ross, Ellen. 1993. "'She Wept and Cried Right Loud for Sorrow and for Pain': Suffering, the Spiritual Journey and Women's Experience in Late Medieval Mysticism." In *Maps of Flesh and Light: The Religious Experience of Medieval Women Mystics.* Ed. Ulrike Wiethaus. New York: Syracuse University Press.

Russell, Jeffrey Burton. 1997. *A History of Heaven: The Singing Silence.* Princeton: Princeton University Press.

Ruud, Jay. 1995. "Julian of Norwich and the Nominalist Question." In *Literary Nominalism and the Theory of Rereading Late Medieval Texts.* Ed. Richard J. Utz. Lewiston: Edwin Meller Press.

Savage, Anne. 1994. "The Translation of the Feminine: Untranslatable Dimensions of the Anchoritic Works." In *The Medieval Translator 4.* New York: Medieval and Renaissance Texts and Studies.

Schmidt, A. V. C. 1980. "Langland and Mystical Tradition." In *The Medieval Mystical Tradition in England: Papers Read at the Exeter Symposium, July, 1980.* Ed. Marion Glasscoe. Exeter: University of Exeter.

Schulenburg, Jane Tibbetts. 1984. "Strict Active Enclosure and Its Effects on the Female Monastic Experience (ca. 500–1100)." In *Distant Echoes: Medieval Religious Women,* Vol. 1. Eds. John A. Nicholls and Lillian Thomas Shank. Kalamazoo: Cistercian Publications.

Smart, Ninian. 1992. "What Would Baddhaghosa Have Made of 'The Cloud of Unknowing'?" In *Mysticism and Language.* Ed. Steven T. Katz. New York: Oxford University Press.

Soja, Edward. 1993. "History: Geography: Modernity." In *The Cultural Reader.* London: Routledge.

Spearing, A. C. 1976. *Medieval Dream-Poetry.* Cambridge: Cambridge University Press.

Sprung, Andrew. 1993. "'We nevyr shall come out of hym': Enclosure and Immanence in Julian of Norwich's Book of Showings." *Mystics Quarterly* 19, no. 2: 47–59.

Stephens, John, and Ruth Waterhouse. 1990. *Literature, Language and Change: From Chaucer to the Present.* London: Routledge.

Szarmach, Paul E., ed. 1984. *An Introduction to the Medieval Mystics of Europe.* Albany: State University of New York Press.

Talbot, Michael. 1991. *The Holographic Universe*. New York: Harper.

Taylor, Cheryl. 2005. "Using and Abusing Language in 'The Cloud of Unknowing.'" *Parergon* 22, no. 2: 31–51.

Thompson, John B. 1991. "Introduction" to *Language and Symbolic Power* by Pierre Bourdieu. Cambridge: Polity Press.

Tixier, Rene. 1990. "'Good Gamesumli Pley': Games of Love in 'The Cloud of Unknowing.'" *Downside Review* 108, no. 373: 235–53.

———. 1997. "'þis louely blinde werk': Contemplation in 'The Cloud of Unknowing' and Related Treatises." In *Mysticism and Spirituality in Medieval England*. Eds. William F. Pollard and Robert Boenig. Woodbridge: D. S. Brewer.

Tobin, Frank. 1995. "Medieval Thought on Visions and Its Resonance in Mechthild von Magdeburg's Flowing Light of the Godhead." In *Vox Mystica: Essays on Medieval Mysticism*. Eds. Anne Clark Bartlett et al. Cambridge: D. S. Brewer.

Torrance, Thomas F. 1969. *Space, Time and Incarnation*. Oxford: Oxford University Press.

Totah, Mary David. 1998. "The Undivided Heart: Another Look at Enclosure." *Cistercian Studies* 33, no. 3: 345–68.

Turner, Victor. 1989. *The Ritual Process*. Ithaca: Cornell University Press. (Orig. pub. 1969.)

———. 1978. *Image and Pilgrimage in Christian Culture*. New York: Columbia University Press.

Underhill, Evelyn. 1995. *Mysticism*. London: Bracken Books. (Orig. pub. 1911.)

Van Gennep, Arnold. 1977. *The Rites of Passage*. London: Routledge & Kegan Paul. (Orig. pub. 1908.)

Voaden, Rosalynn, ed. 1996. *Prophets Abroad: The Reception of Continental Holy Women in Late Medieval England*. Cambridge: D. S. Brewer.

Wakelin, M. F. 1980. "English Mysticism and the English Homiletic Tradition." In *The Medieval Mystical Tradition in England: Papers Read at the Exeter Symposium, July, 1980*. Ed. Marion Glasscoe. Exeter: University of Exeter.

Warner, Marina. 1985. *Alone of All Her Sex*. London: Picador.

Warren, Ann K. 1984. "The Nun as Anchoress: England 1100–1500." In *Distant Echoes: Medieval Religious Women*, Vol. 1. Eds. John A. Nicholls and Lillian Thomas Shank. Kalamazoo: Cistercian Publications.

———. 1985. *Anchorites and Their Patrons in Medieval England*. Berkeley and Los Angeles: University of California Press.

Watson, Nicholas. 1987. "The Methods and Objectives of Thirteenth-Century Anchoritic Devotion." In *The Medieval Mystical Tradition in England: Exeter Symposium IV. Papers Read at Dartington Hall, July, 1987*. Ed. Marion Glasscoe. Cambridge: D. S. Brewer.

———. 1991. *Richard Rolle and the Invention of Authority*. Cambridge: Cambridge University Press.

———. 1992. "The Trinitarian Hermeneutic in Julian of Norwich's *Revelation of Love.*" In *The Medieval Mystical Tradition in England: Exeter Symposium V. Papers Read at the Devon Centre, Dartington Hall, July, 1992.* Ed. Marion Glasscoe. Cambridge: D. S. Brewer.

———. 1993. "The Composition of Julian of Norwich's *Revelation of Love.*" *Speculum: A Journal of Medieval Studies* 68: 637–83.

———. 1995. "Censorship and Cultural Change in Late-Medieval England: Vernacular Theology, the Oxford Translation Debate, and Arundel's Constitution of 1409." *Speculum: A Journal of Medieval Studies* 70, no. 4: 822–64.

———. 1996. "Melting into God the English Way: Deification in the Middle English Version of Marguerite Porete's 'Mirouer des simples ames anienties.'" In *Prophets Abroad: The Reception of Continental Holy Women in Late Medieval England.* Ed. Rosalynn Voaden. Cambridge: D. S. Brewer.

Wenzel, Siegfried. 1978. *Fasciculum morum and Its Middle English Poems.* Cambridge: Medieval Academy of America.

Wertheim, Margaret. 1999. *The Pearly Gates of Cyberspace: A History of Space from Dante to the Internet.* Sydney: Doubleday.

Whitehead, Christiana. 1998. "Regarding the Ark: Revisions of Architectural Imagery in the Writings of the Cloud Author." *Downside Review* 116, no. 404: 195–212.

———. 2003. *Castles of the Mind.* Cardiff: University of Wales Press.

Wiethaus, Ulrike, ed. 1993. *Maps of Flesh and Light: The Religious Experience of Medieval Women Mystics.* New York: Syracuse University Press.

Wilson, R. M. 1970. *The Lost Literature of Medieval England.* London: Methuen & Co.

Windeatt, B. A. 1980. "The Art of Mystical Loving: Julian of Norwich." In *The Medieval Mystical Tradition in England: Papers Read at the Exeter Symposium, July, 1980.* Ed. Marion Glasscoe. Exeter: University of Exeter.

Wogan-Browne, Jocelyn. 1994. "Wreaths of Thyme: The Female Translator in Anglo-Norman Hagiography." In *The Medieval Translator 4.* New York: Medieval and Renaissance Texts and Studies.

Yates, Frances. 1966. *The Art of Memory.* Chicago: University of Chicago Press.

Ziegler, Joanna E. 1993. "Reality as Imitation. The Role of Religious Imagery among the Beguines of the Low Countries." In *Maps of Flesh and Light: The Religious Experience of Medieval Women Mystics.* Ed. Ulrike Wiethaus. New York: Syracuse University Press.

Zum Brunn, Emilie, and Georgette Epiney-Burgard. 1989. *Women Mystics in Medieval Europe.* New York: Paragon House.

INDEX

Abyss, 6–7, 178, 196, 202

Albertus Magnus, on astrology, 29n13

Allen, Hope Emily, 13, 82n48, 154; edition of Rolle's English works, 14

Allen, Rosamund, 145, 146

Anchorholds: archaeology, 94; as enclosure, 55–56; geography of reclusorium, 4

Anchorites and anchoresses, 4; as liminal, 92; numbers in medieval England, 63; patronage of, 31n16; texts for, 33

Ancrene Wisse, 11n9, 55

Anselm of Canterbury, Saint, 7

Aquinas, Saint Thomas, 108, 111, 118n26

Architectural imagery. *See* Space

Architecture, 17, 39, 45,75; Cistercian, 35n28; Gothic, 45; and Scholasticism, 44

Ark of the Covenant: as image of temple, 39; as image of text, 43

Aristotle, 1; theories of, 8, 11, 22, 23, 27, 56

Athanasius, Saint: on Saint Antony, 92

Athomus, 131

Auctor, 103

Augustine, Saint: on book as metaphor, 103; on desire, 211; on fire, 164; on geometry, 128–29; and *habitus,* 62n4; on music, 170; on social dimension of Christian life, 65; on spatial notion of God, 36; theory of perception, 184n10, 186

Averroës, 23

Baker, Denise, 32, 51n57, 69, 154

Bakhtin, Mikhail, 17, 59; and the *grotesque,* 17, 52–54; on space and the medieval cosmos, 25, 164

Bernard of Clairvaux, 152, 165

Boenig, Robert, 170, 175

Boethius: *De Musica,* 170; view of the universe, 25

Body: as site of mystical experience, 52; spatial associations with mysticism, 47–57

Body-space and soul-space, 8, 54, 68, 141, 142, 156, 158, 169, 170, 199–201, 207, 216, 219, 223, 228, 229, 237, 244

Bourdieu, Pierre, 17; and *habitus,* 62–63, 78–79; study of illness, 86–87, 215n2

Bradwardine: *Treatise on Proportions,* 23

Brown, Peter, 65, 88

Buccal perception, theory of, 167

Bynum, Caroline Walker: on Christ as mother, 239–40; on medieval society, 63–64; on saints as social models, 72, 89

Caldwell, Ellen, 204

Carthusians, 34n24, 180

Casey, Edward, 22n1, 23

Cassiodorus, 170

Cecelia, Saint, 69

Chalcidius, 171–72

Chaucer, Geoffrey: *Troilus and Criseyde,* 21, 25, 171

Chewning, Susannah Mary, 93

Cicero: *Ad Herrenium,* 43n41

Cistercians: architecture of, 35; female communities, 30

Clay, Rotha Mary, 63

Clement of Alexandria, 2n1

Cloisters, 35

Clothing: Christ as, 220; medieval, 82–84; metaphor, 85

Cloud, image of, 191–96

Cloud author, 9, 13; associations with Carthusians, 34n24, 179–80; cloud

267

Mysticism & Space: Space and Spatiality in the Works of Richard Rolle, The Cloud of Unknowing *Author, and Julian of Norwich* was designed and typeset in Garamond Premier Pro by Kachergis Book Design of Pittsboro, North Carolina. It was printed on 60-pound Natures Natural and bound by Thomson-Shore of Dexter, Michigan.